A NEW JERUSALEM

Written and illustrated by
Benjamin Dickson

A New Jerusalem

First published in 2018 by
New Internationalist
The Old Music Hall
106-108 Cowley Road
Oxford OX4 1JE
newint.org

Printed and bound in the Czech Republic by PBtisk, who hold environmental
accreditation ISO 14001.

[FSC symbol]

British Library Cataloguing-in-Publication Data
A catalogue record for this book is available from the British Library.
Library of Congress Cataloging-in-Publication Data
A catalog record for this book is available from the Library of Congress.

ISBN 978-1-78026-442-4

Introduction
by the author

One evening over dinner, about ten years ago, I started asking my father about his childhood memories of post-war Britain.

My father was born in Merseyside, just after VE Day. Like most of his generation, he grew up surrounded by devastation and deprivation; he was aware from a very young age that there had been a war, but it was not until much later he became aware that this was not normal. His route to school included several bombsites, and he spent many hours playing in them. They were, by his account, the greatest playgrounds imaginable. Places to climb up, places to crawl through... and, best of all, they were enormously dangerous.

'...and your parents let you play there?!' I asked.

'Of course', replied my father.

'But... weren't they worried about your safety?!'

'Not really. It wasn't like today; in the 1950s it was inconceivable that a child wasn't safe to play outside wherever he wanted. As far as they were concerned, if the Luftwaffe weren't bombing us any more, then we were safe.'

There's nothing quite like a war to shift your sense of perspective.

It's difficult to contemplate just how dark the future could have been; a future that Britain and its allies had only narrowly averted. In the same way a man who narrowly avoids death will find himself reassessing what's important in life, Britain collectively found itself questioning what kind of world it wanted its children to grow up in. Things that were politically impossible before the war suddenly became possible. Out of that optimism and sense of unity came Britain's National Health Service, its welfare state, and many other things that are still treasured today. The Post-War Settlement, as it came to be known, was far from perfect; but in the years following the war, as rationing finally ended and the bombsites were cleared, Britain became a far more equal society than it had ever been before.

People gave thanks and paid tribute to those who had paid for this future with their lives. But the cost to those who actually did come home was often not discussed.

Post-Traumatic Stress Disorder (PTSD) is a condition that, at the time, was not really understood. There was certainly an awareness of a condition which seemed to affect soldiers – often referred to as 'shell shock' - and that it seemed to affect some more than others. We now know that any traumatic event we experience can cause mental health problems; you certainly don't need to go to war to experience it. But we also now know that 99 per cent of any given population would develop PTSD if left in the field of battle for long enough. The only people immune to it are psychopaths.

Britain likes to pride itself on being a stoic nation; our national memory of how we coped during the war ('Keep calm and carry on!') reflects this very clearly. But stoicism and PTSD really don't mix well. Many of those who fought simply refused to speak about their experiences, and became withdrawn. Those who did speak found that few could understand how they felt, their families especially. Many became angry and resentful of this fact.

This is a story about all of the above. The initial idea came when, during that dinner with my father, I wondered what kind of things he and his friends might have found in the rubble of those bombsites. Perhaps they might have found something that set them on an adventure, like so many children's detective stories. Or perhaps they might have found some kind of buried treasure. But the idea ended up going in a radically different direction after watching Ken Loach's documentary *The Spirit of '45* (a film about the emergence of the Post-War Settlement and subsequent attempts to destroy it), and seeing a YouTube video of Patrick Stewart talking about his experiences with his father – a war veteran – who suffered from severe PTSD. I realied there was a lot to say about this point in time; things that, in my opinion at least, are in danger of being forgotten.

This book is a snapshot of life in Britain immediately after the war; a unique moment in British history between two defining eras, where the war had been won, but the nation had not yet decided what its future should be. But it's also about the freedoms, rights and privileges Britain takes for granted today, and just how hard-won they were.

As Ralph's father says: 'It's not enough to win a war. You have to make it mean something.'

Benjamin Dickson
May 2018

I will not cease from mental fight
Nor shall my sword sleep in my hand
Till we have built Jerusalem
In England's green and pleasant land

– William Blake

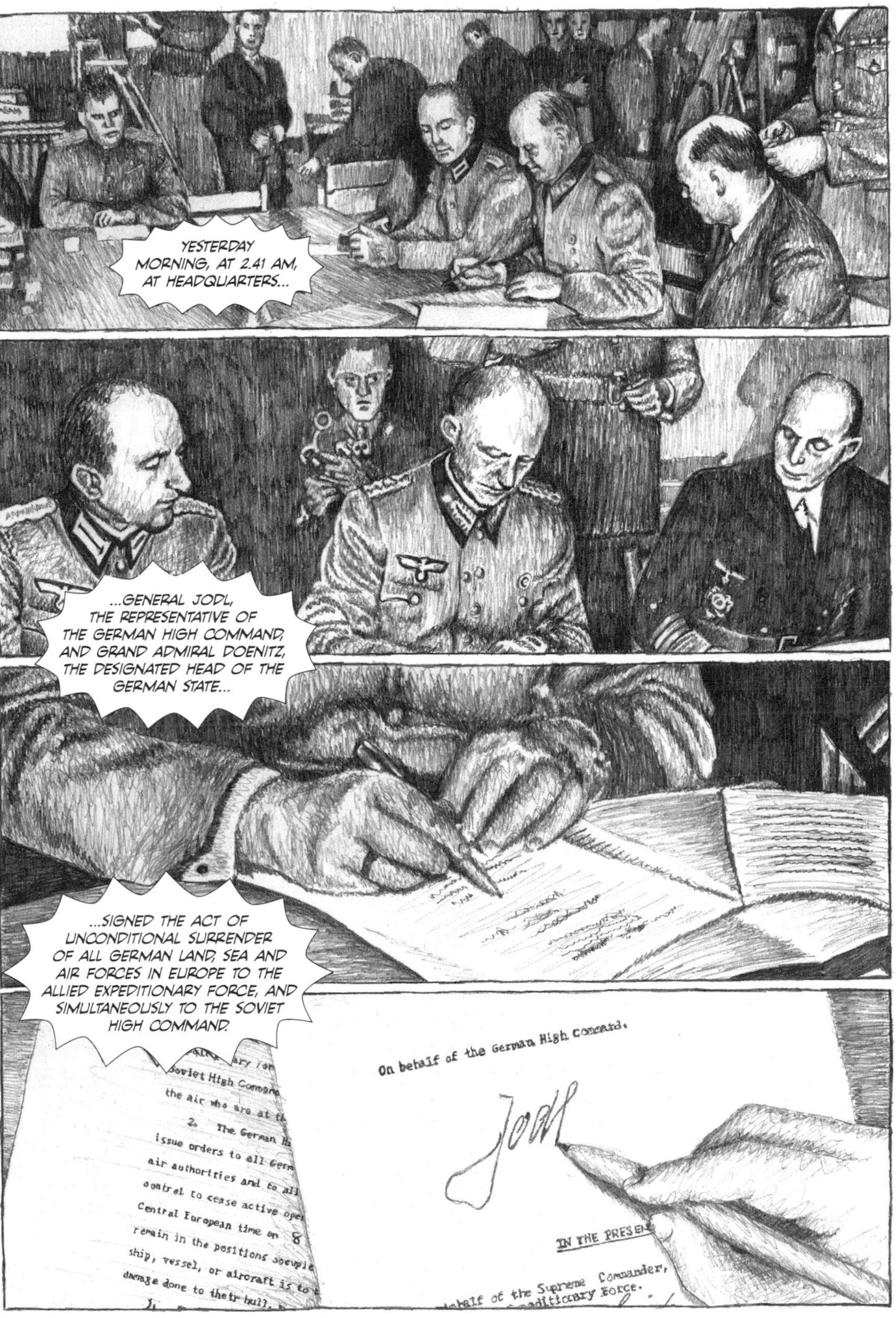

YESTERDAY MORNING, AT 2.41 AM, AT HEADQUARTERS...
...GENERAL JODL, THE REPRESENTATIVE OF THE GERMAN HIGH COMMAND, AND GRAND ADMIRAL DOENITZ, THE DESIGNATED HEAD OF THE GERMAN STATE...
...SIGNED THE ACT OF UNCONDITIONAL SURRENDER OF ALL GERMAN LAND, SEA AND AIR FORCES IN EUROPE TO THE ALLIED EXPEDITIONARY FORCE, AND SIMULTANEOUSLY TO THE SOVIET HIGH COMMAND.
On behalf of the German High Command.

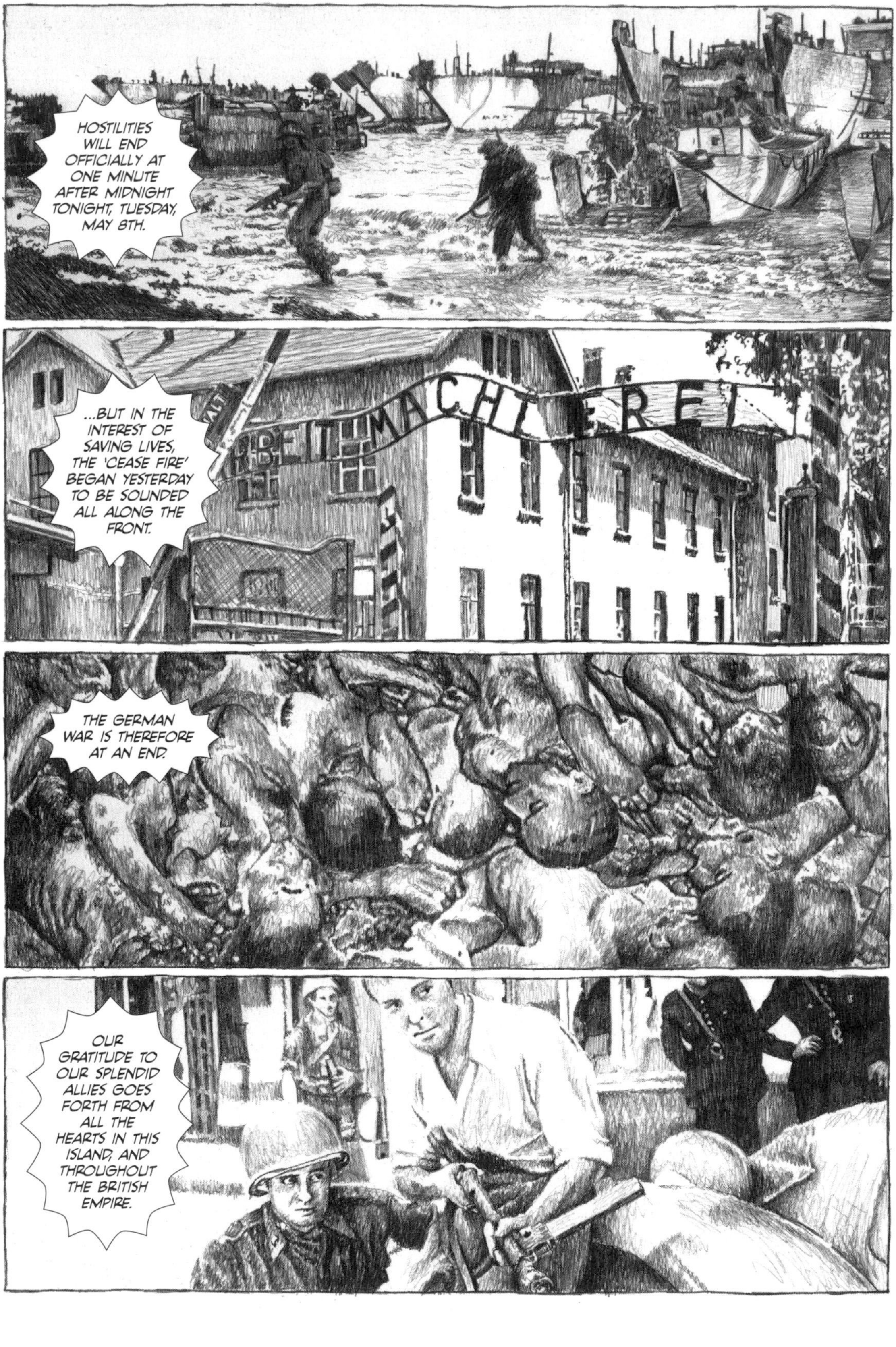
HOSTILITIES WILL END OFFICIALLY AT ONE MINUTE AFTER MIDNIGHT TONIGHT, TUESDAY, MAY 8TH.
...BUT IN THE INTEREST OF SAVING LIVES, THE 'CEASE FIRE' BEGAN YESTERDAY TO BE SOUNDED ALL ALONG THE FRONT.
THE GERMAN WAR IS THEREFORE AT AN END.
OUR GRATITUDE TO OUR SPLENDID ALLIES GOES FORTH FROM ALL THE HEARTS IN THIS ISLAND, AND THROUGHOUT THE BRITISH EMPIRE.

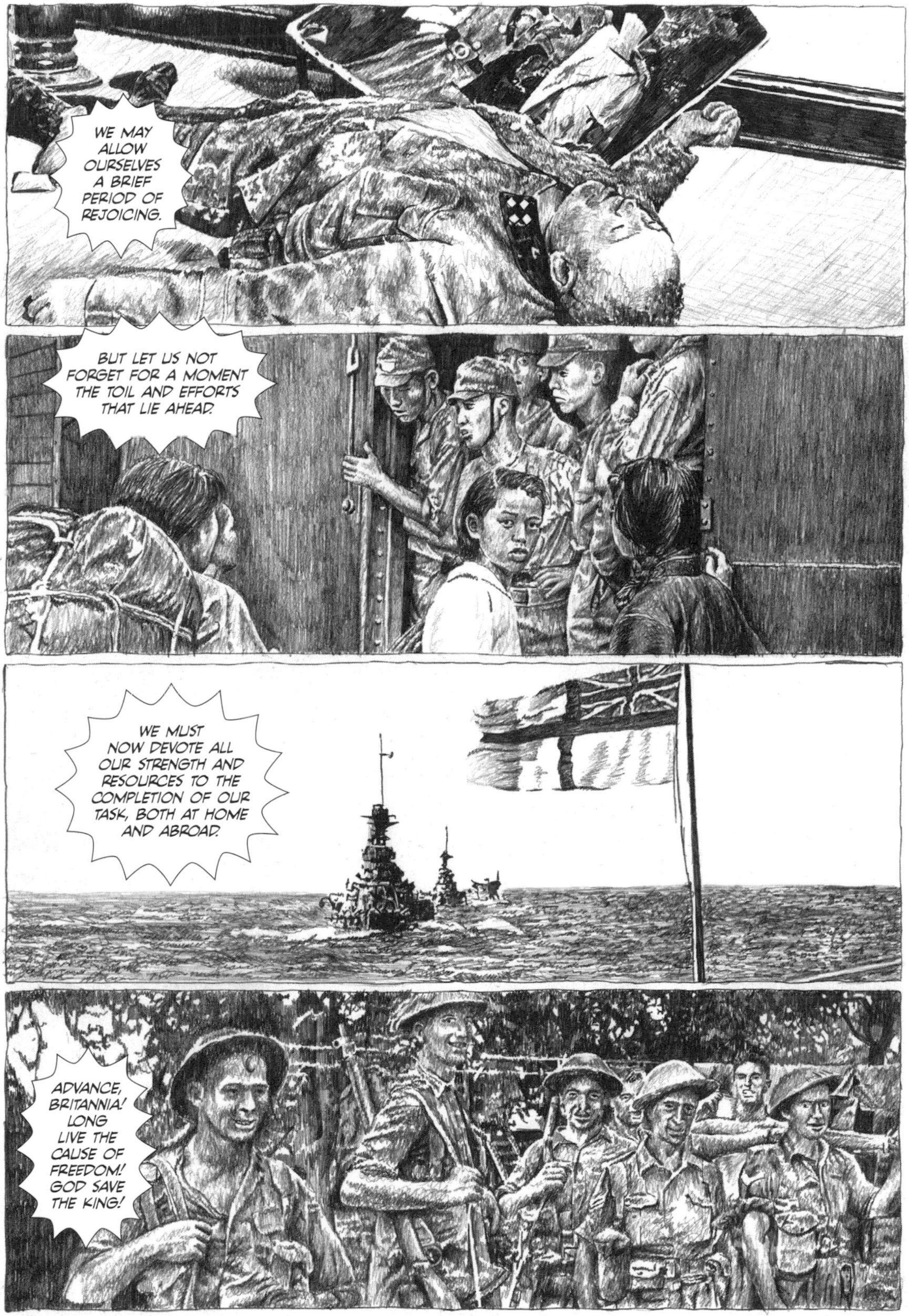
WE MAY ALLOW OURSELVES A BRIEF PERIOD OF REJOICING.
BUT LET US NOT FORGET FOR A MOMENT THE TOIL AND EFFORTS THAT LIE AHEAD.
WE MUST NOW DEVOTE ALL OUR STRENGTH AND RESOURCES TO THE COMPLETION OF OUR TASK, BOTH AT HOME AND ABROAD.
ADVANCE, BRITANNIA! LONG LIVE THE CAUSE OF FREEDOM! GOD SAVE THE KING!

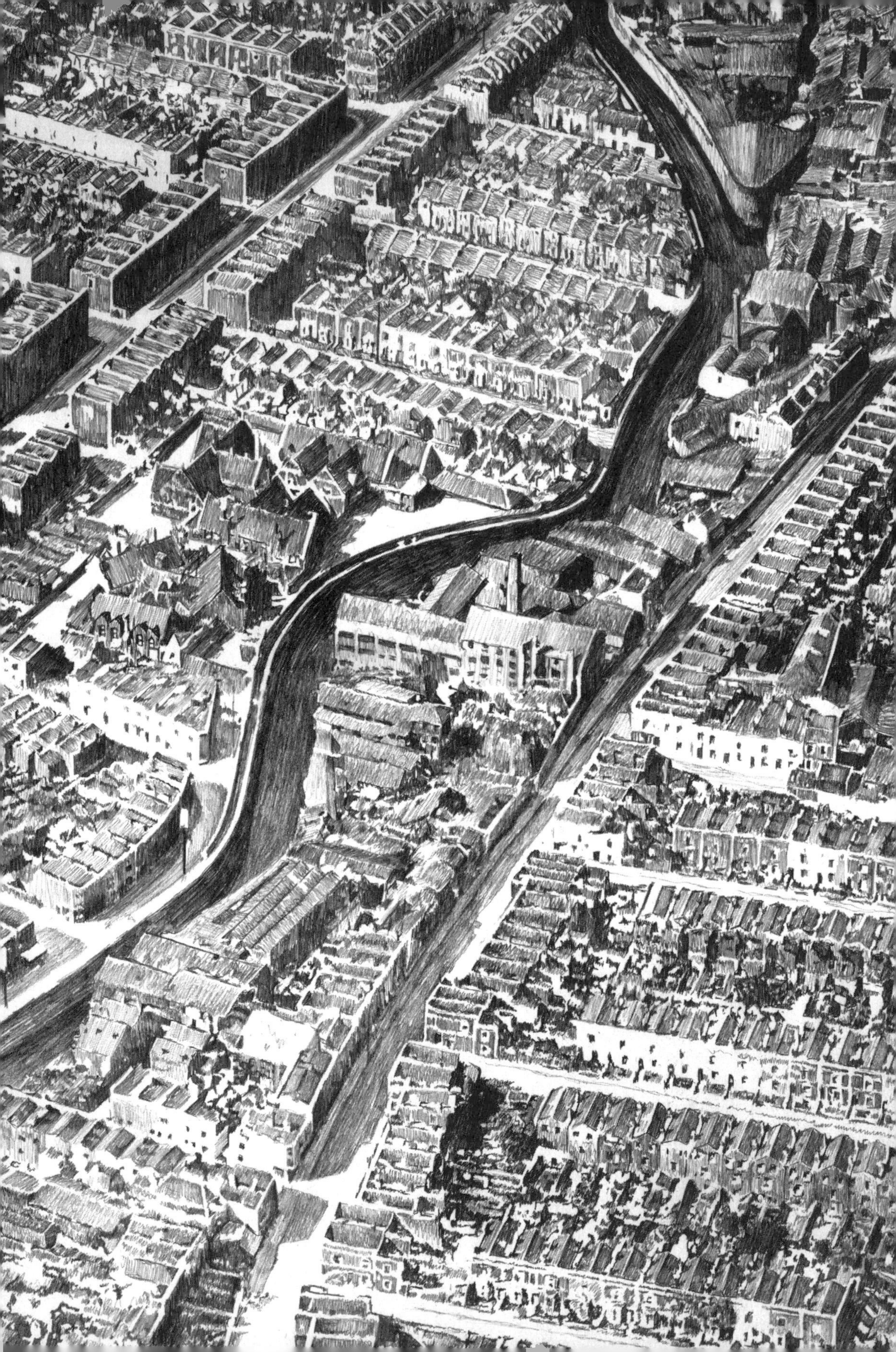

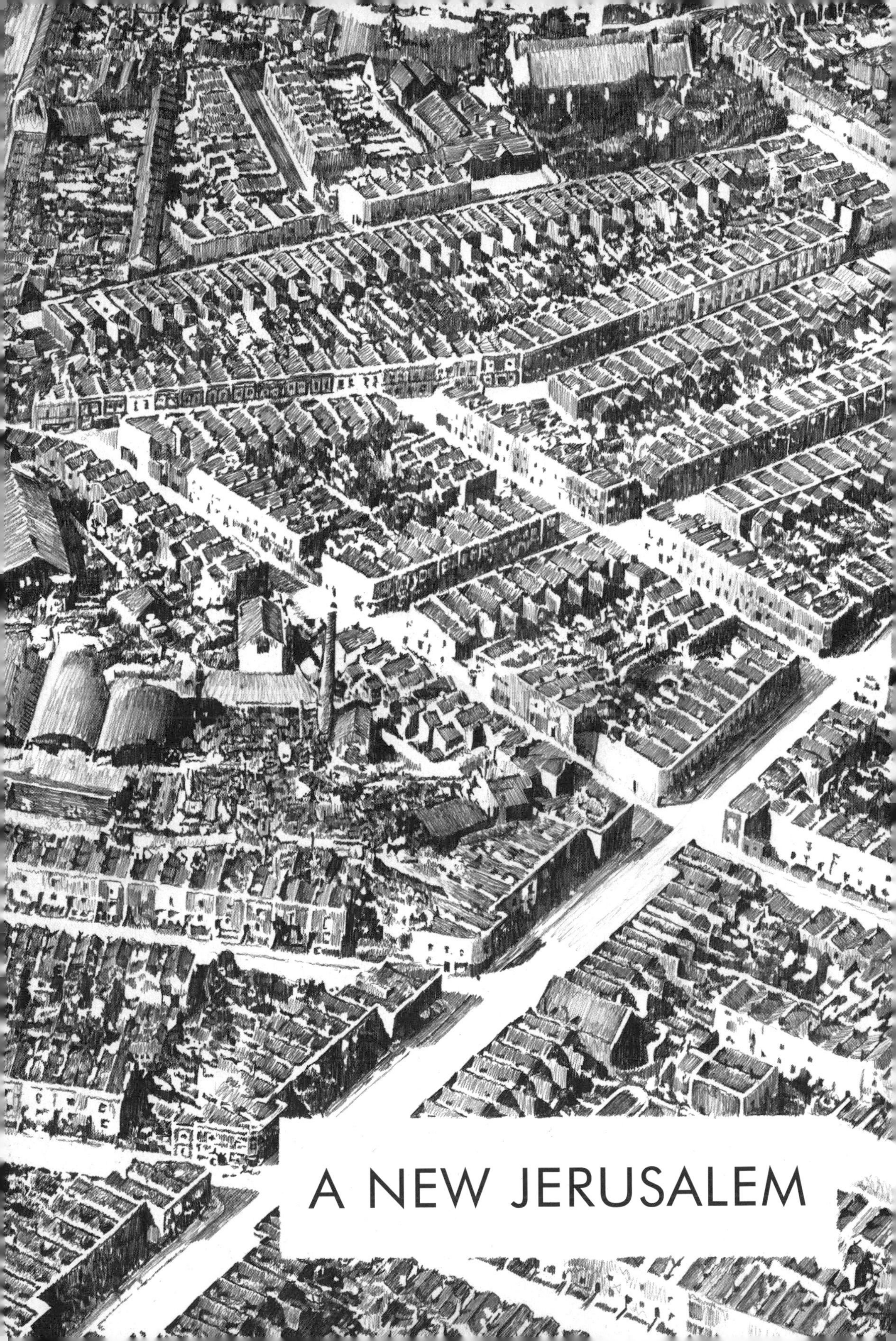

A NEW JERUSALEM

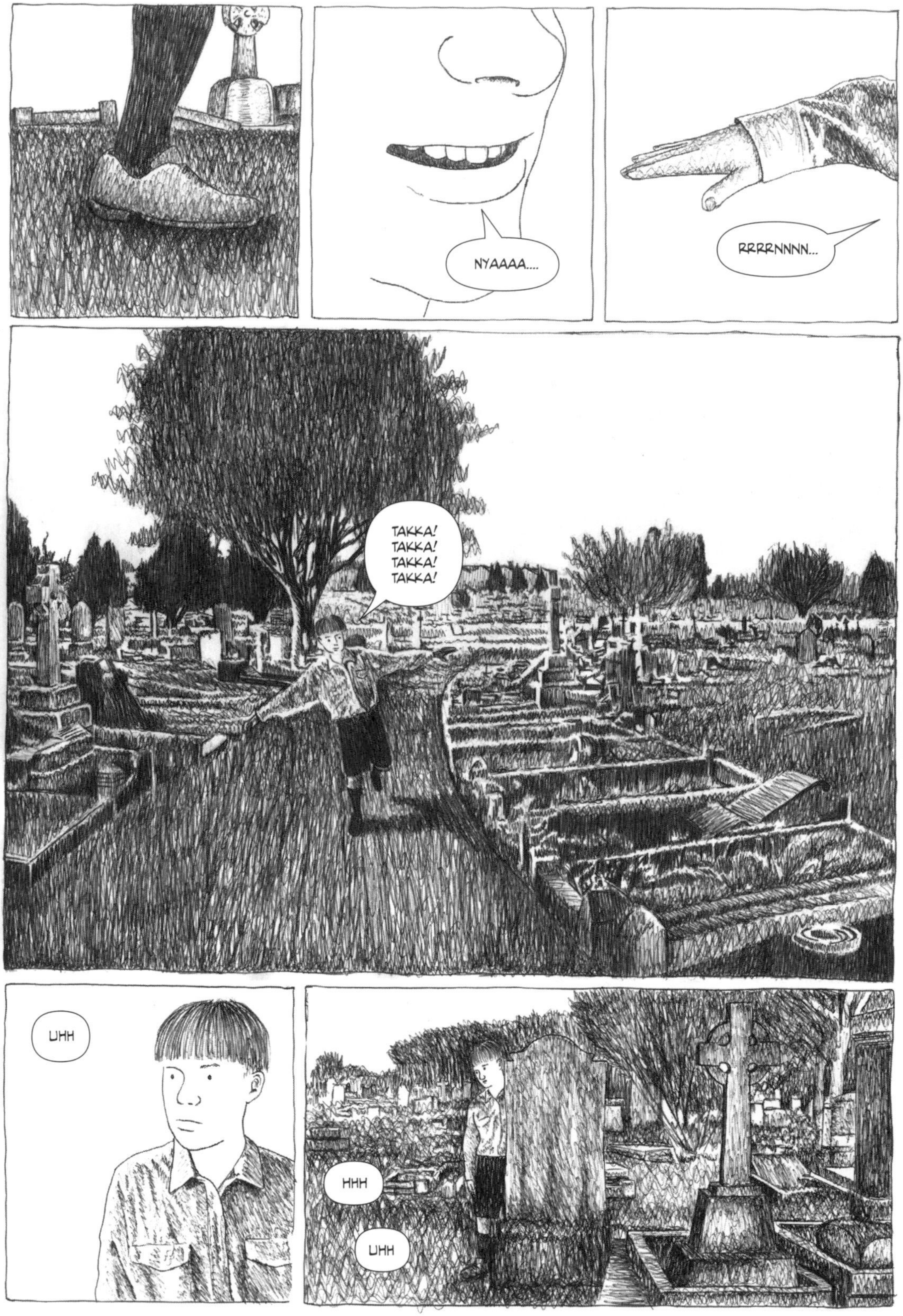
NYAAAA....
RRRRNNNN...
TAKKA! TAKKA! TAKKA! TAKKA!
UHH
HHH
UHH

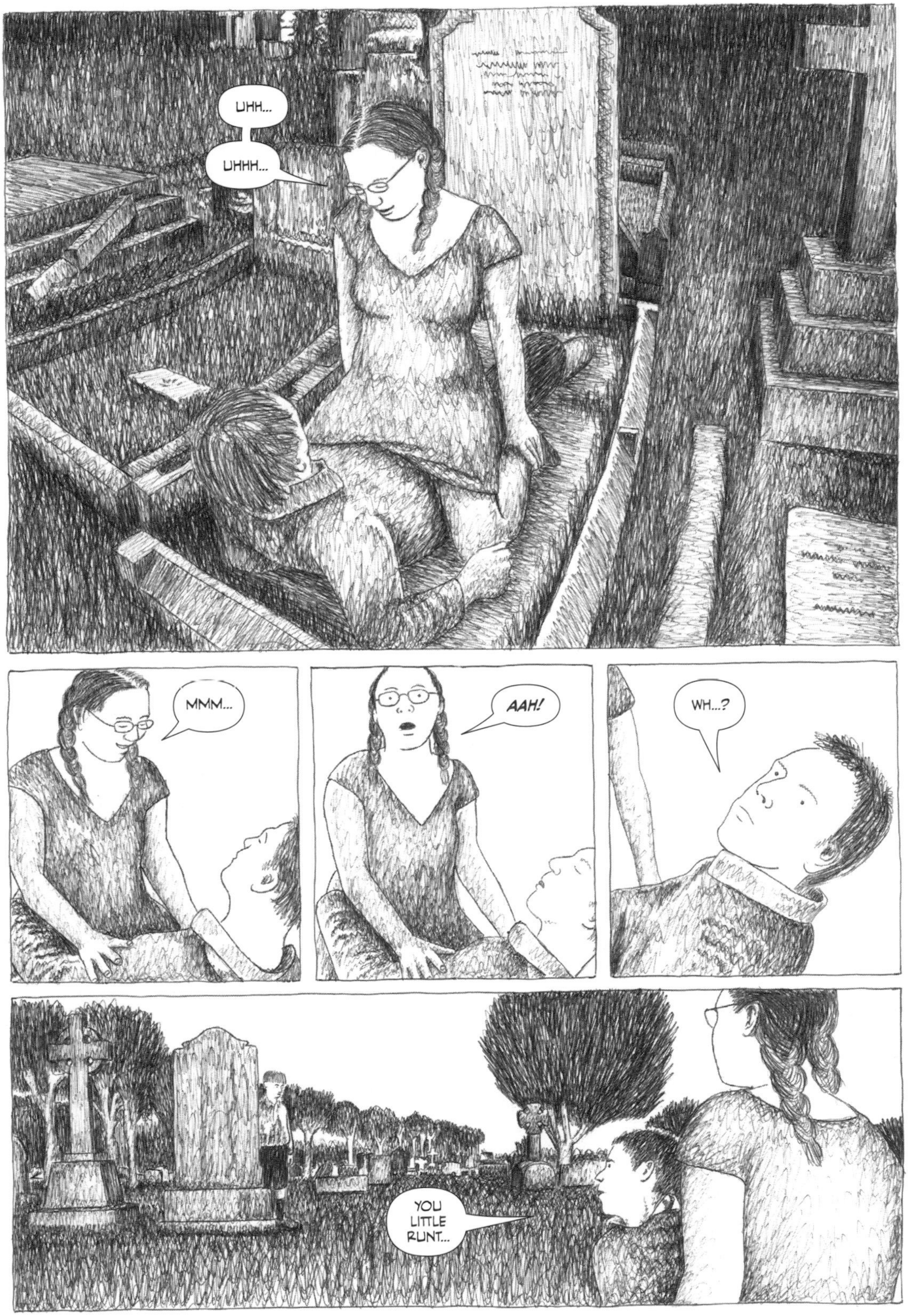
UHH...
UHHH...
MMM...
AAH!
WH...?
YOU LITTLE RUNT...

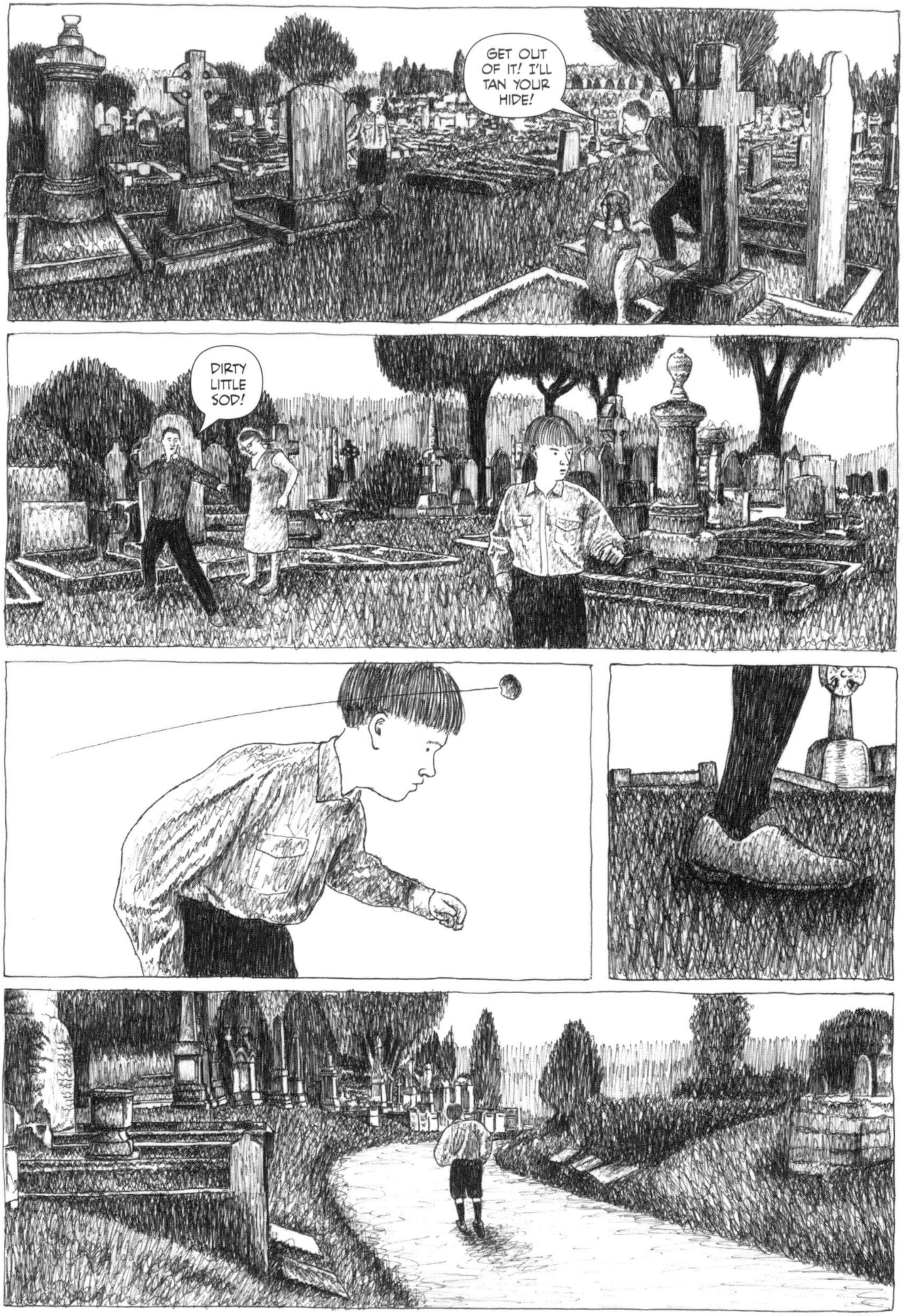
GET OUT OF IT! I'LL TAN YOUR HIDE!
DIRTY LITTLE SOD!

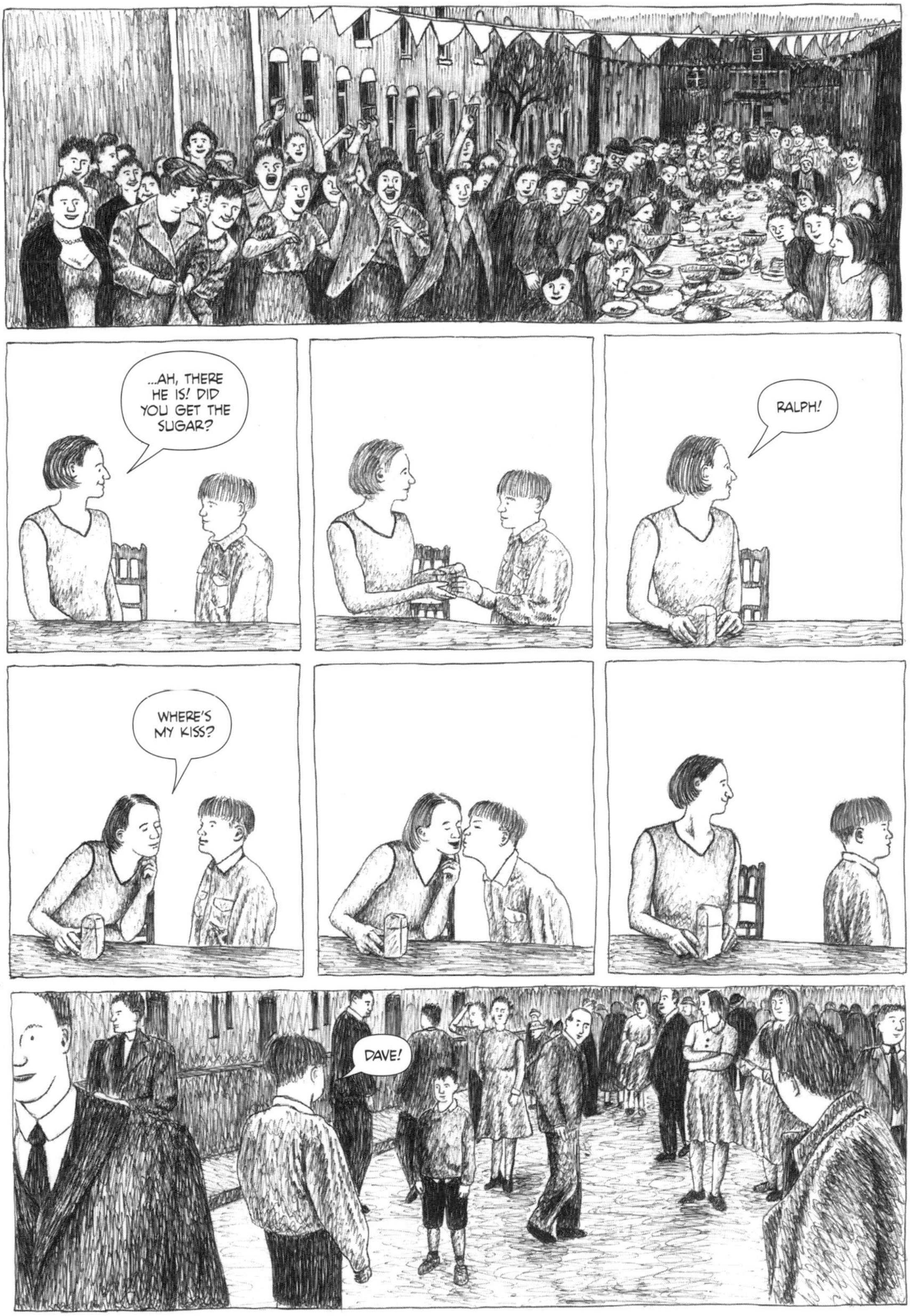
...AH, THERE HE IS! DID YOU GET THE SUGAR?
RALPH!
WHERE'S MY KISS?
DAVE!

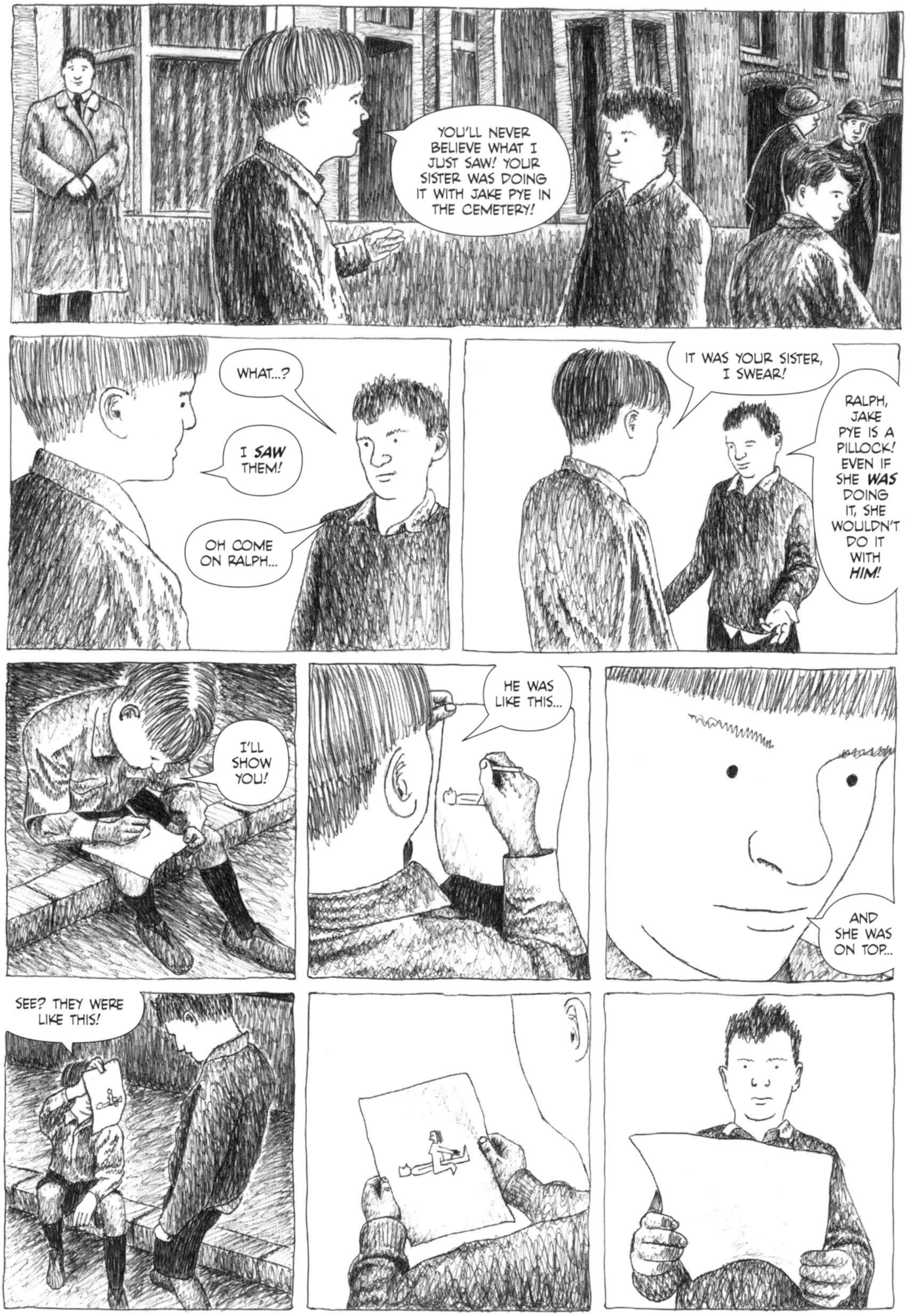
YOU'LL NEVER BELIEVE WHAT I JUST SAW! YOUR SISTER WAS DOING IT WITH JAKE PYE IN THE CEMETERY!
WHAT...?
I SAW THEM!
OH COME ON RALPH...
IT WAS YOUR SISTER, I SWEAR!
RALPH, JAKE PYE IS A PILLOCK! EVEN IF SHE WAS DOING IT, SHE WOULDN'T DO IT WITH HIM!
I'LL SHOW YOU!
HE WAS LIKE THIS...
AND SHE WAS ON TOP...
SEE? THEY WERE LIKE THIS!

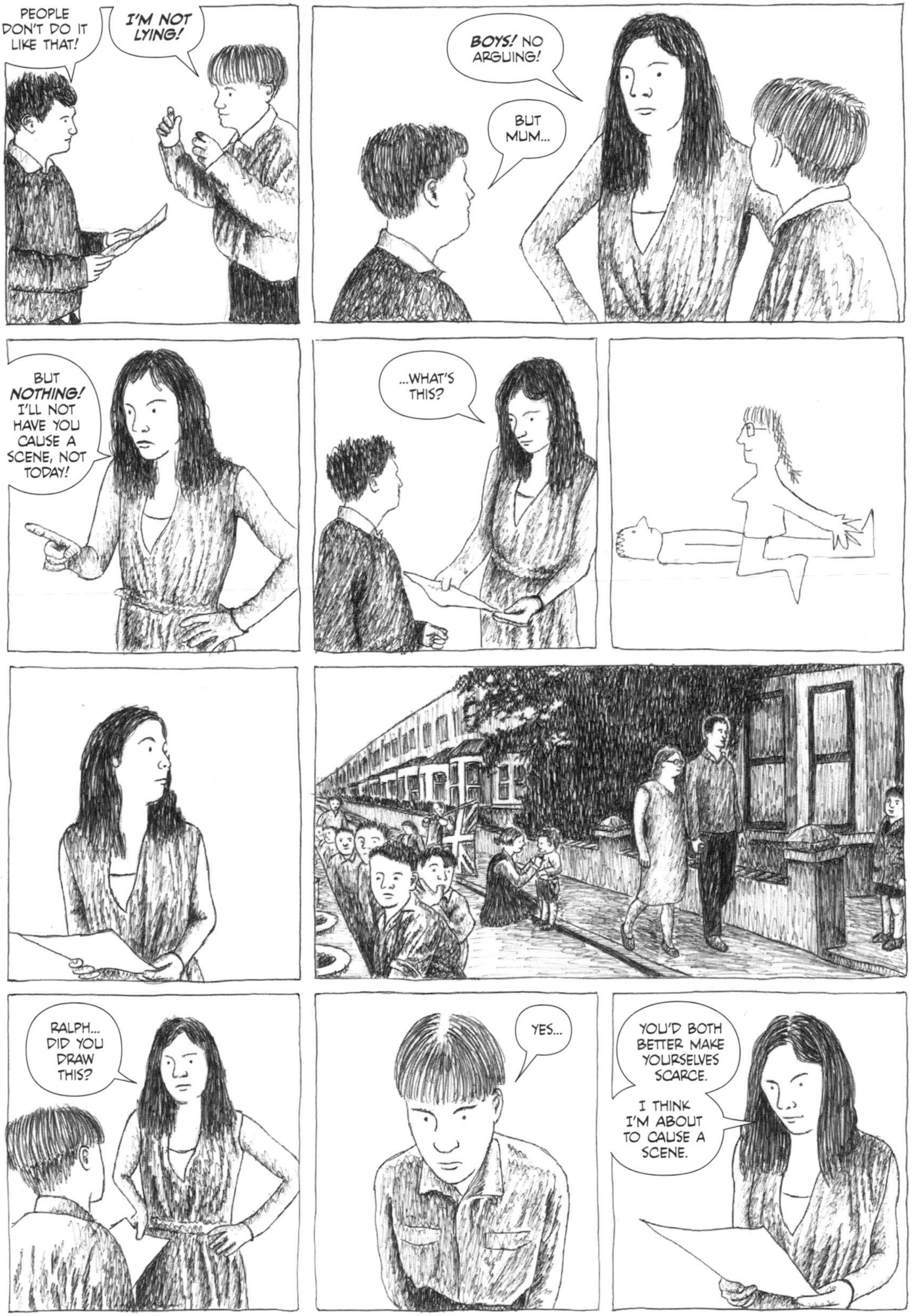
PEOPLE DON'T DO IT LIKE THAT!
I'M NOT LYING!
BOYS! NO ARGUING!
BUT MUM...
BUT NOTHING! I'LL NOT HAVE YOU CAUSE A SCENE, NOT TODAY!
...WHAT'S THIS?
RALPH... DID YOU DRAW THIS?
YES...
YOU'D BOTH BETTER MAKE YOURSELVES SCARCE.
I THINK I'M ABOUT TO CAUSE A SCENE.

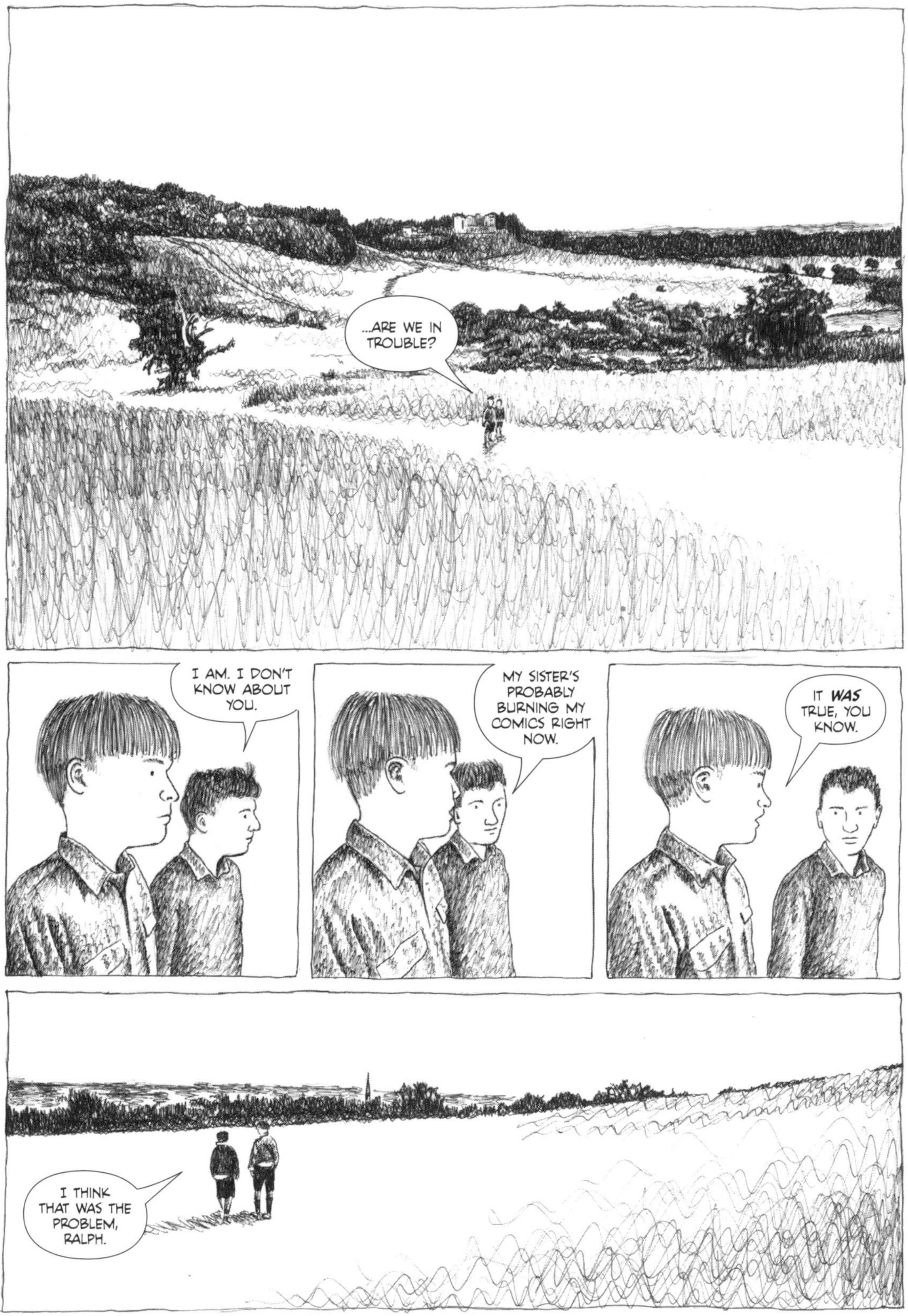
...ARE WE IN TROUBLE?
I AM. I DON'T KNOW ABOUT YOU.
MY SISTER'S PROBABLY BURNING MY COMICS RIGHT NOW.
IT **WAS** TRUE, YOU KNOW.
I THINK THAT WAS THE PROBLEM, RALPH.

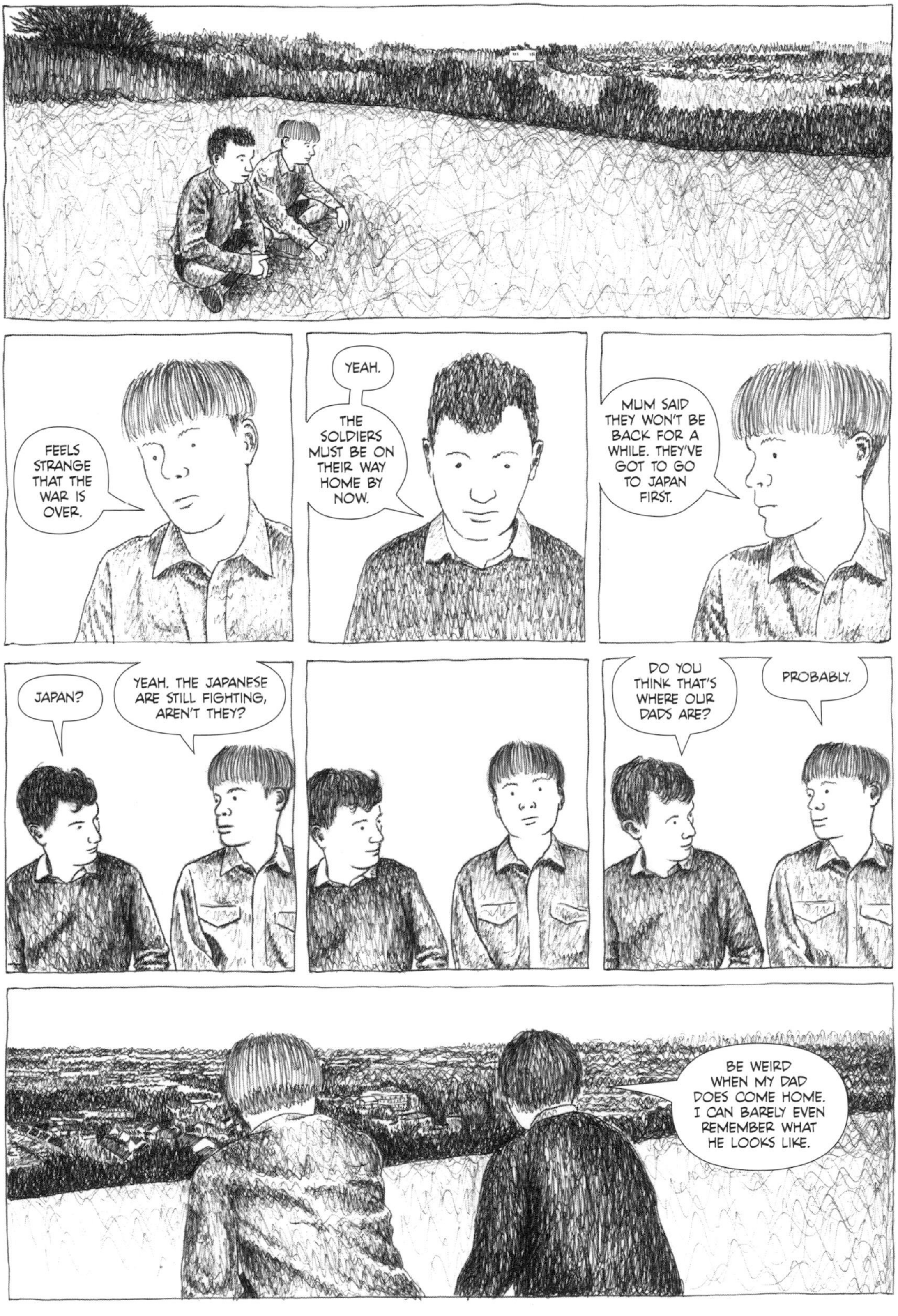
FEELS STRANGE THAT THE WAR IS OVER.
YEAH.
THE SOLDIERS MUST BE ON THEIR WAY HOME BY NOW.
MUM SAID THEY WON'T BE BACK FOR A WHILE. THEY'VE GOT TO GO TO JAPAN FIRST.
JAPAN?
YEAH. THE JAPANESE ARE STILL FIGHTING, AREN'T THEY?
DO YOU THINK THAT'S WHERE OUR DADS ARE?
PROBABLY.
BE WEIRD WHEN MY DAD DOES COME HOME. I CAN BARELY EVEN REMEMBER WHAT HE LOOKS LIKE.

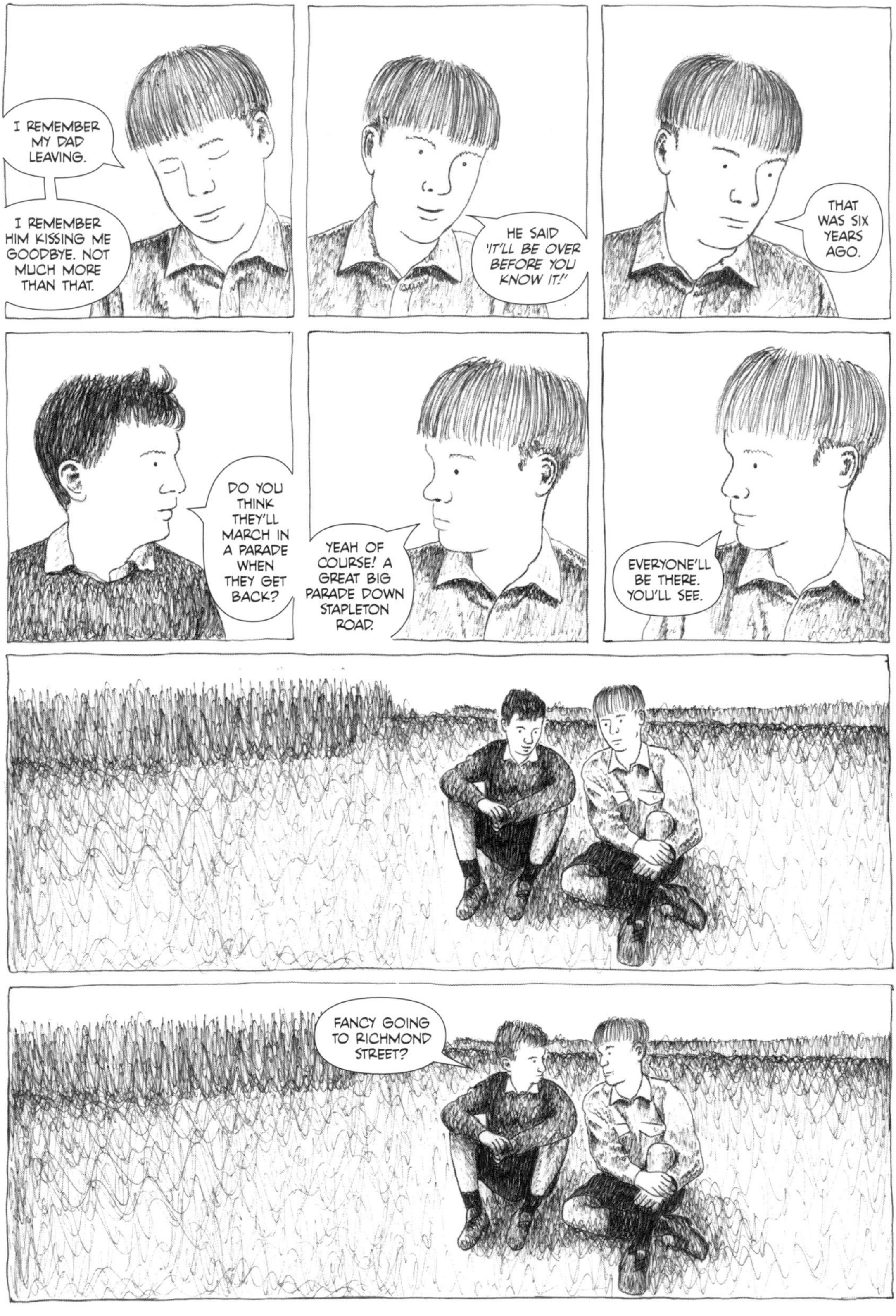
I REMEMBER MY DAD LEAVING.
I REMEMBER HIM KISSING ME GOODBYE. NOT MUCH MORE THAN THAT.
HE SAID 'IT'LL BE OVER BEFORE YOU KNOW IT!'
THAT WAS SIX YEARS AGO.
DO YOU THINK THEY'LL MARCH IN A PARADE WHEN THEY GET BACK?
YEAH OF COURSE! A GREAT BIG PARADE DOWN STAPLETON ROAD.
EVERYONE'LL BE THERE. YOU'LL SEE.
FANCY GOING TO RICHMOND STREET?

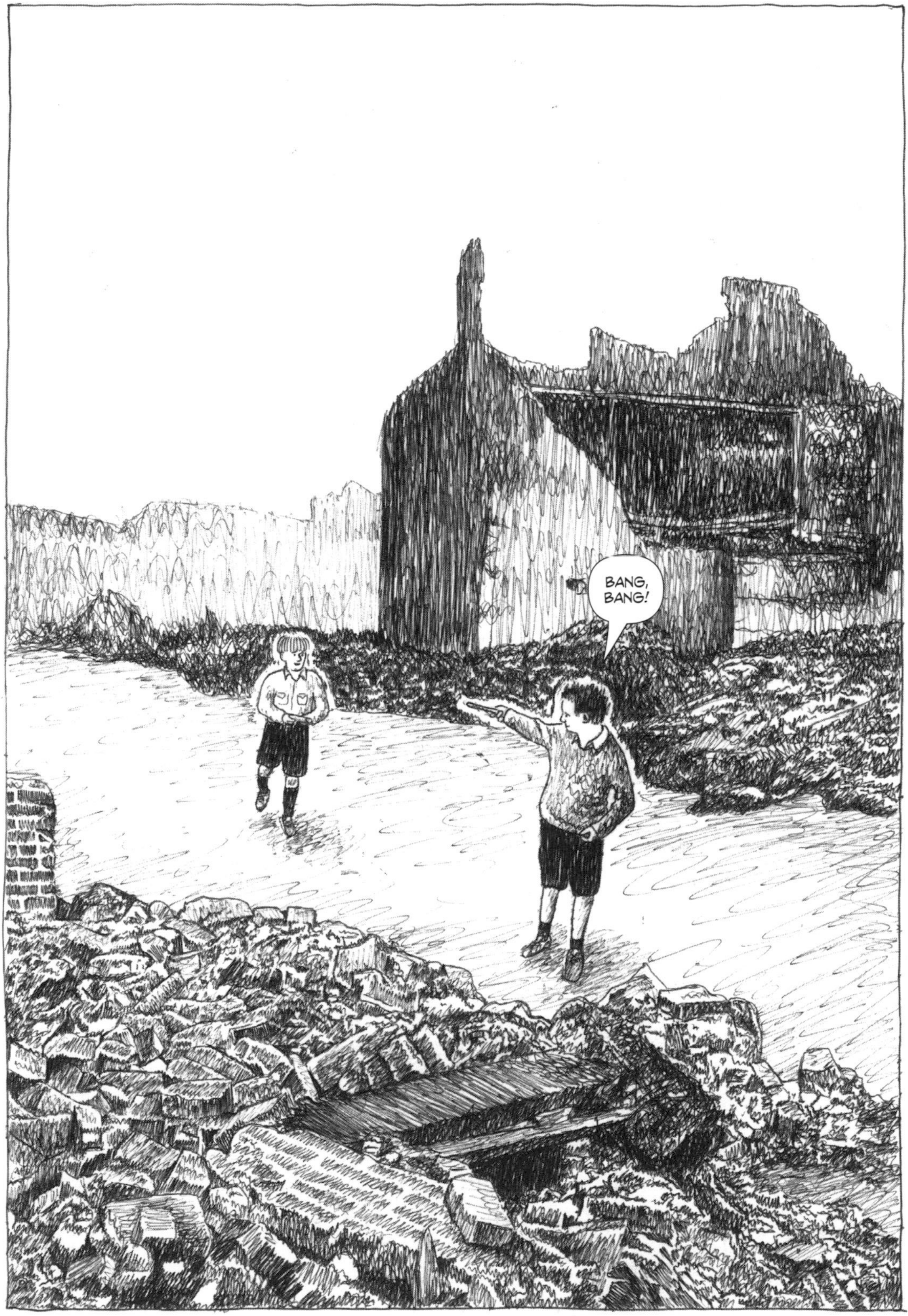
BANG, BANG!

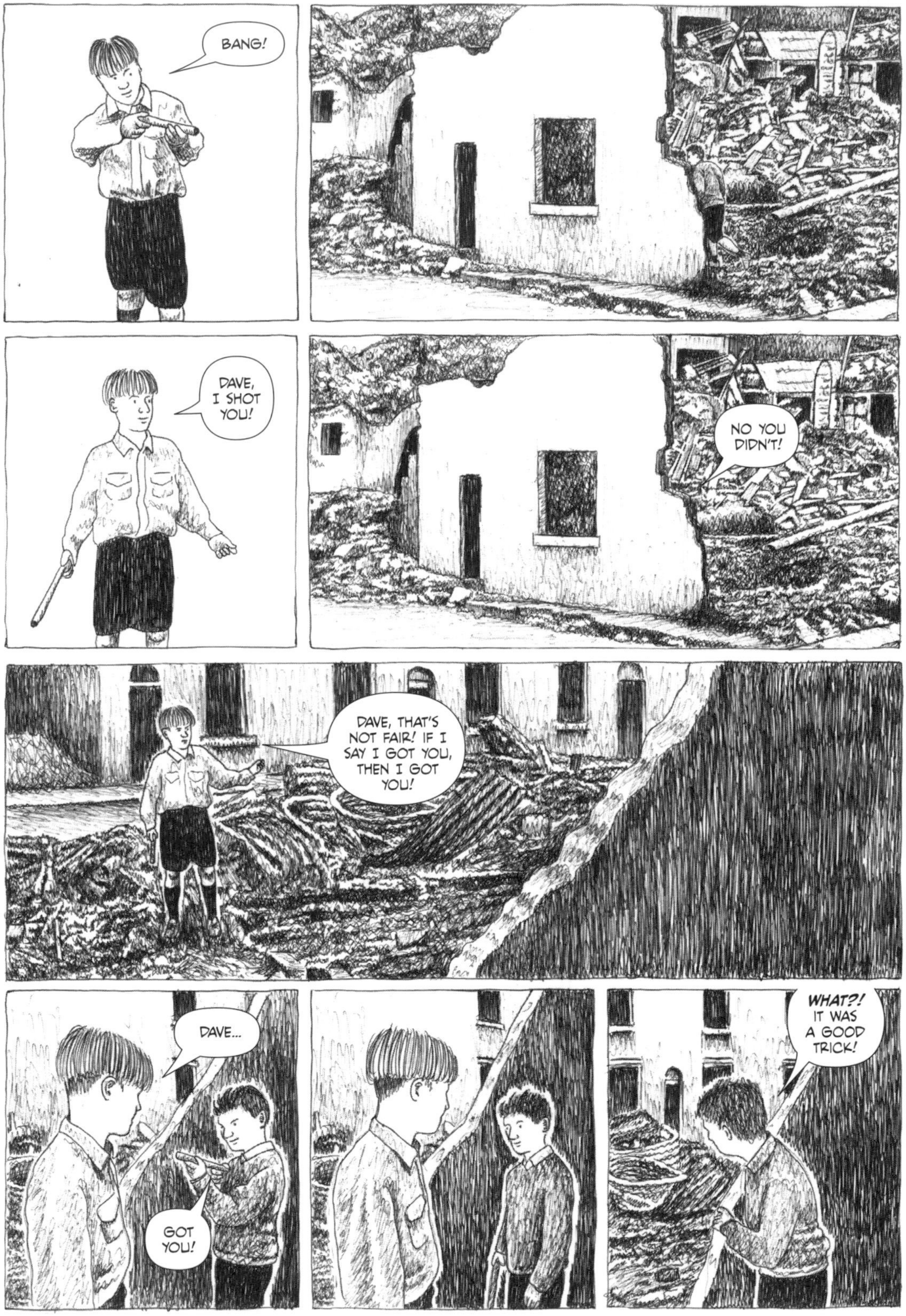
BANG!
DAVE, I SHOT YOU!
NO YOU DIDN'T!
DAVE, THAT'S NOT FAIR! IF I SAY I GOT YOU, THEN I GOT YOU!
DAVE...
GOT YOU!
WHAT?! IT WAS A GOOD TRICK!

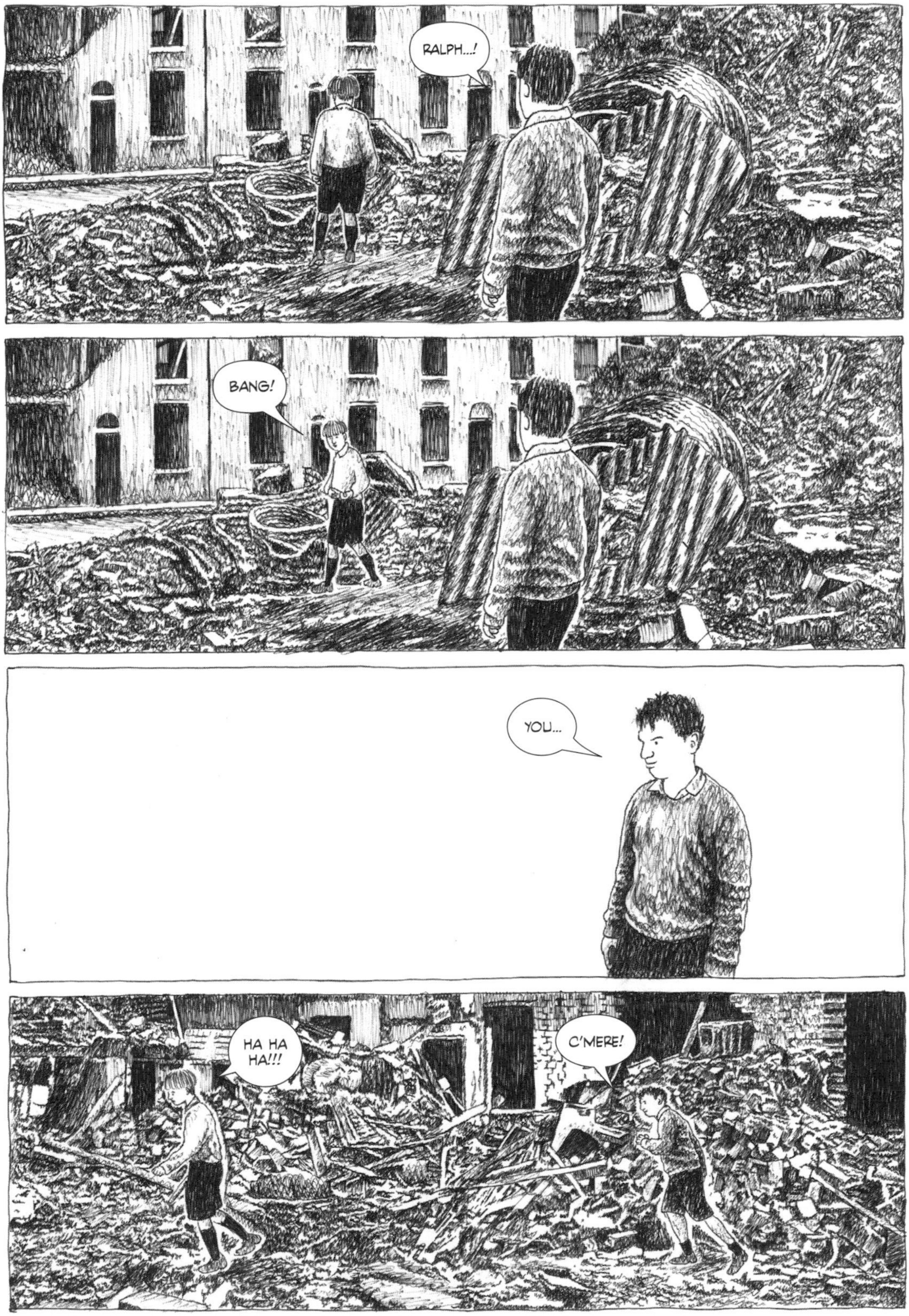
RALPH...!
BANG!
YOU...
HA HA HA!!!
C'MERE!

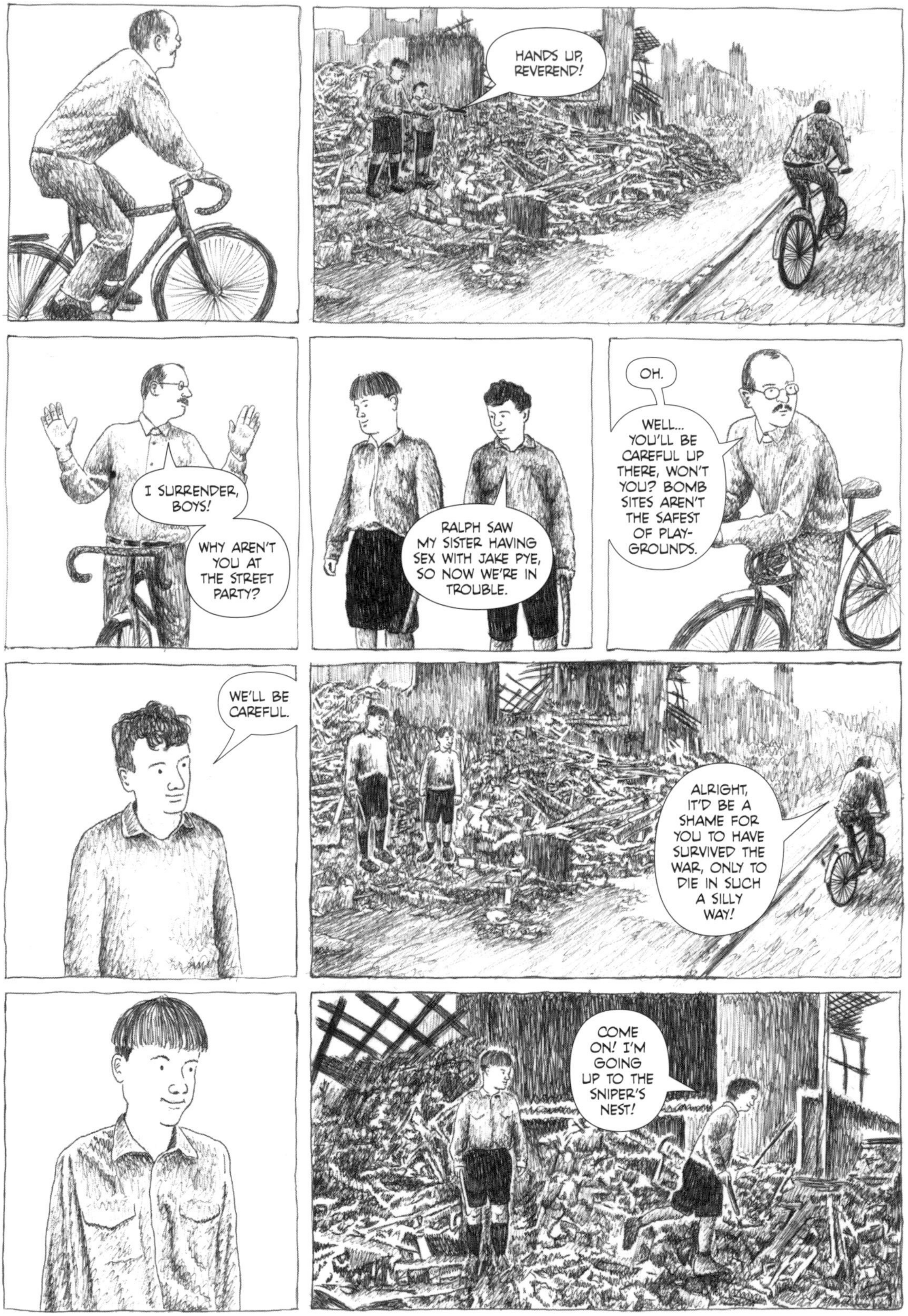
HANDS UP, REVEREND!
I SURRENDER, BOYS!
WHY AREN'T YOU AT THE STREET PARTY?
RALPH SAW MY SISTER HAVING SEX WITH JAKE PYE, SO NOW WE'RE IN TROUBLE.
OH.
WELL... YOU'LL BE CAREFUL UP THERE, WON'T YOU? BOMB SITES AREN'T THE SAFEST OF PLAY-GROUNDS.
WE'LL BE CAREFUL.
ALRIGHT, IT'D BE A SHAME FOR YOU TO HAVE SURVIVED THE WAR, ONLY TO DIE IN SUCH A SILLY WAY!
COME ON! I'M GOING UP TO THE SNIPER'S NEST!

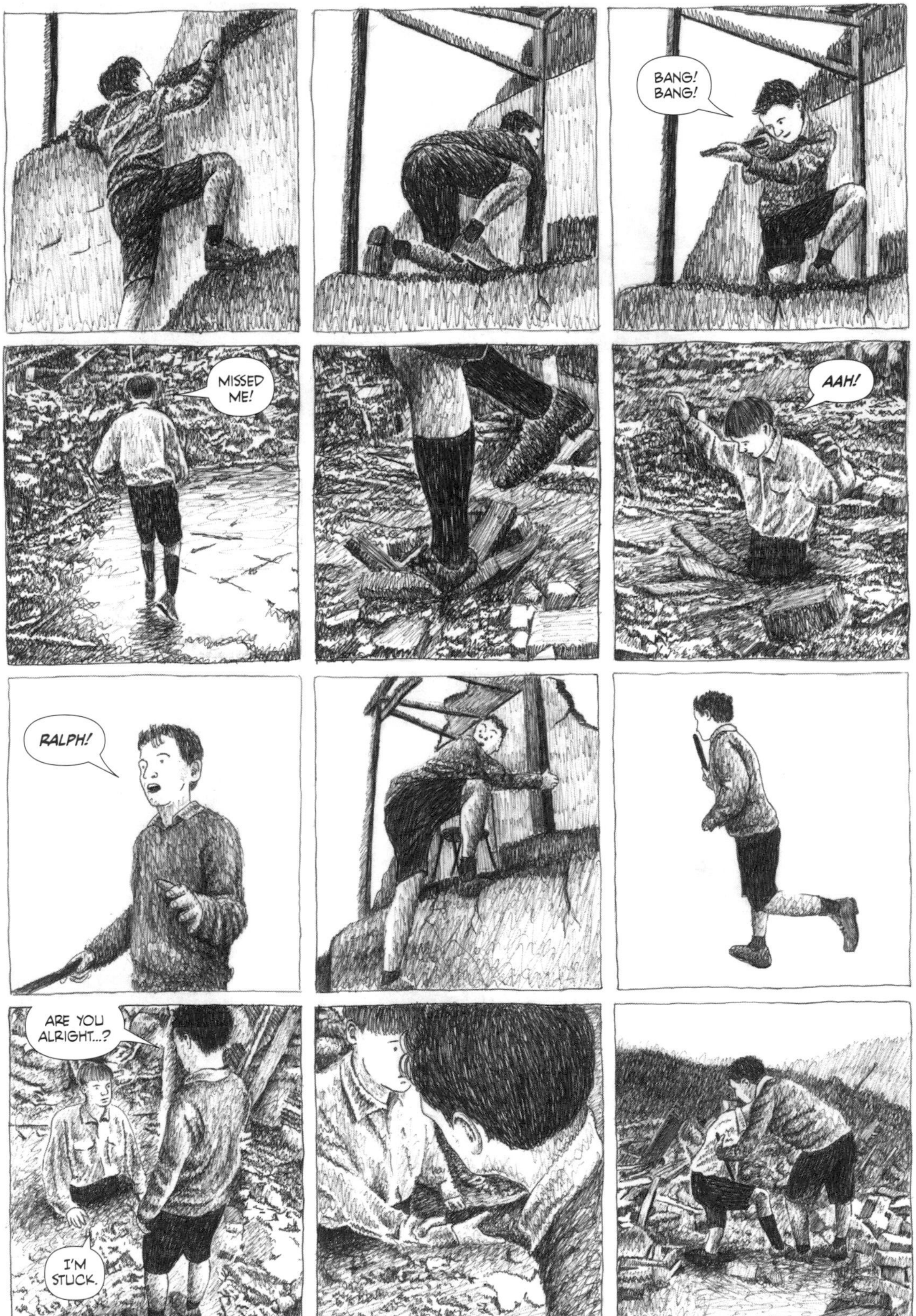
BANG! BANG!
MISSED ME!
AAH!
RALPH!
ARE YOU ALRIGHT...?
I'M STUCK.

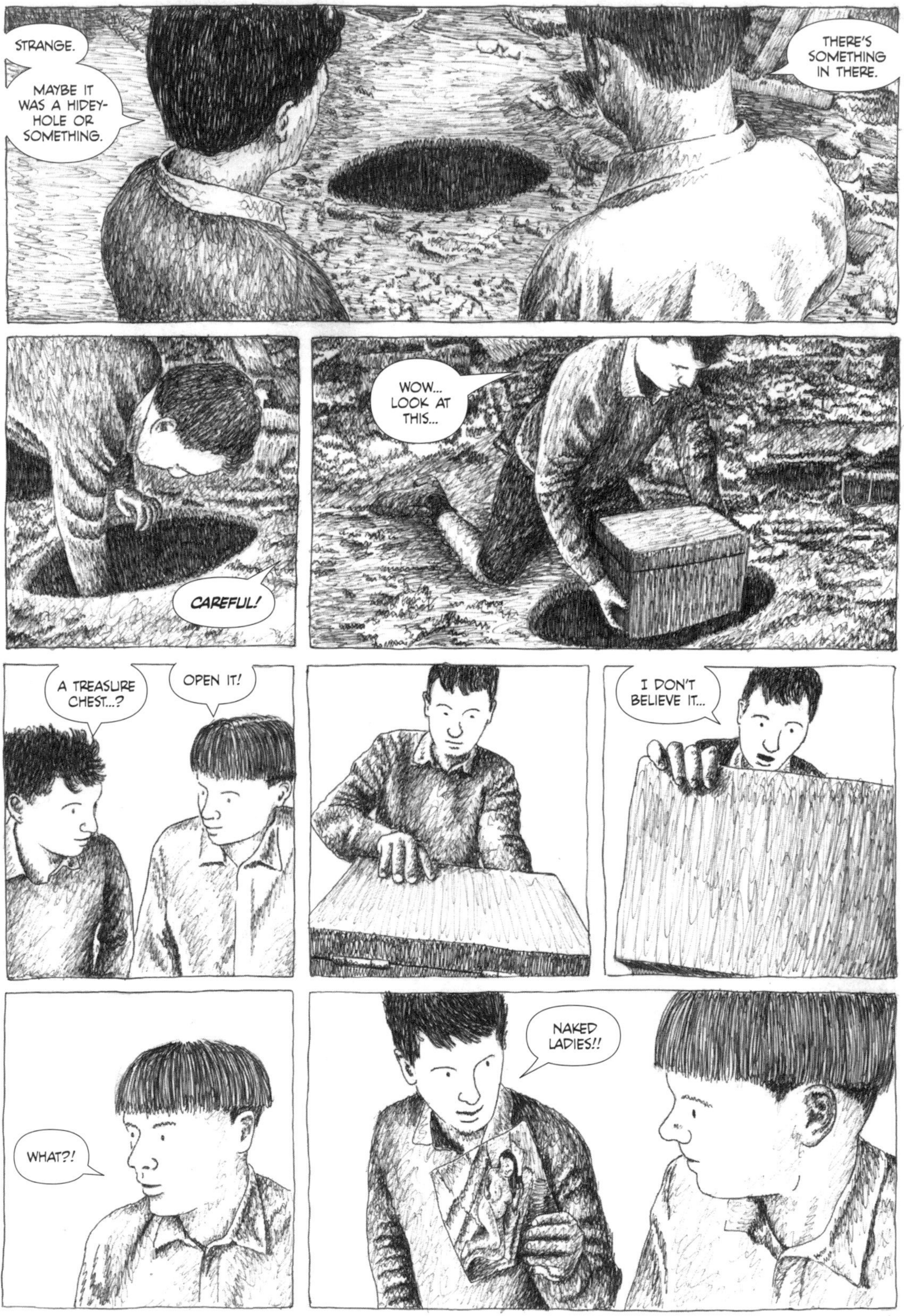
STRANGE.
MAYBE IT WAS A HIDEY-HOLE OR SOMETHING.
THERE'S SOMETHING IN THERE.
CAREFUL!
WOW... LOOK AT THIS...
A TREASURE CHEST...?
OPEN IT!
I DON'T BELIEVE IT...
WHAT?!
NAKED LADIES!!

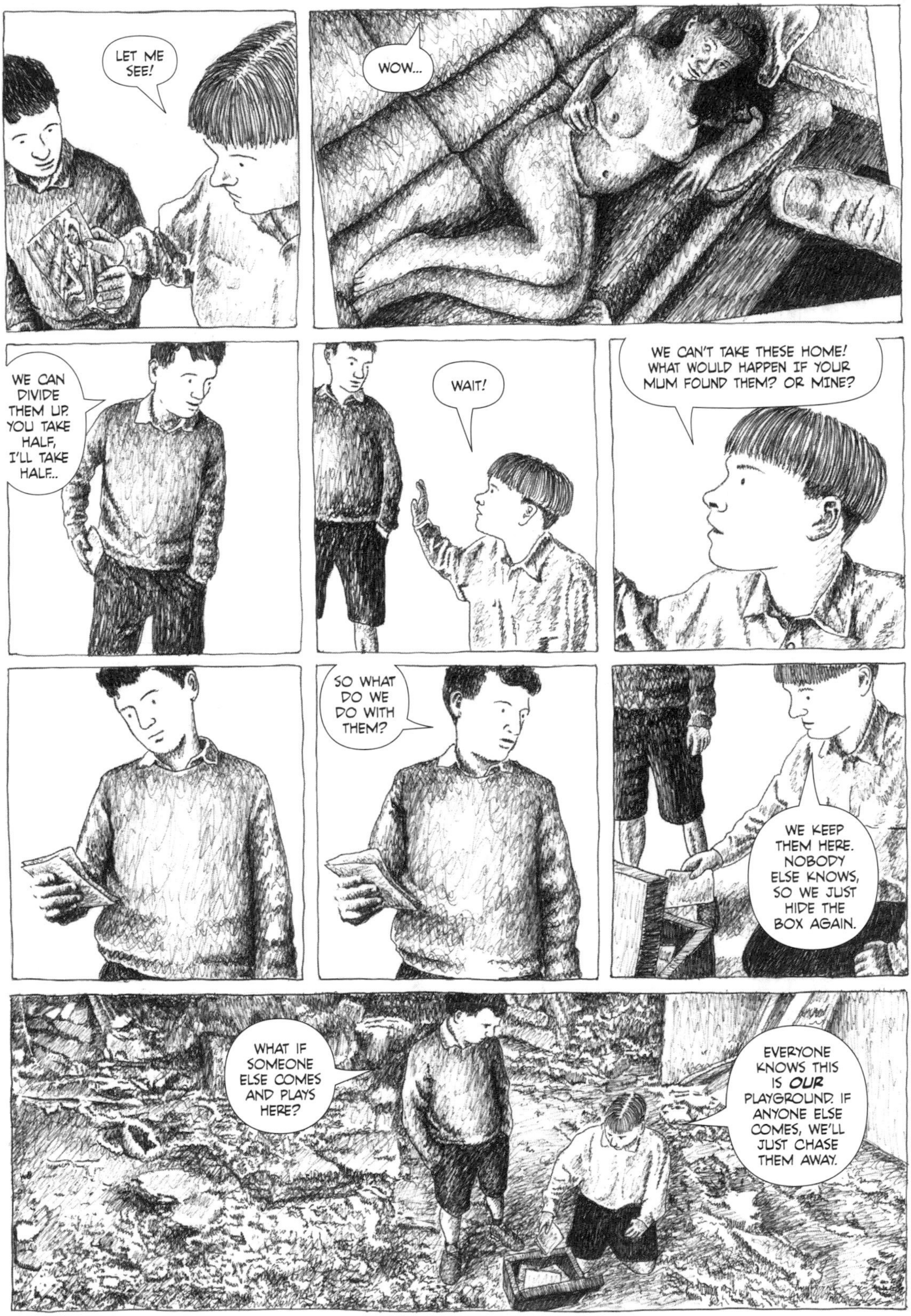
LET ME SEE!
WOW...
WE CAN DIVIDE THEM UP. YOU TAKE HALF, I'LL TAKE HALF...
WAIT!
WE CAN'T TAKE THESE HOME! WHAT WOULD HAPPEN IF YOUR MUM FOUND THEM? OR MINE?
SO WHAT DO WE DO WITH THEM?
WE KEEP THEM HERE. NOBODY ELSE KNOWS, SO WE JUST HIDE THE BOX AGAIN.
WHAT IF SOMEONE ELSE COMES AND PLAYS HERE?
EVERYONE KNOWS THIS IS ***OUR*** PLAYGROUND. IF ANYONE ELSE COMES, WE'LL JUST CHASE THEM AWAY.

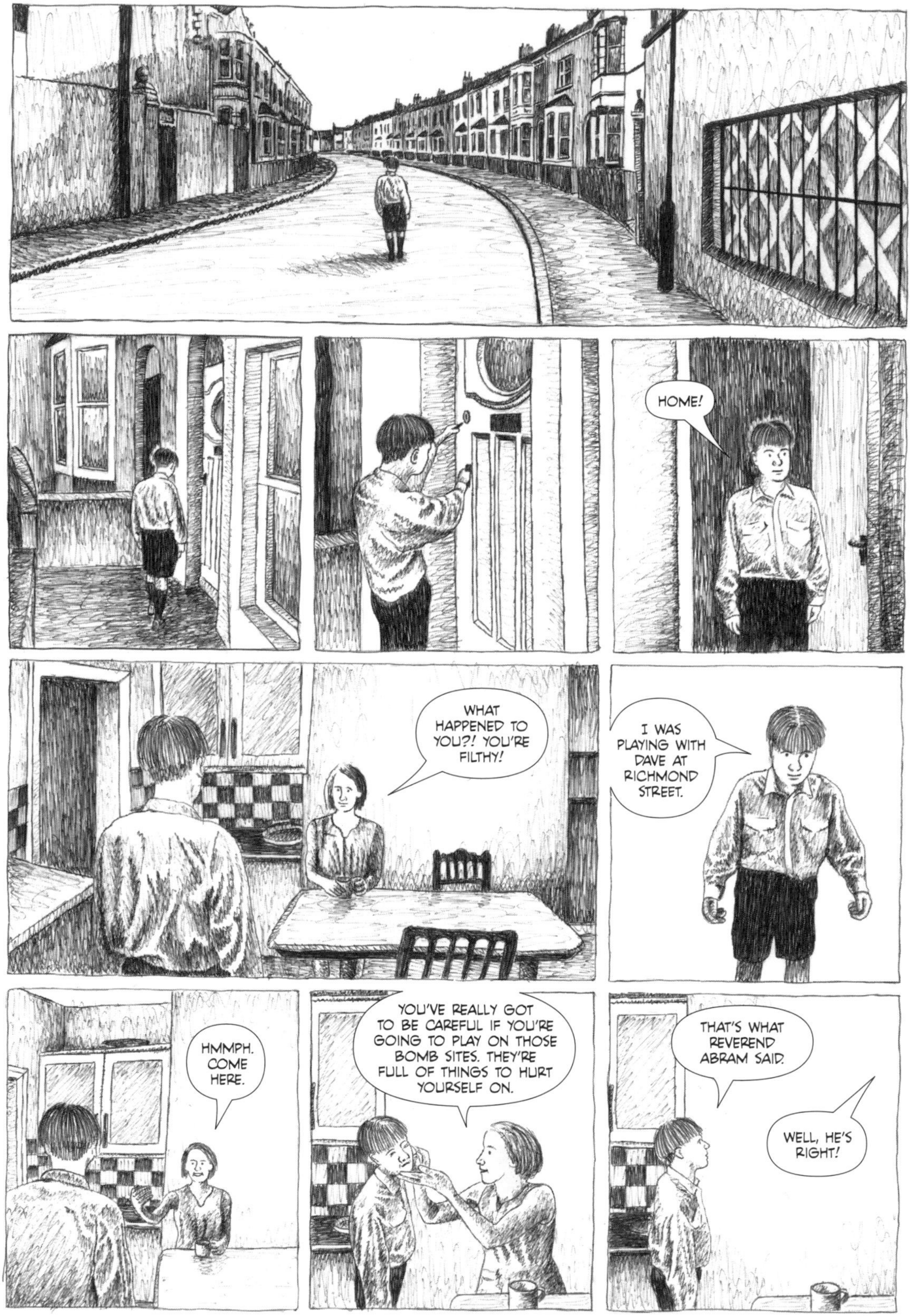
HOME!
WHAT HAPPENED TO YOU?! YOU'RE FILTHY!
I WAS PLAYING WITH DAVE AT RICHMOND STREET.
HMMPH. COME HERE.
YOU'VE REALLY GOT TO BE CAREFUL IF YOU'RE GOING TO PLAY ON THOSE BOMB SITES. THEY'RE FULL OF THINGS TO HURT YOURSELF ON.
THAT'S WHAT REVEREND ABRAM SAID.
WELL, HE'S RIGHT!

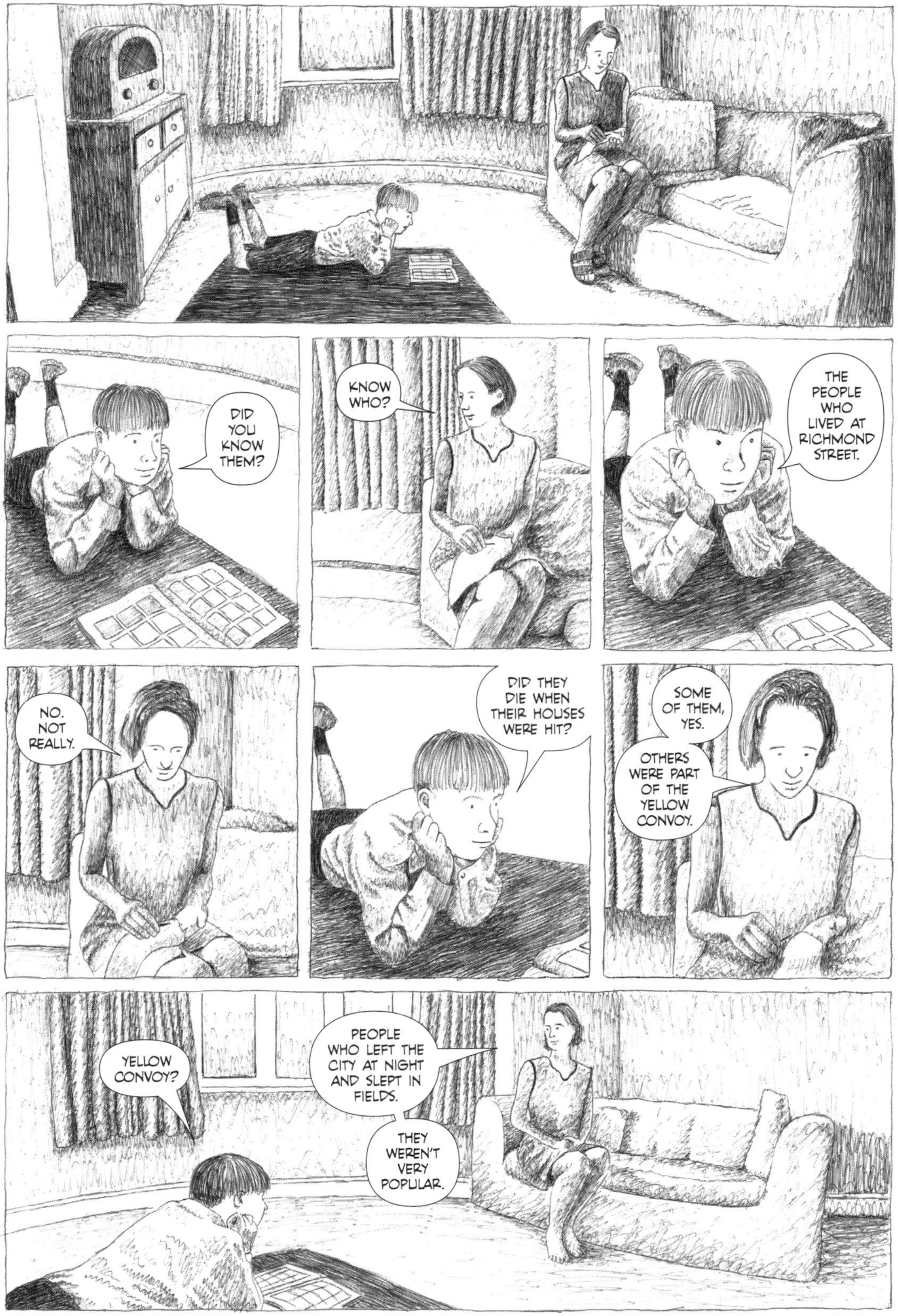
DID YOU KNOW THEM?
KNOW WHO?
THE PEOPLE WHO LIVED AT RICHMOND STREET.
NO. NOT REALLY.
DID THEY DIE WHEN THEIR HOUSES WERE HIT?
SOME OF THEM, YES.
OTHERS WERE PART OF THE YELLOW CONVOY.
YELLOW CONVOY?
PEOPLE WHO LEFT THE CITY AT NIGHT AND SLEPT IN FIELDS.
THEY WEREN'T VERY POPULAR.

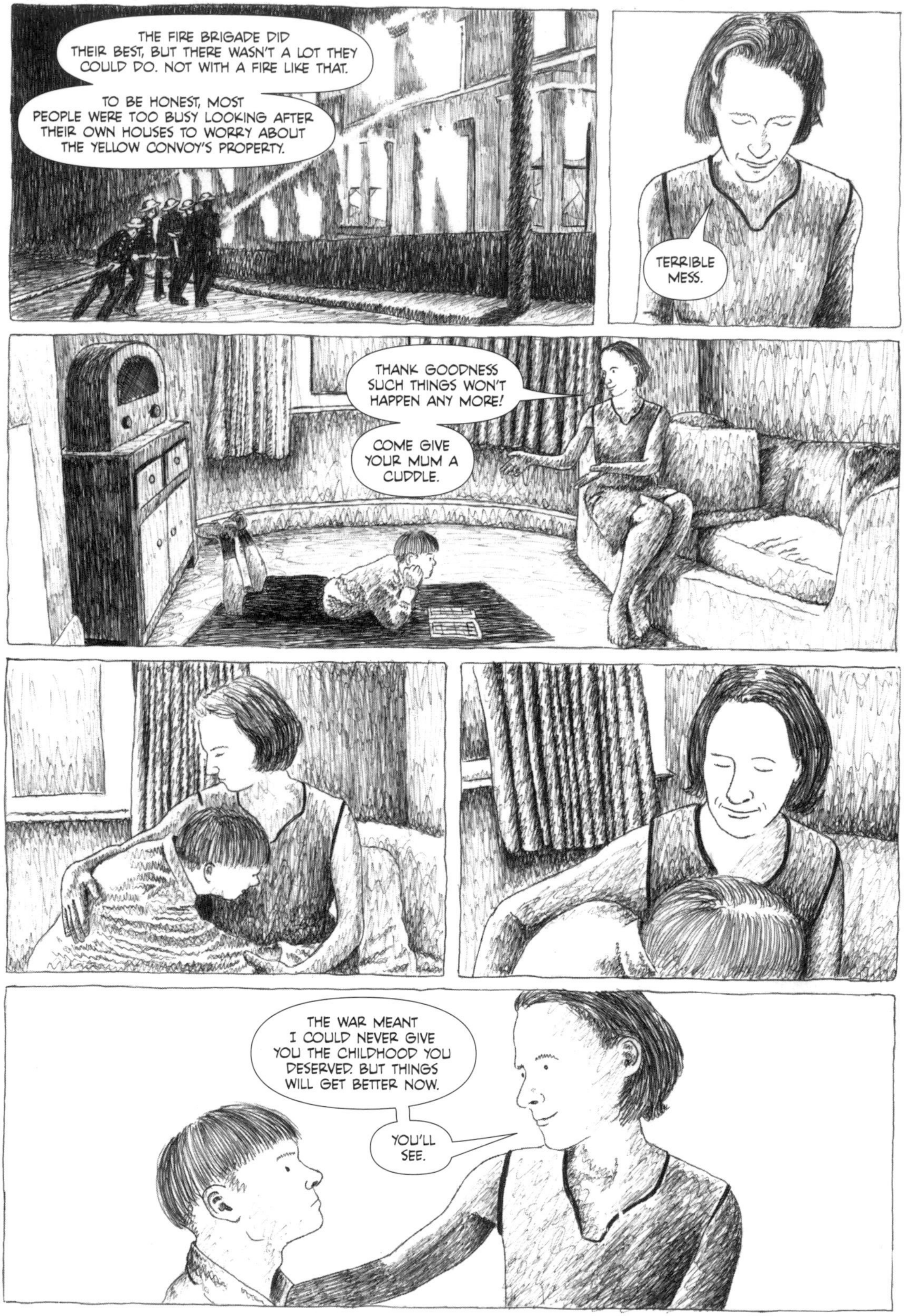
THE FIRE BRIGADE DID THEIR BEST, BUT THERE WASN'T A LOT THEY COULD DO. NOT WITH A FIRE LIKE THAT.
TO BE HONEST, MOST PEOPLE WERE TOO BUSY LOOKING AFTER THEIR OWN HOUSES TO WORRY ABOUT THE YELLOW CONVOY'S PROPERTY.
TERRIBLE MESS.
THANK GOODNESS SUCH THINGS WON'T HAPPEN ANY MORE!
COME GIVE YOUR MUM A CUDDLE.
THE WAR MEANT I COULD NEVER GIVE YOU THE CHILDHOOD YOU DESERVED. BUT THINGS WILL GET BETTER NOW.
YOU'LL SEE.

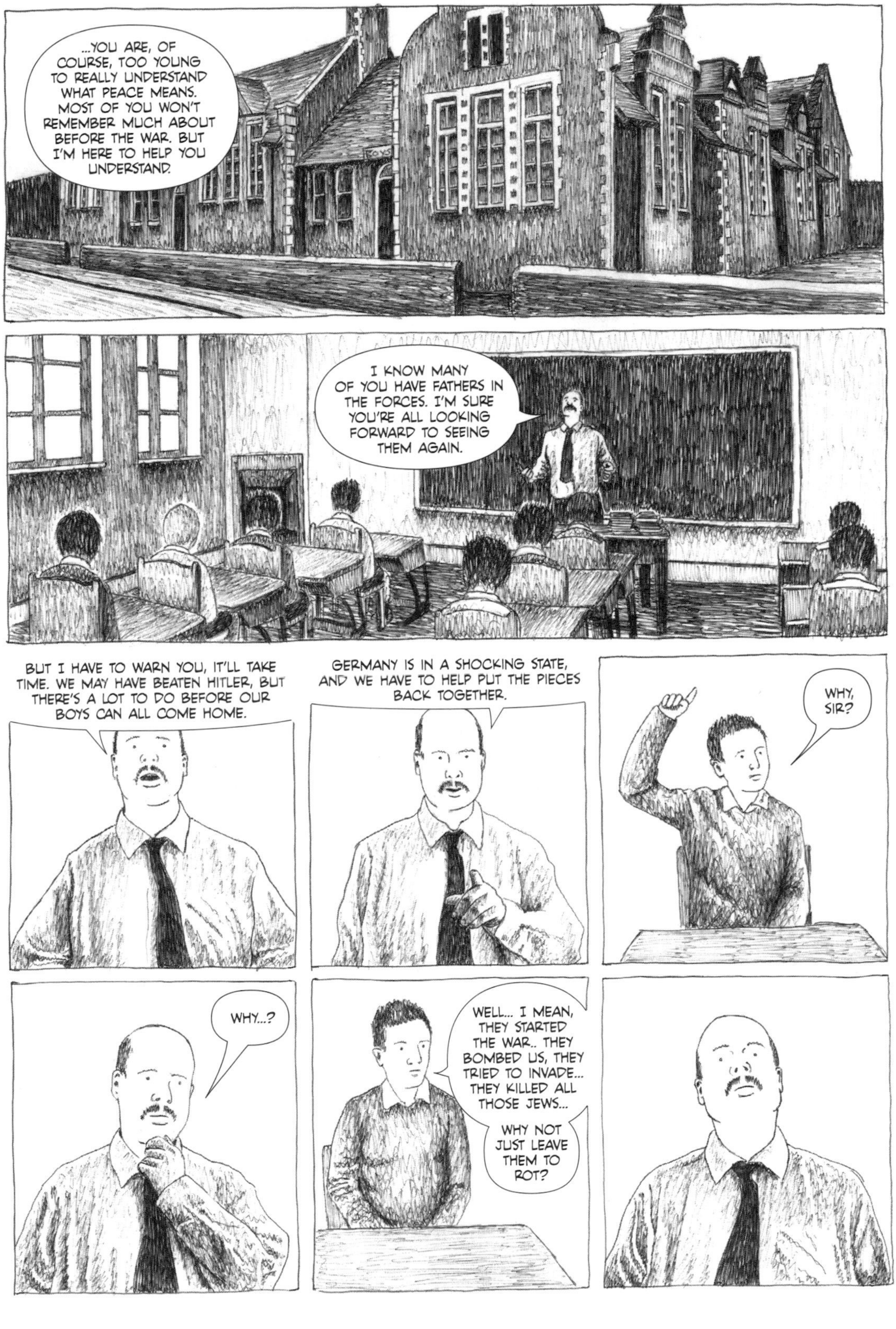
...YOU ARE, OF COURSE, TOO YOUNG TO REALLY UNDERSTAND WHAT PEACE MEANS. MOST OF YOU WON'T REMEMBER MUCH ABOUT BEFORE THE WAR. BUT I'M HERE TO HELP YOU UNDERSTAND.
I KNOW MANY OF YOU HAVE FATHERS IN THE FORCES. I'M SURE YOU'RE ALL LOOKING FORWARD TO SEEING THEM AGAIN.
BUT I HAVE TO WARN YOU, IT'LL TAKE TIME. WE MAY HAVE BEATEN HITLER, BUT THERE'S A LOT TO DO BEFORE OUR BOYS CAN ALL COME HOME.
GERMANY IS IN A SHOCKING STATE, AND WE HAVE TO HELP PUT THE PIECES BACK TOGETHER.
WHY, SIR?
WHY...?
WELL... I MEAN, THEY STARTED THE WAR.. THEY BOMBED US, THEY TRIED TO INVADE... THEY KILLED ALL THOSE JEWS...
WHY NOT JUST LEAVE THEM TO ROT?

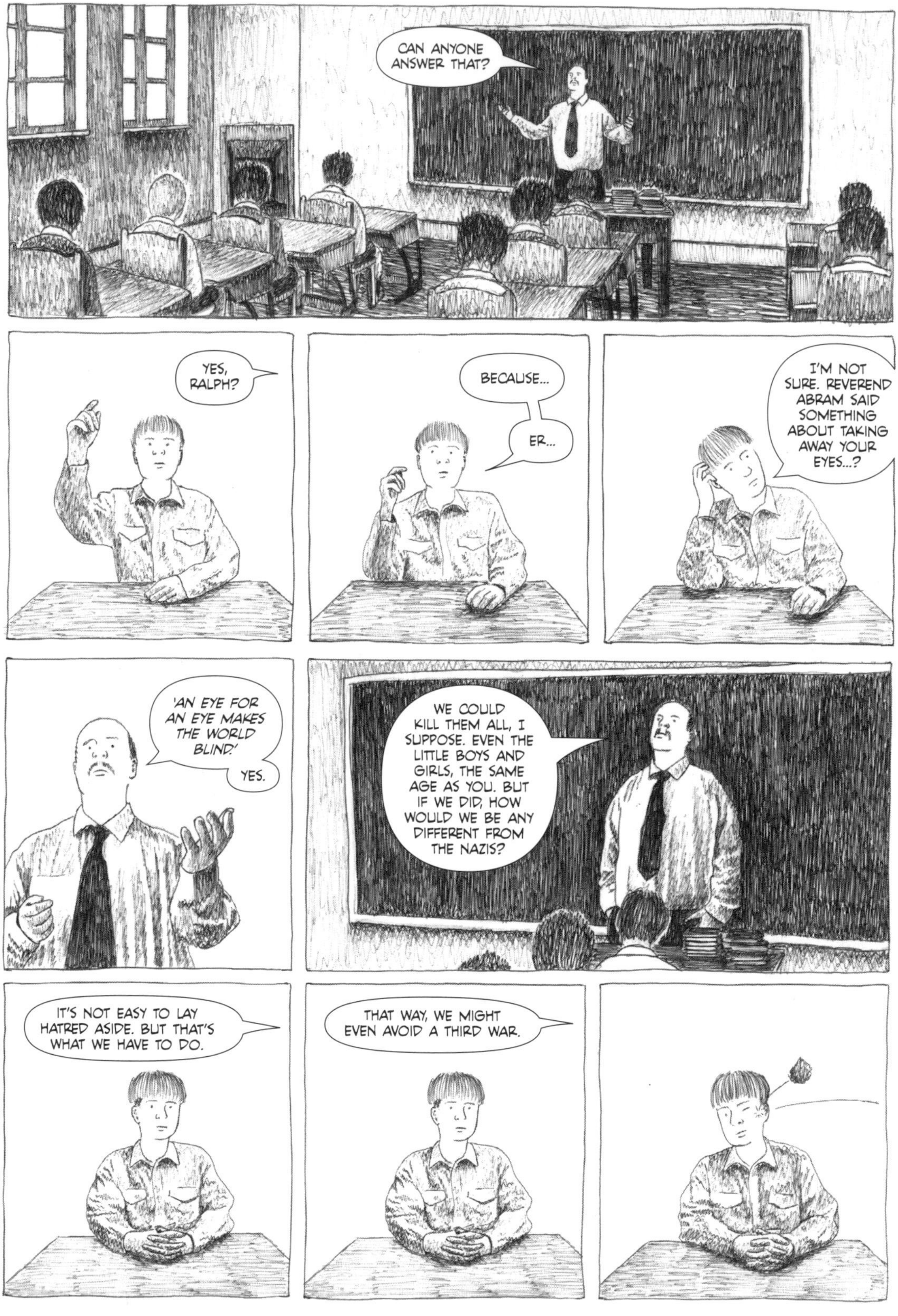
CAN ANYONE ANSWER THAT?
YES, RALPH?
BECAUSE...
ER...
I'M NOT SURE. REVEREND ABRAM SAID SOMETHING ABOUT TAKING AWAY YOUR EYES...?
'AN EYE FOR AN EYE MAKES THE WORLD BLIND.'
YES.
WE COULD KILL THEM ALL, I SUPPOSE. EVEN THE LITTLE BOYS AND GIRLS, THE SAME AGE AS YOU. BUT IF WE DID, HOW WOULD WE BE ANY DIFFERENT FROM THE NAZIS?
IT'S NOT EASY TO LAY HATRED ASIDE. BUT THAT'S WHAT WE HAVE TO DO.
THAT WAY, WE MIGHT EVEN AVOID A THIRD WAR.

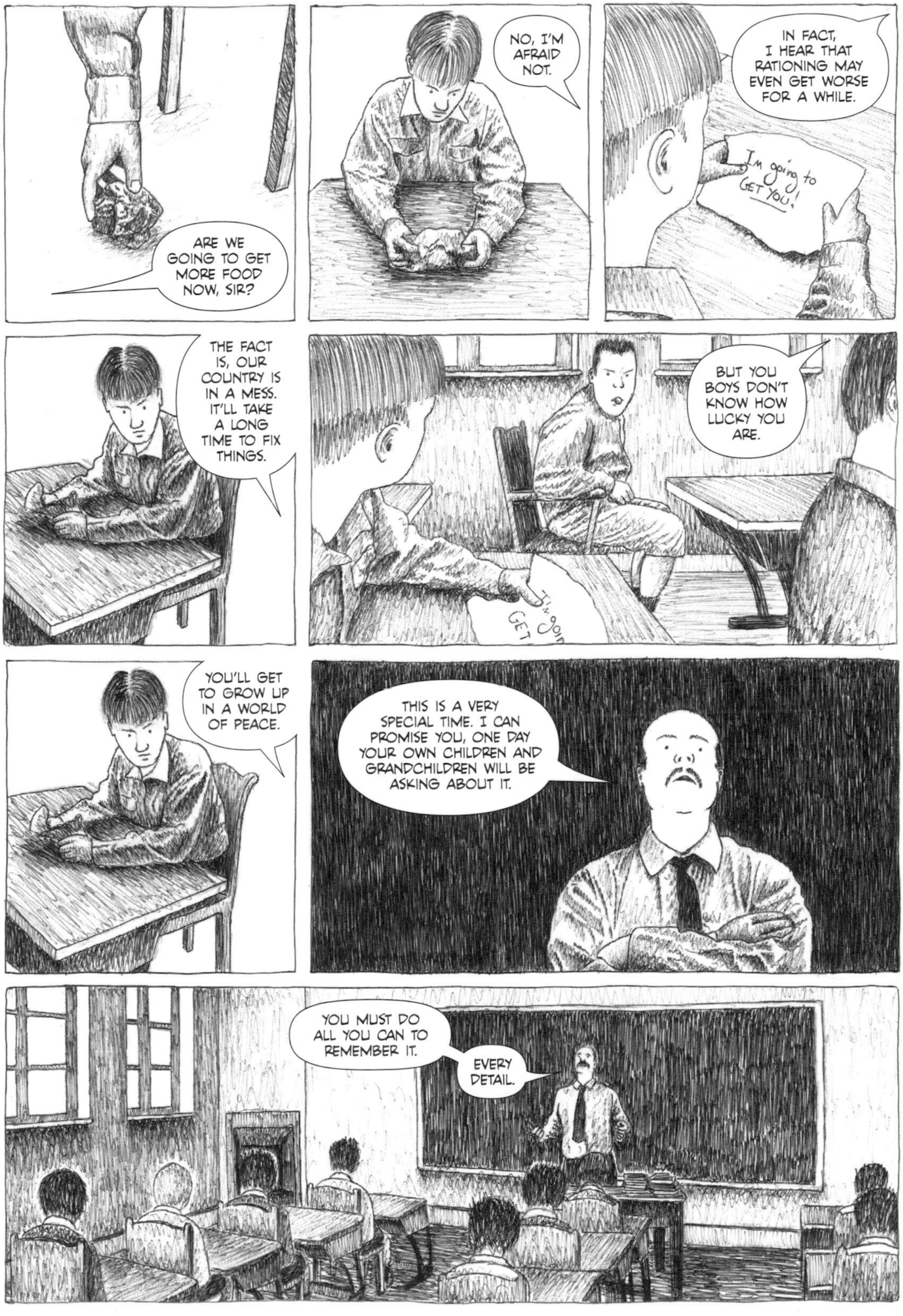
ARE WE GOING TO GET MORE FOOD NOW, SIR?
NO, I'M AFRAID NOT.
IN FACT, I HEAR THAT RATIONING MAY EVEN GET WORSE FOR A WHILE.
I'm going to GET YOU!
THE FACT IS, OUR COUNTRY IS IN A MESS. IT'LL TAKE A LONG TIME TO FIX THINGS.
BUT YOU BOYS DON'T KNOW HOW LUCKY YOU ARE.
YOU'LL GET TO GROW UP IN A WORLD OF PEACE.
THIS IS A VERY SPECIAL TIME. I CAN PROMISE YOU, ONE DAY YOUR OWN CHILDREN AND GRANDCHILDREN WILL BE ASKING ABOUT IT.
YOU MUST DO ALL YOU CAN TO REMEMBER IT.
EVERY DETAIL.

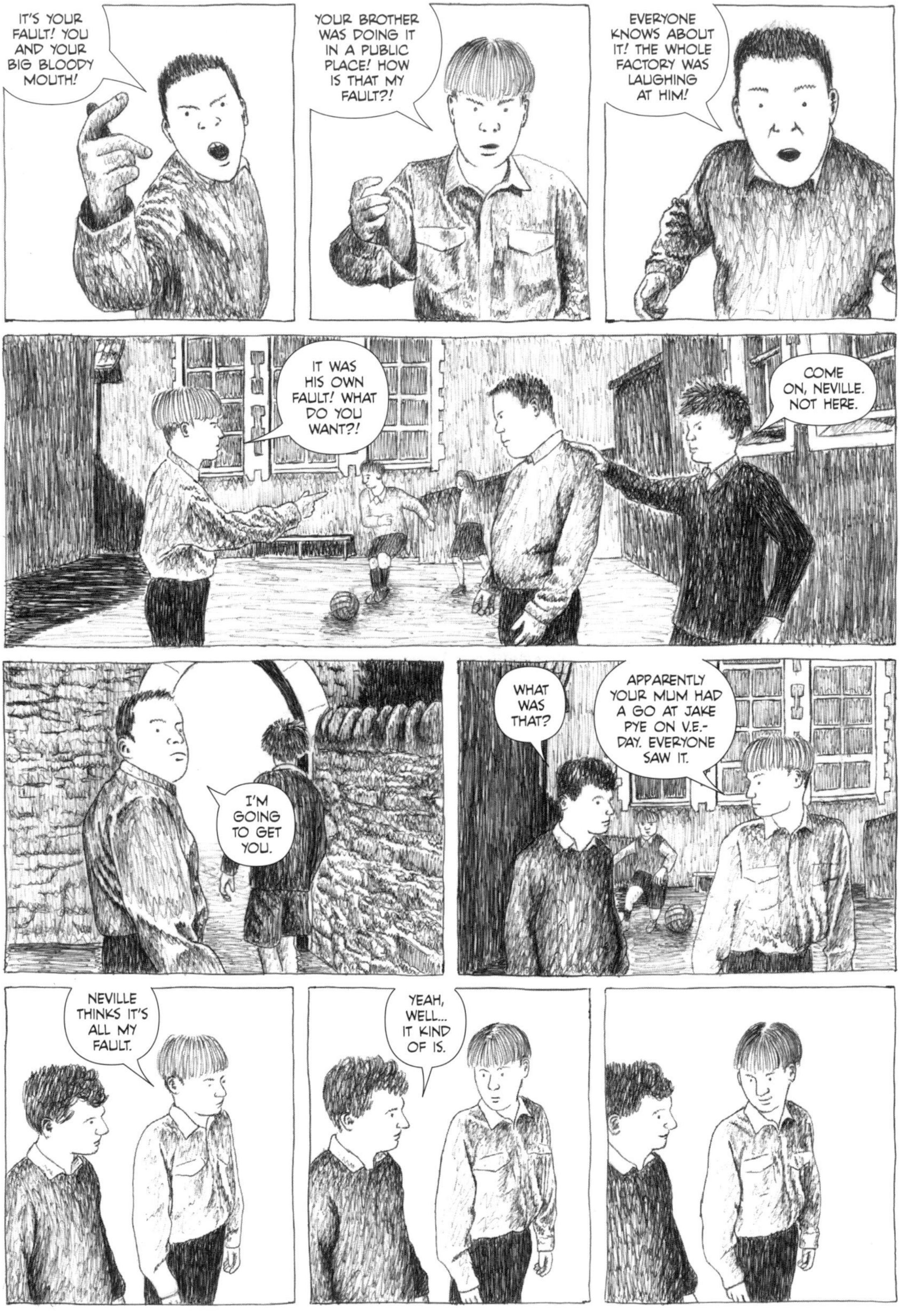
IT'S YOUR FAULT! YOU AND YOUR BIG BLOODY MOUTH!
YOUR BROTHER WAS DOING IT IN A PUBLIC PLACE! HOW IS THAT MY FAULT?!
EVERYONE KNOWS ABOUT IT! THE WHOLE FACTORY WAS LAUGHING AT HIM!
IT WAS HIS OWN FAULT! WHAT DO YOU WANT?!
COME ON, NEVILLE. NOT HERE.
I'M GOING TO GET YOU.
WHAT WAS THAT?
APPARENTLY YOUR MUM HAD A GO AT JAKE PYE ON V.E.-DAY. EVERYONE SAW IT.
NEVILLE THINKS IT'S ALL MY FAULT.
YEAH, WELL... IT KIND OF IS.

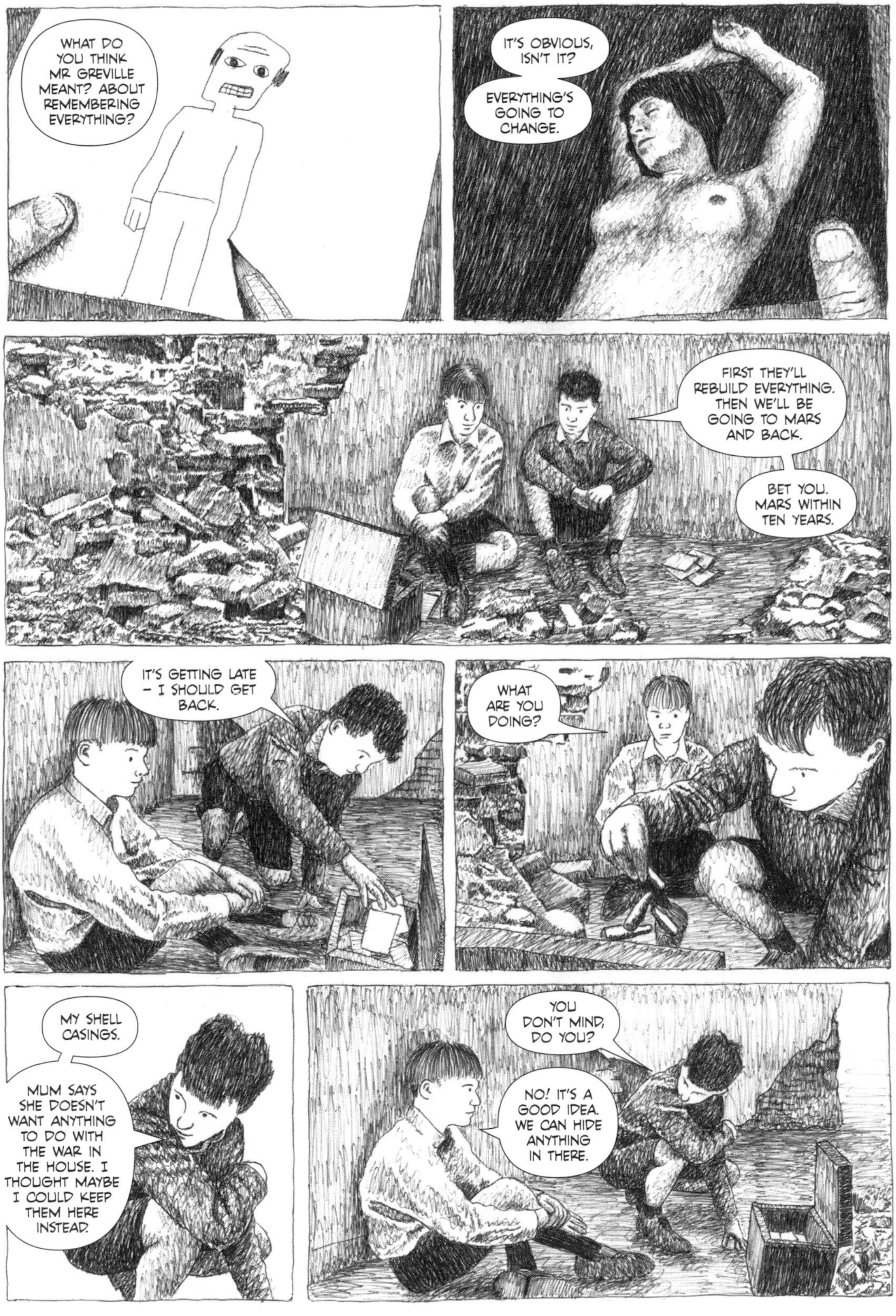
WHAT DO YOU THINK MR GREVILLE MEANT? ABOUT REMEMBERING EVERYTHING?
IT'S OBVIOUS, ISN'T IT?
EVERYTHING'S GOING TO CHANGE.
FIRST THEY'LL REBUILD EVERYTHING. THEN WE'LL BE GOING TO MARS AND BACK.
BET YOU. MARS WITHIN TEN YEARS.
IT'S GETTING LATE – I SHOULD GET BACK.
WHAT ARE YOU DOING?
MY SHELL CASINGS.
MUM SAYS SHE DOESN'T WANT ANYTHING TO DO WITH THE WAR IN THE HOUSE. I THOUGHT MAYBE I COULD KEEP THEM HERE INSTEAD.
YOU DON'T MIND, DO YOU?
NO! IT'S A GOOD IDEA. WE CAN HIDE ANYTHING IN THERE.

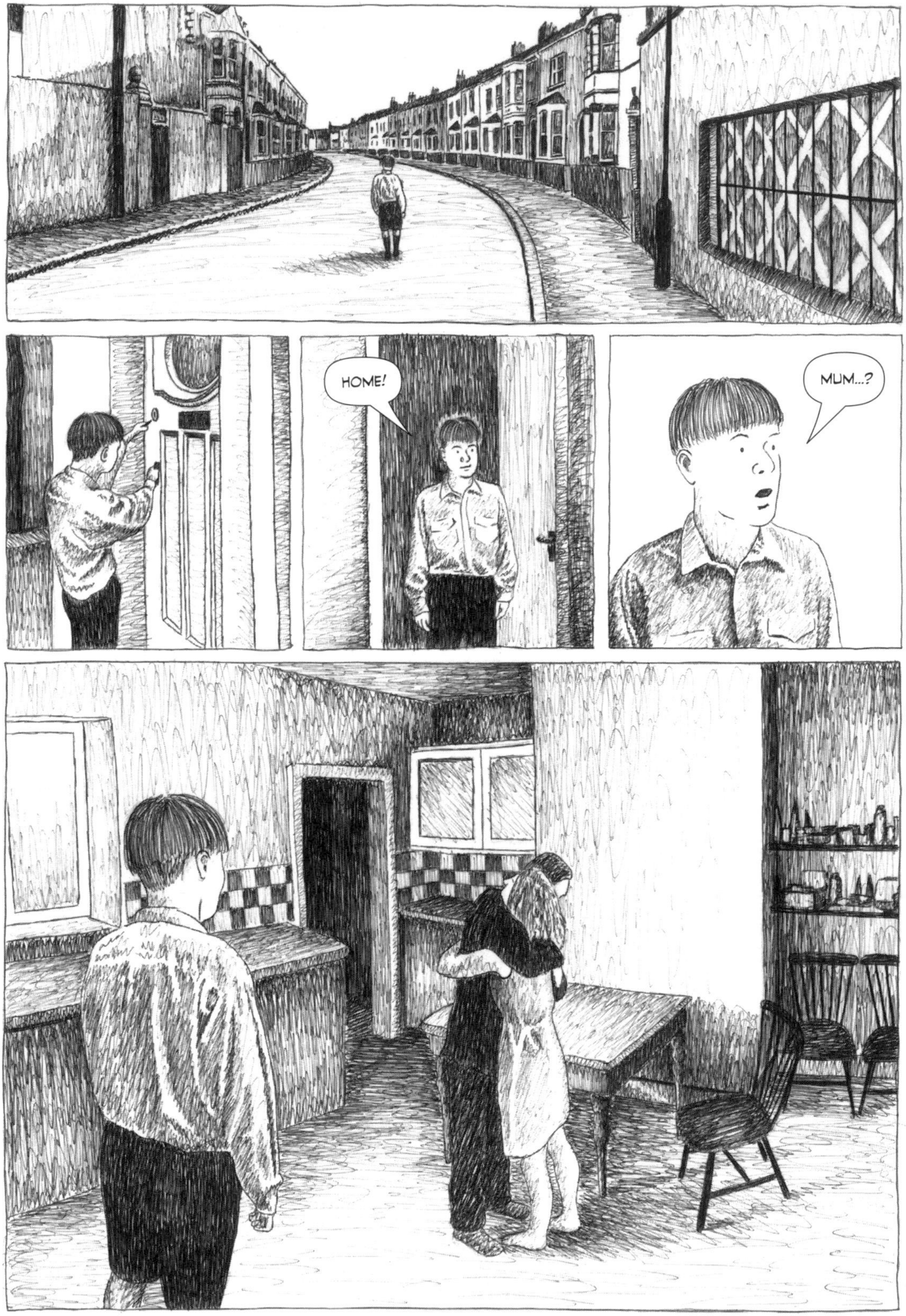
HOME!
MUM...?

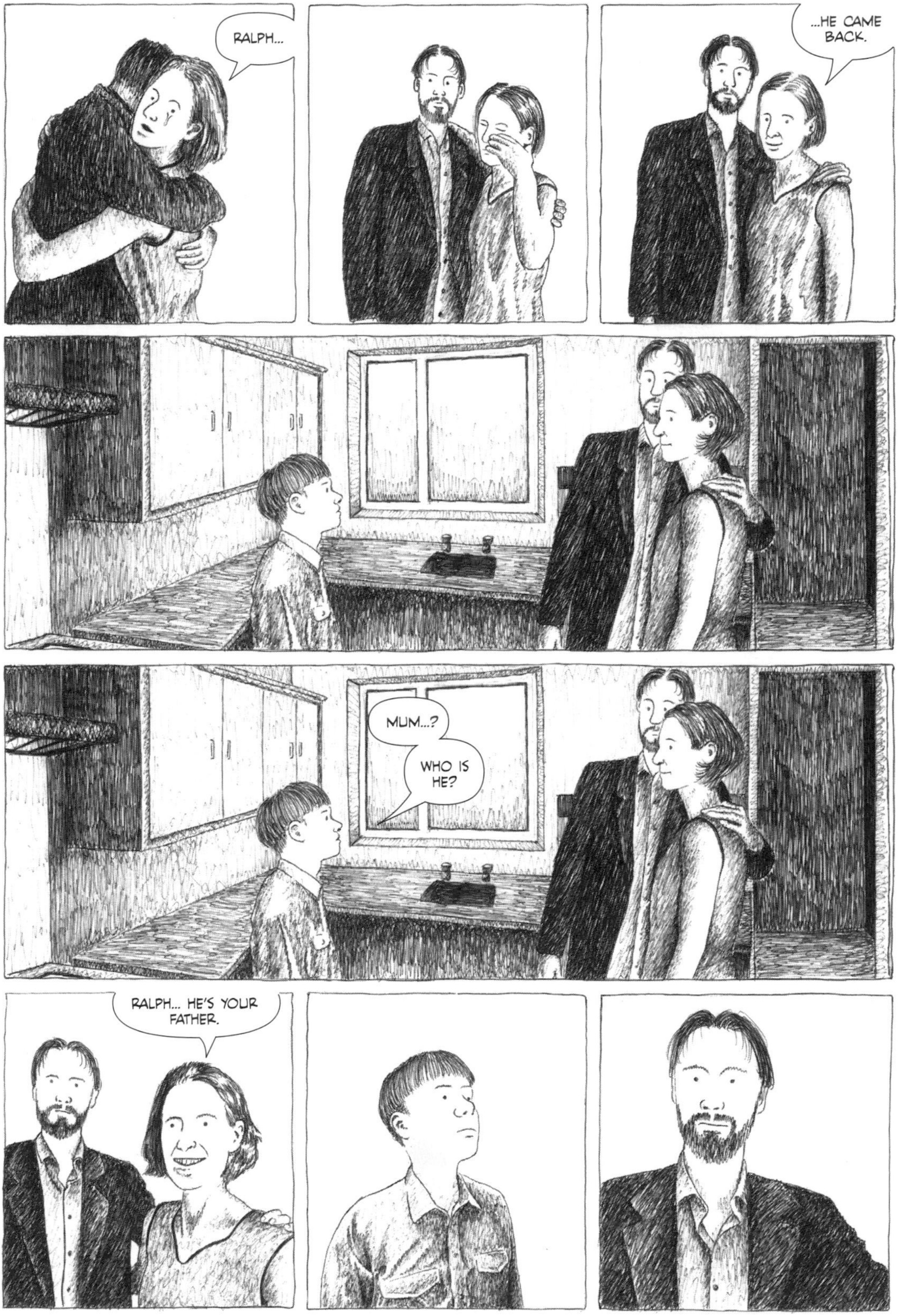
RALPH...
...HE CAME BACK.
MUM...?
WHO IS HE?
RALPH... HE'S YOUR FATHER.

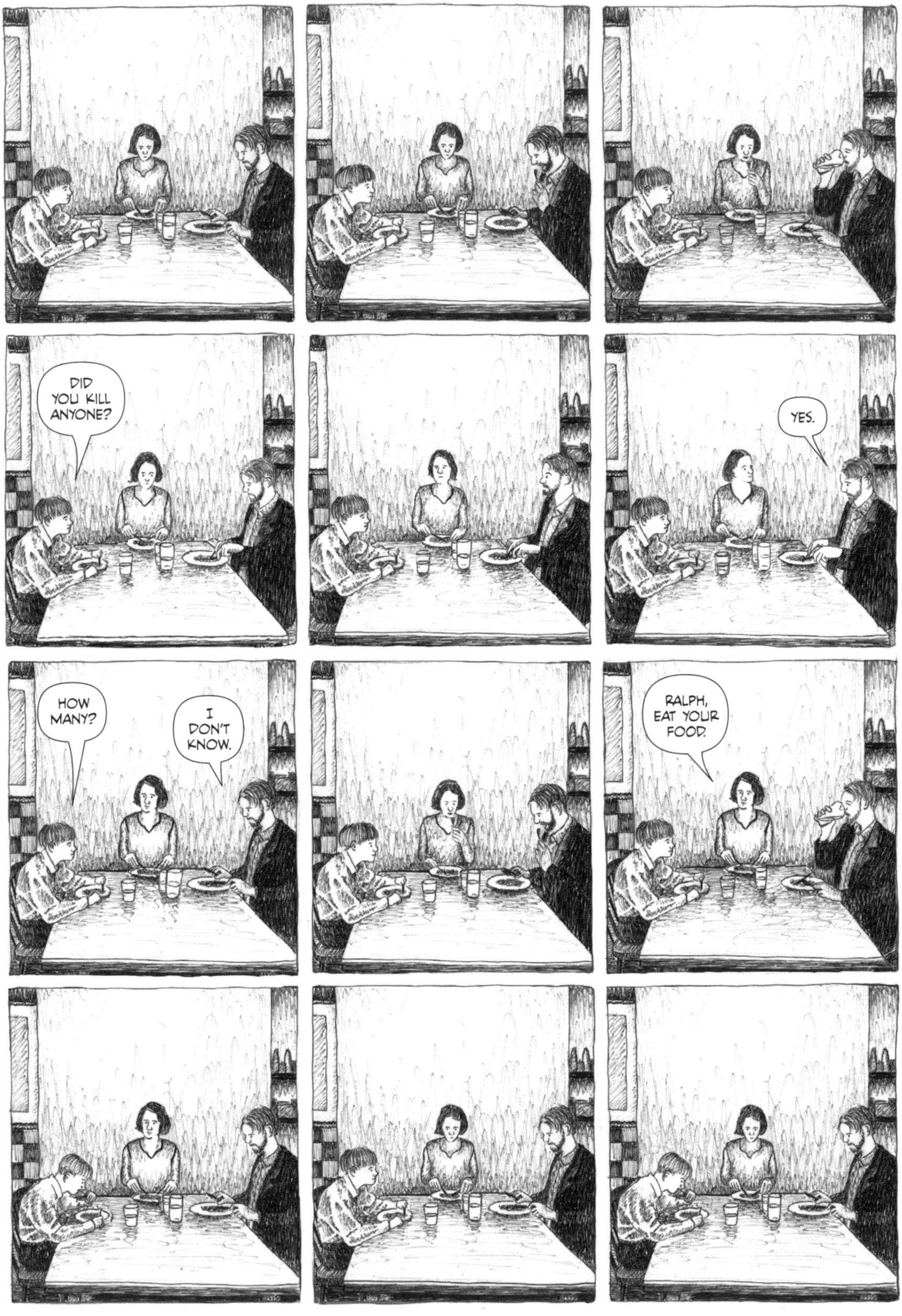
DID YOU KILL ANYONE?
YES.
HOW MANY?
I DON'T KNOW.
RALPH, EAT YOUR FOOD.

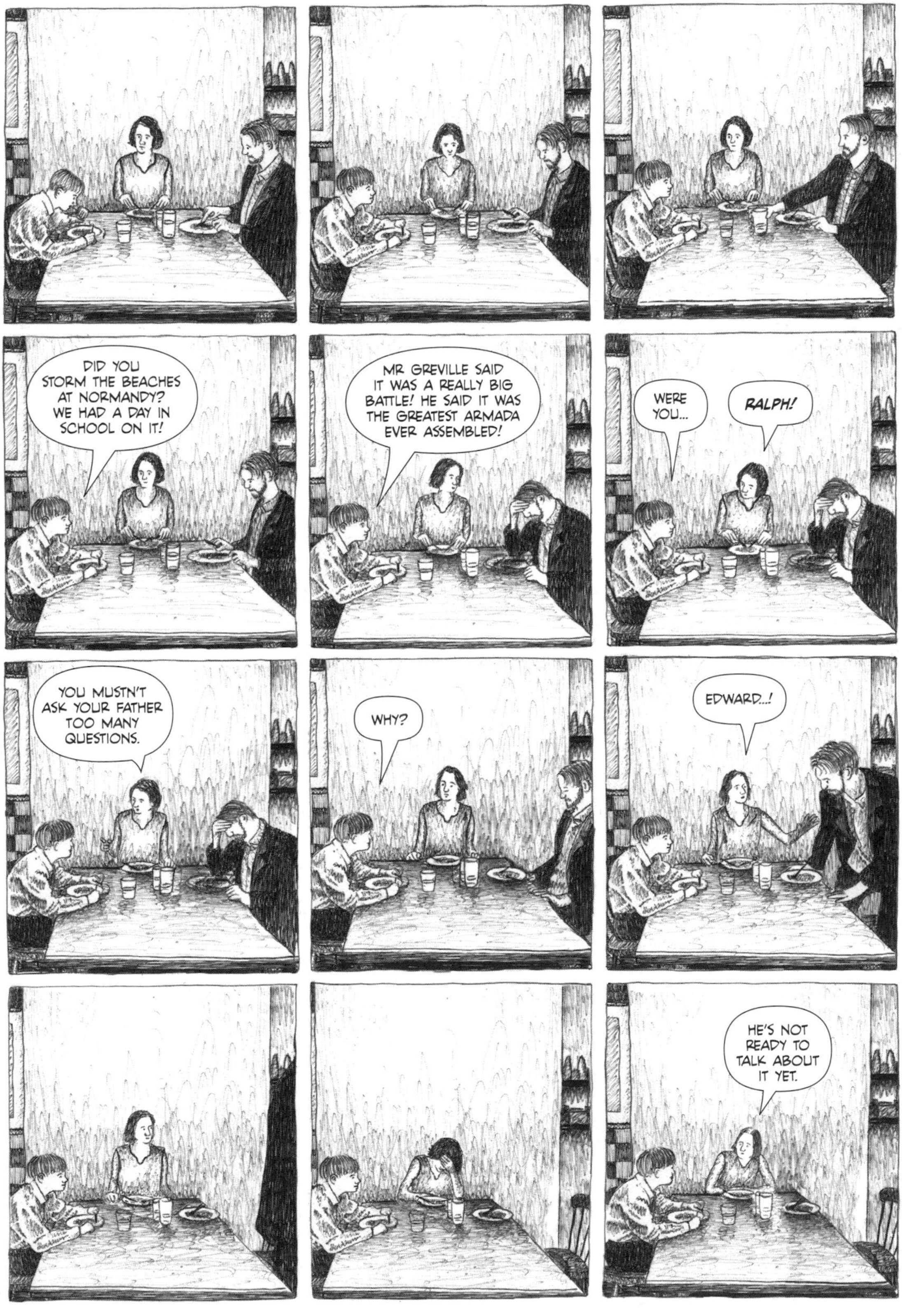
DID YOU STORM THE BEACHES AT NORMANDY? WE HAD A DAY IN SCHOOL ON IT!
MR GREVILLE SAID IT WAS A REALLY BIG BATTLE! HE SAID IT WAS THE GREATEST ARMADA EVER ASSEMBLED!
WERE YOU...
RALPH!
YOU MUSTN'T ASK YOUR FATHER TOO MANY QUESTIONS.
WHY?
EDWARD...!
HE'S NOT READY TO TALK ABOUT IT YET.

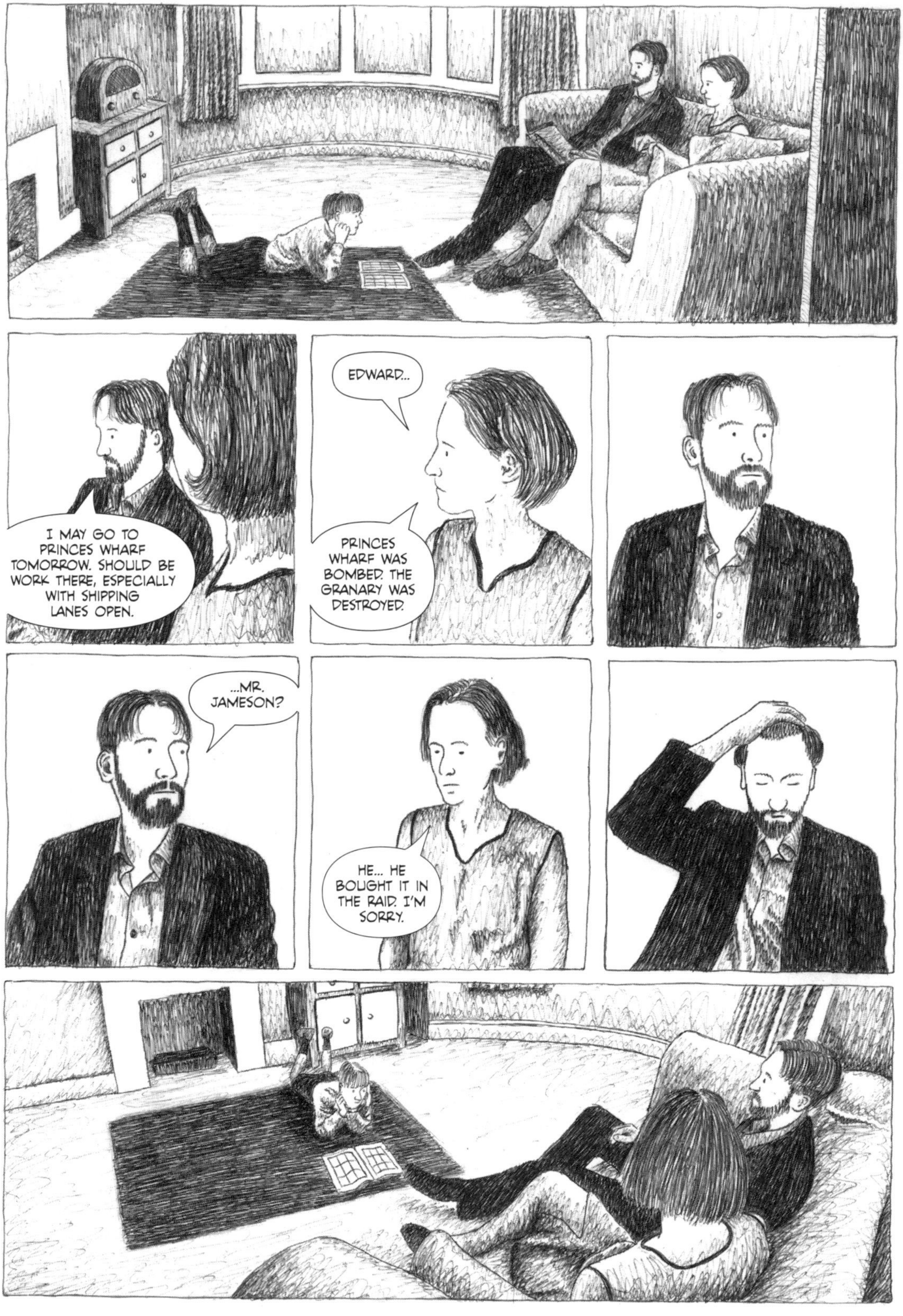
I MAY GO TO PRINCES WHARF TOMORROW. SHOULD BE WORK THERE, ESPECIALLY WITH SHIPPING LANES OPEN.
EDWARD...
PRINCES WHARF WAS BOMBED. THE GRANARY WAS DESTROYED.
...MR. JAMESON?
HE... HE BOUGHT IT IN THE RAID. I'M SORRY.

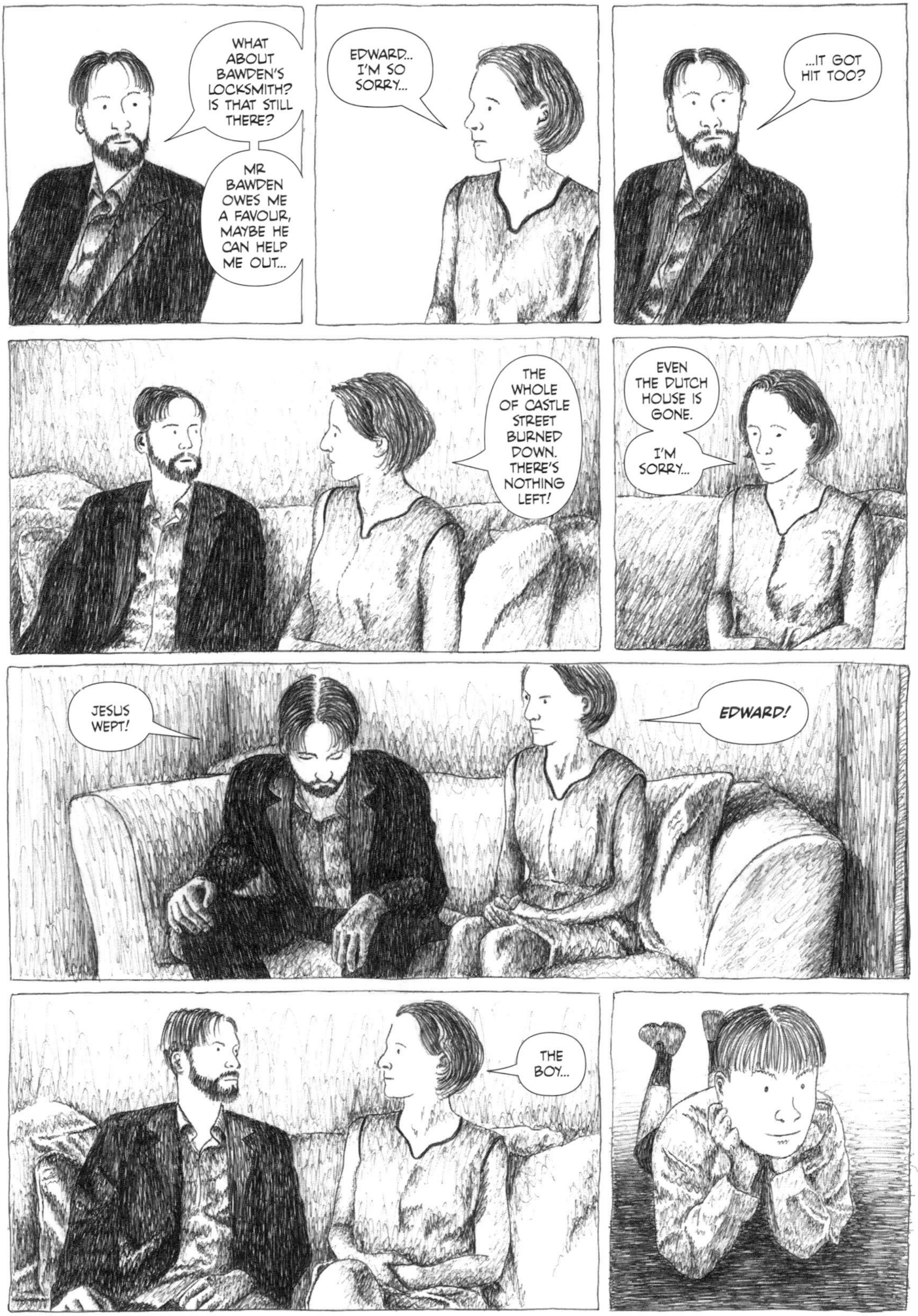
WHAT ABOUT BAWDEN'S LOCKSMITH? IS THAT STILL THERE?
MR BAWDEN OWES ME A FAVOUR, MAYBE HE CAN HELP ME OUT...
EDWARD... I'M SO SORRY...
...IT GOT HIT TOO?
THE WHOLE OF CASTLE STREET BURNED DOWN. THERE'S NOTHING LEFT!
EVEN THE DUTCH HOUSE IS GONE.
I'M SORRY...
JESUS WEPT!
EDWARD!
THE BOY...

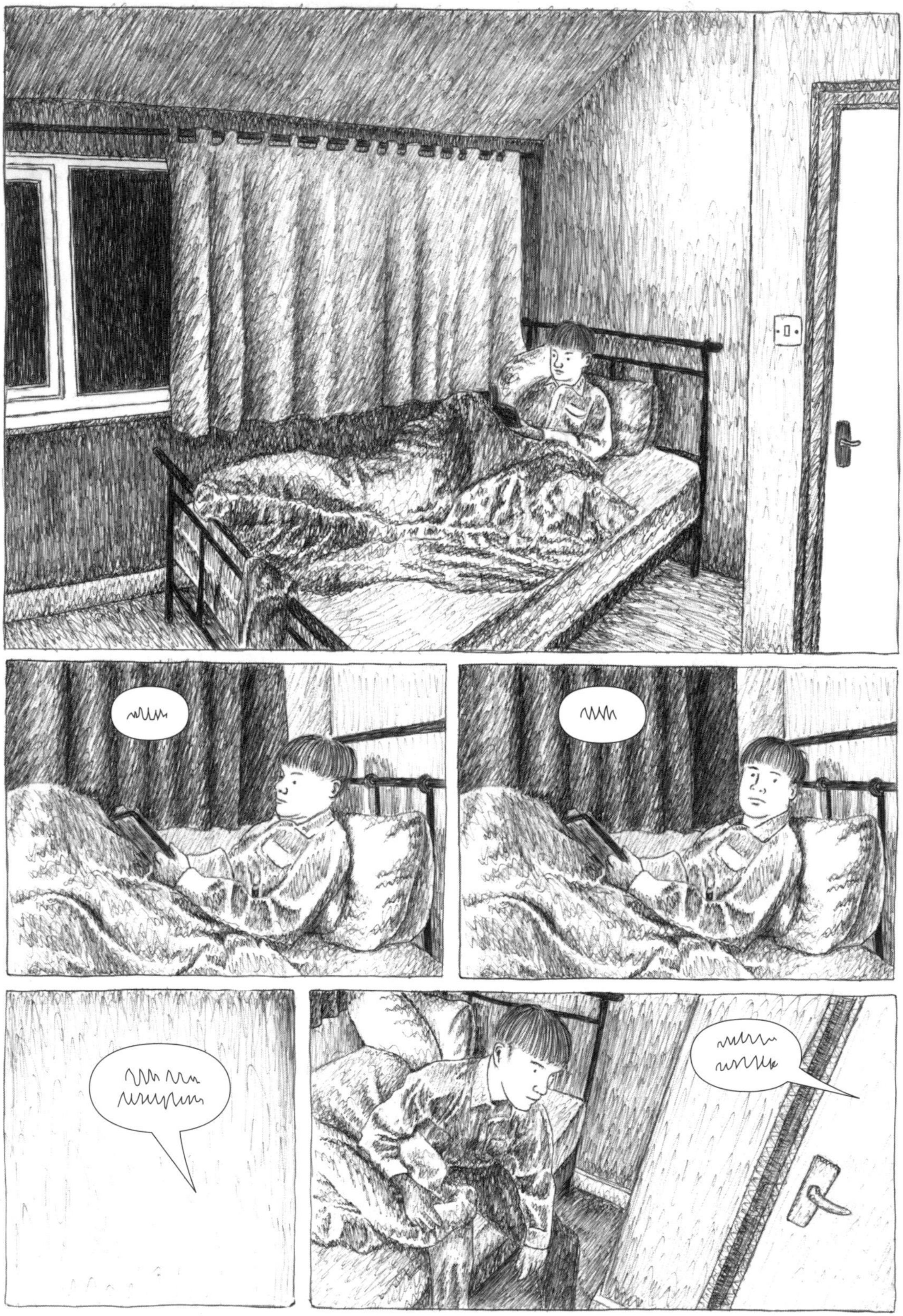

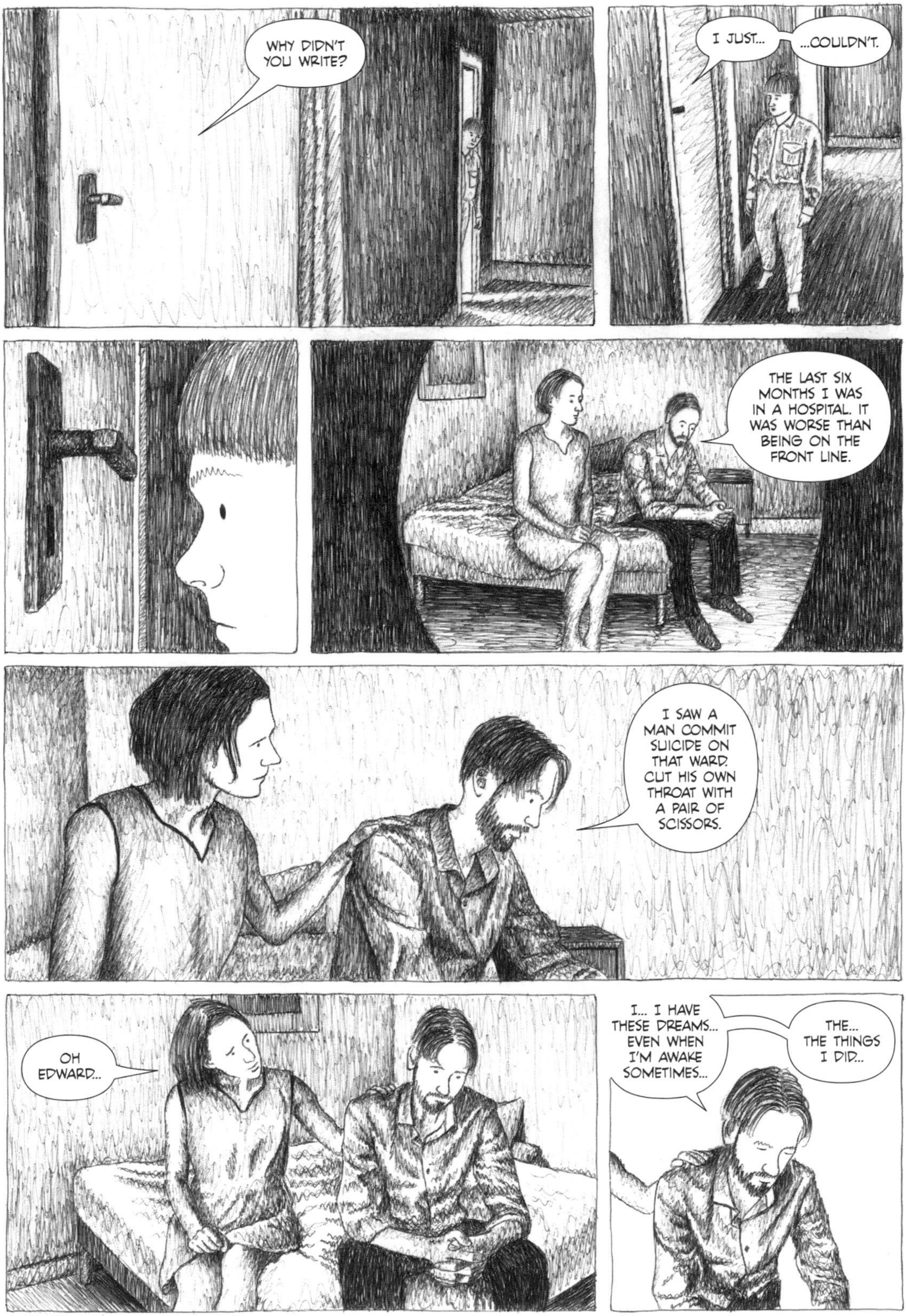
WHY DIDN'T YOU WRITE?
I JUST...
...COULDN'T.
THE LAST SIX MONTHS I WAS IN A HOSPITAL. IT WAS WORSE THAN BEING ON THE FRONT LINE.
I SAW A MAN COMMIT SUICIDE ON THAT WARD. CUT HIS OWN THROAT WITH A PAIR OF SCISSORS.
OH EDWARD...
I... I HAVE THESE DREAMS... EVEN WHEN I'M AWAKE SOMETIMES...
THE... THE THINGS I DID...

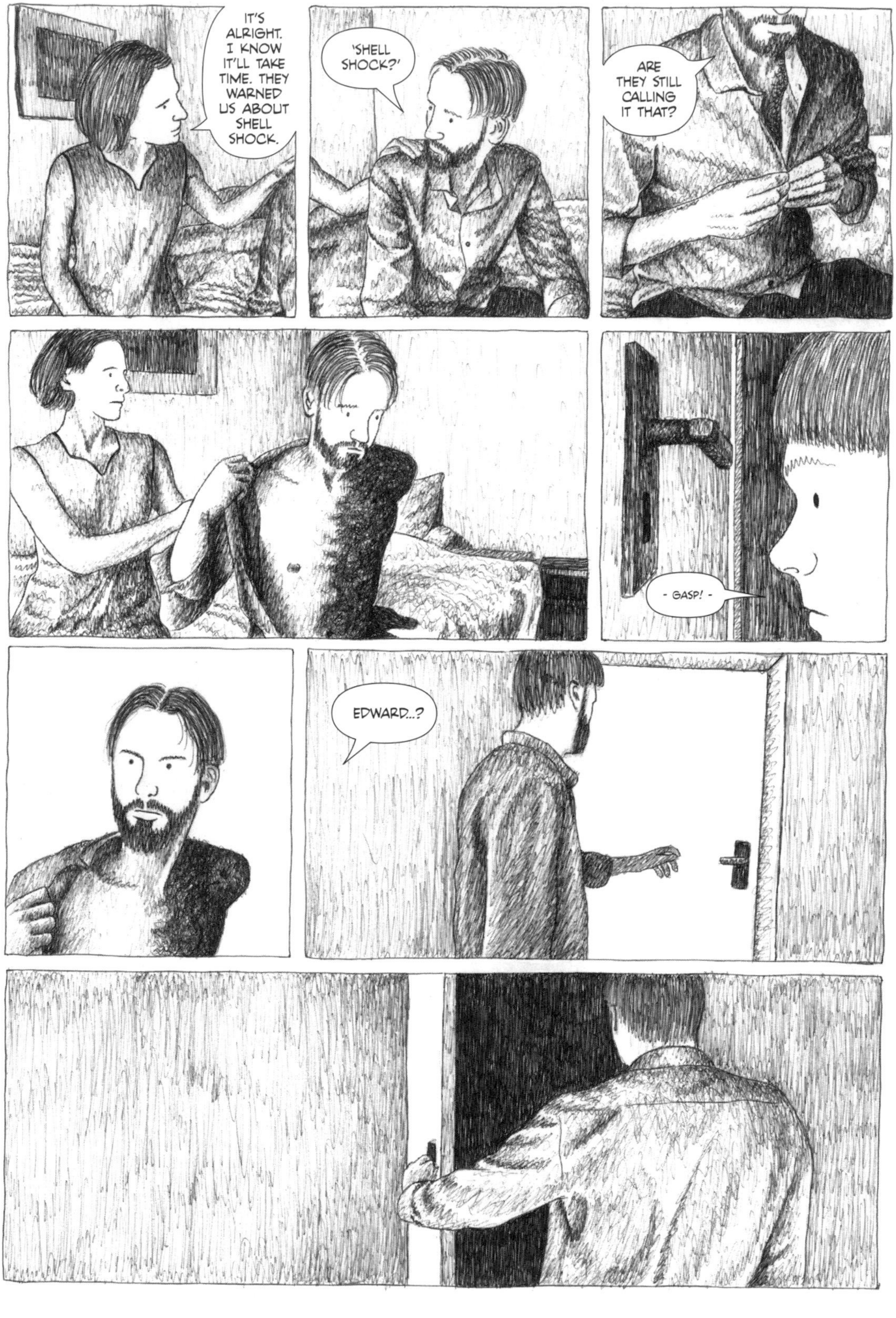
IT'S ALRIGHT. I KNOW IT'LL TAKE TIME. THEY WARNED US ABOUT SHELL SHOCK.
'SHELL SHOCK?'
ARE THEY STILL CALLING IT THAT?
- GASP! -
EDWARD...?

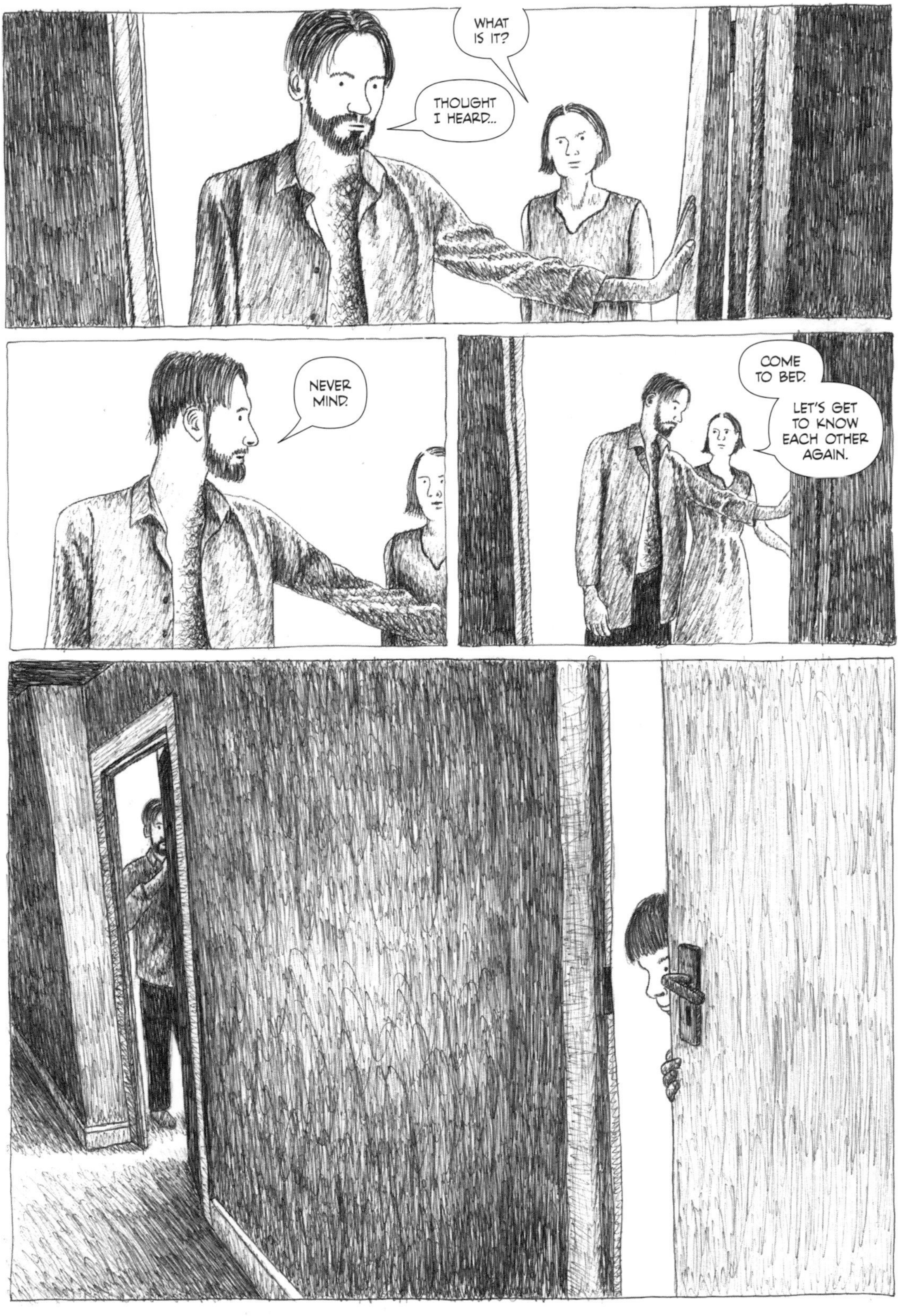
WHAT IS IT?
THOUGHT I HEARD...
NEVER MIND.
COME TO BED.
LET'S GET TO KNOW EACH OTHER AGAIN.

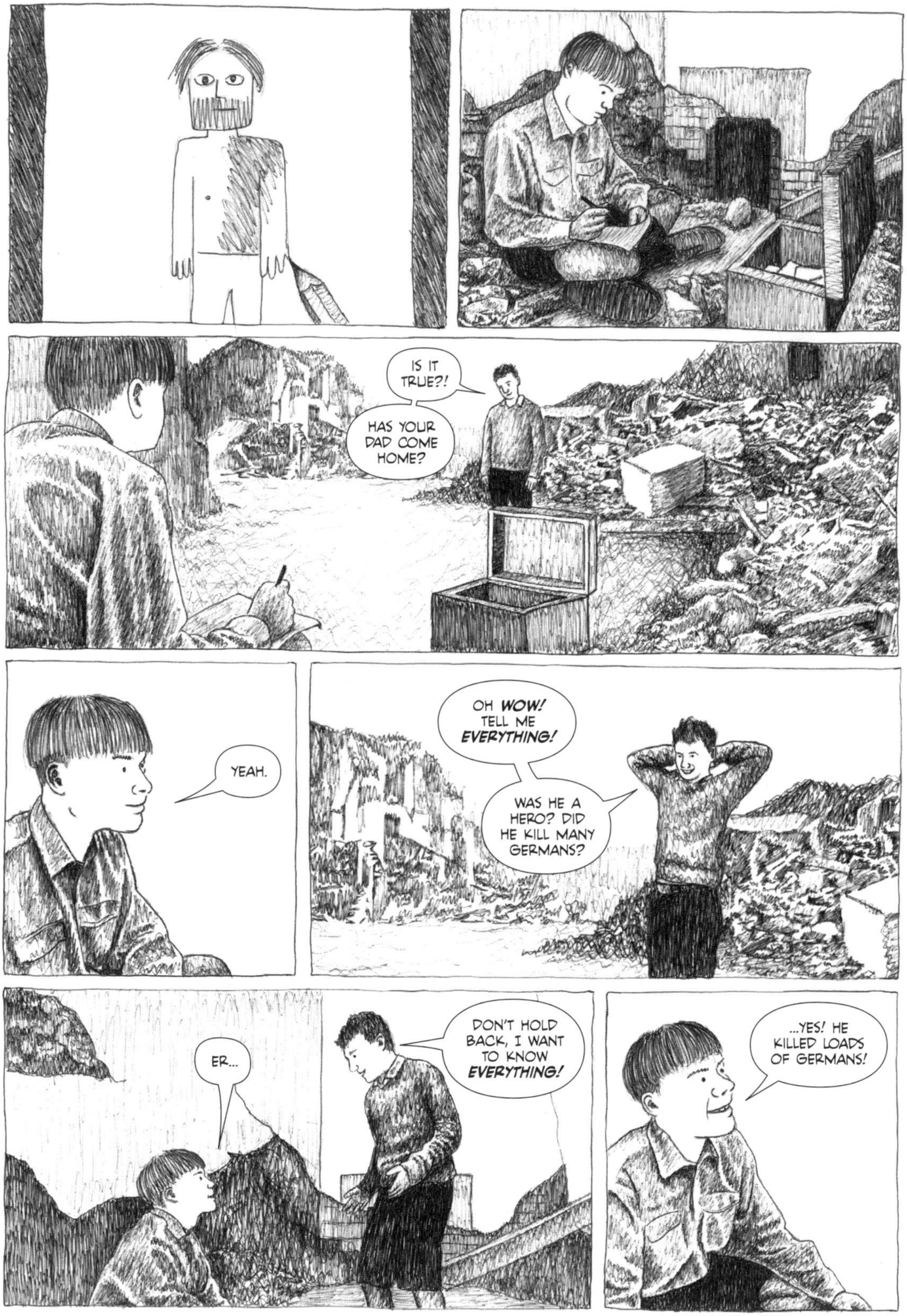
IS IT TRUE?!
HAS YOUR DAD COME HOME?
YEAH.
OH WOW! TELL ME EVERYTHING!
WAS HE A HERO? DID HE KILL MANY GERMANS?
ER...
DON'T HOLD BACK, I WANT TO KNOW EVERYTHING!
...YES! HE KILLED LOADS OF GERMANS!

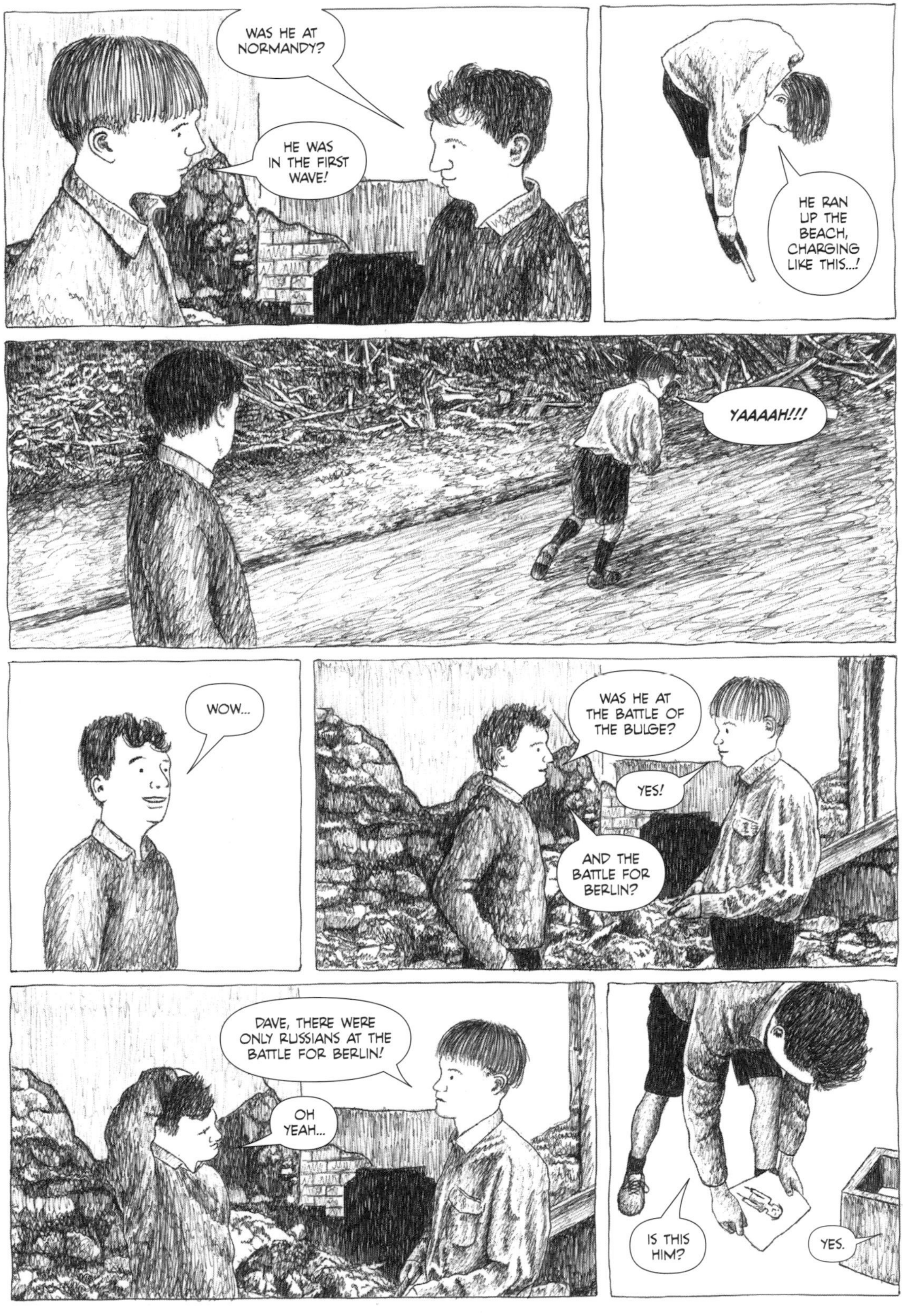
WAS HE AT NORMANDY?
HE WAS IN THE FIRST WAVE!
HE RAN UP THE BEACH, CHARGING LIKE THIS...!
YAAAAH!!!
WOW...
WAS HE AT THE BATTLE OF THE BULGE?
YES!
AND THE BATTLE FOR BERLIN?
DAVE, THERE WERE ONLY RUSSIANS AT THE BATTLE FOR BERLIN!
OH YEAH...
IS THIS HIM?
YES.

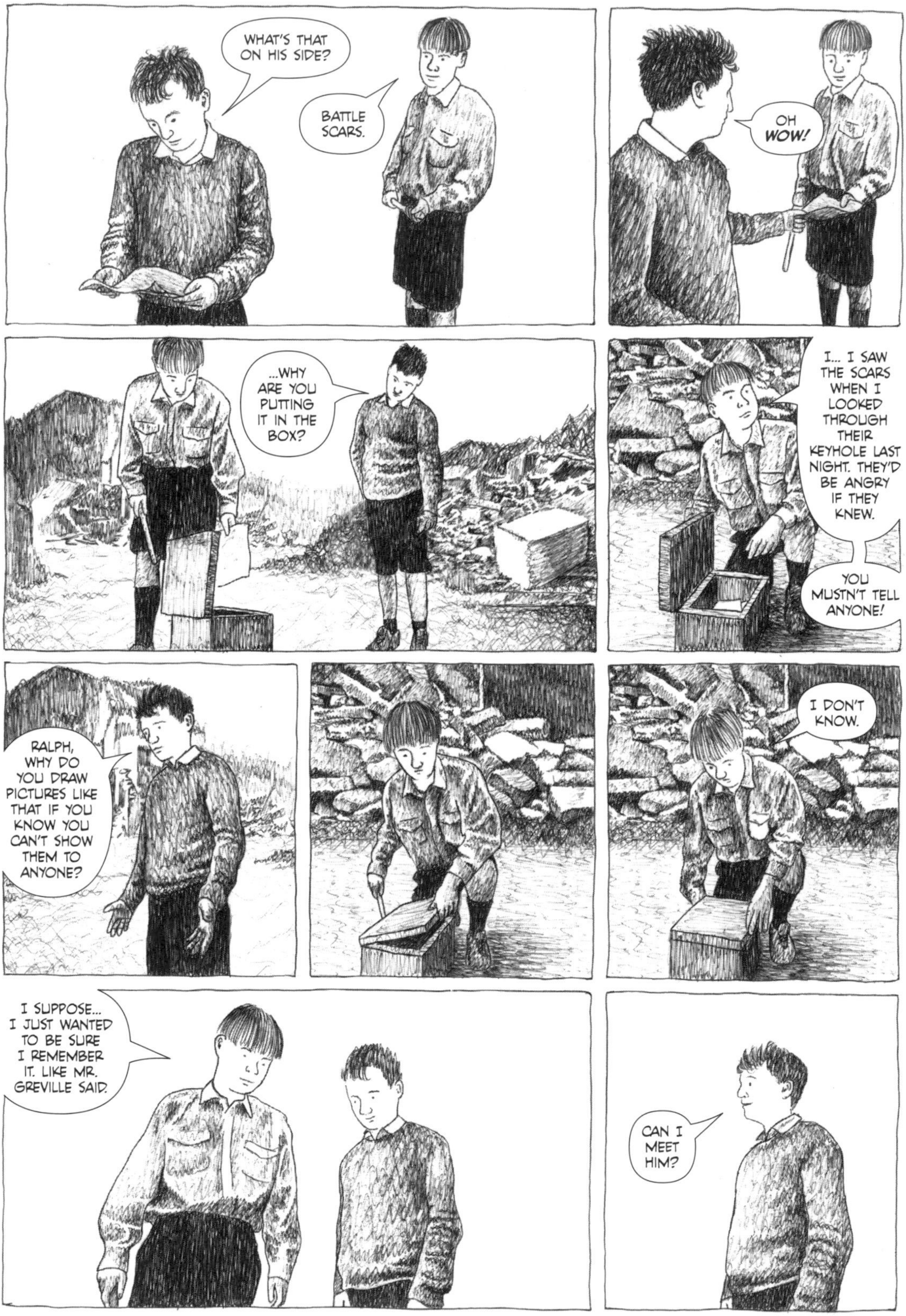

WHAT'S THAT ON HIS SIDE?
BATTLE SCARS.
OH WOW!
...WHY ARE YOU PUTTING IT IN THE BOX?
I... I SAW THE SCARS WHEN I LOOKED THROUGH THEIR KEYHOLE LAST NIGHT. THEY'D BE ANGRY IF THEY KNEW.
YOU MUSTN'T TELL ANYONE!
RALPH, WHY DO YOU DRAW PICTURES LIKE THAT IF YOU KNOW YOU CAN'T SHOW THEM TO ANYONE?
I DON'T KNOW.
I SUPPOSE... I JUST WANTED TO BE SURE I REMEMBER IT. LIKE MR. GREVILLE SAID.
CAN I MEET HIM?

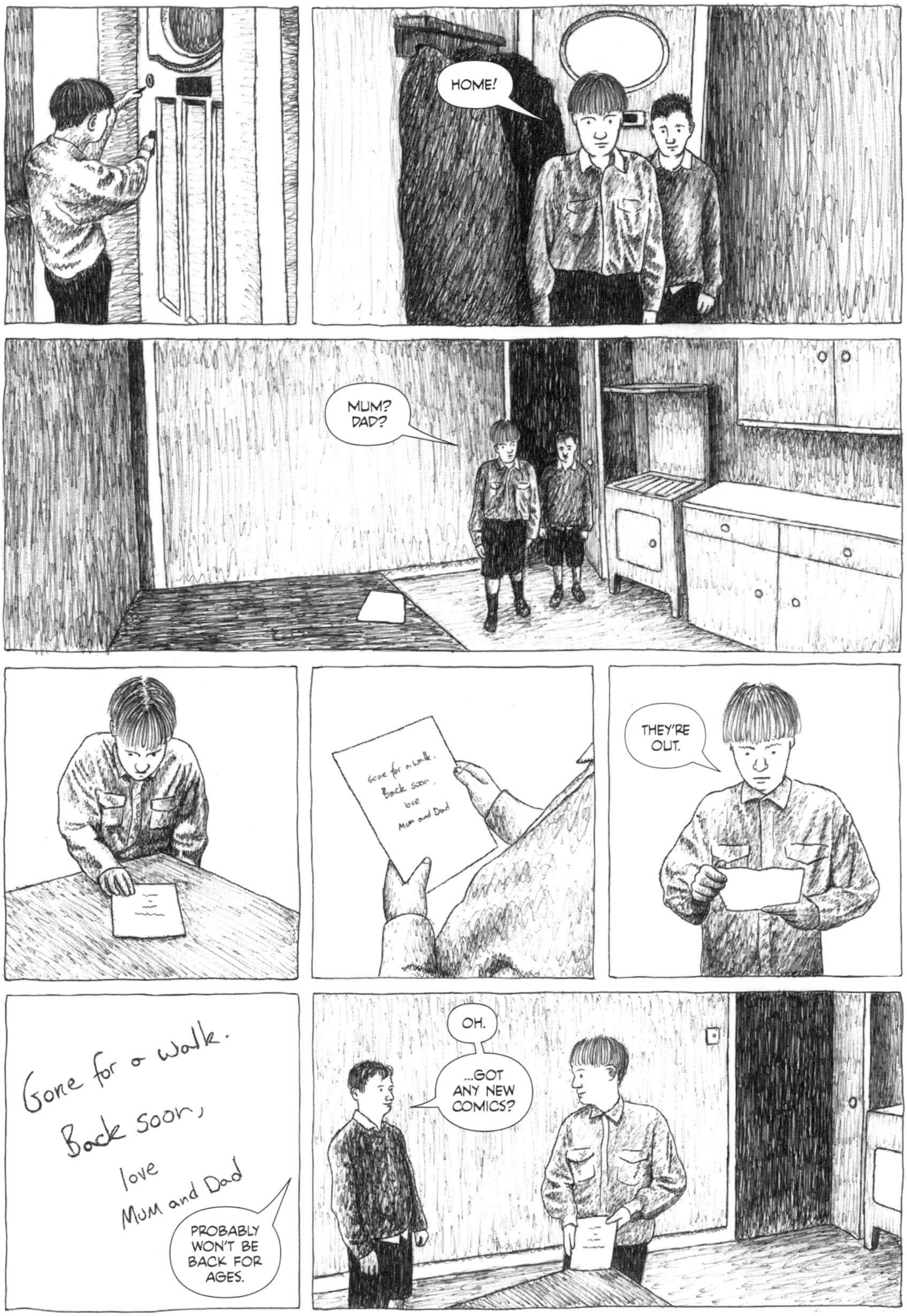
HOME!
MUM? DAD?
Gone for a walk. Back soon, love Mum and Dad
THEY'RE OUT.
Gone for a walk. Back soon, love Mum and Dad
PROBABLY WON'T BE BACK FOR AGES.
OH.
...GOT ANY NEW COMICS?

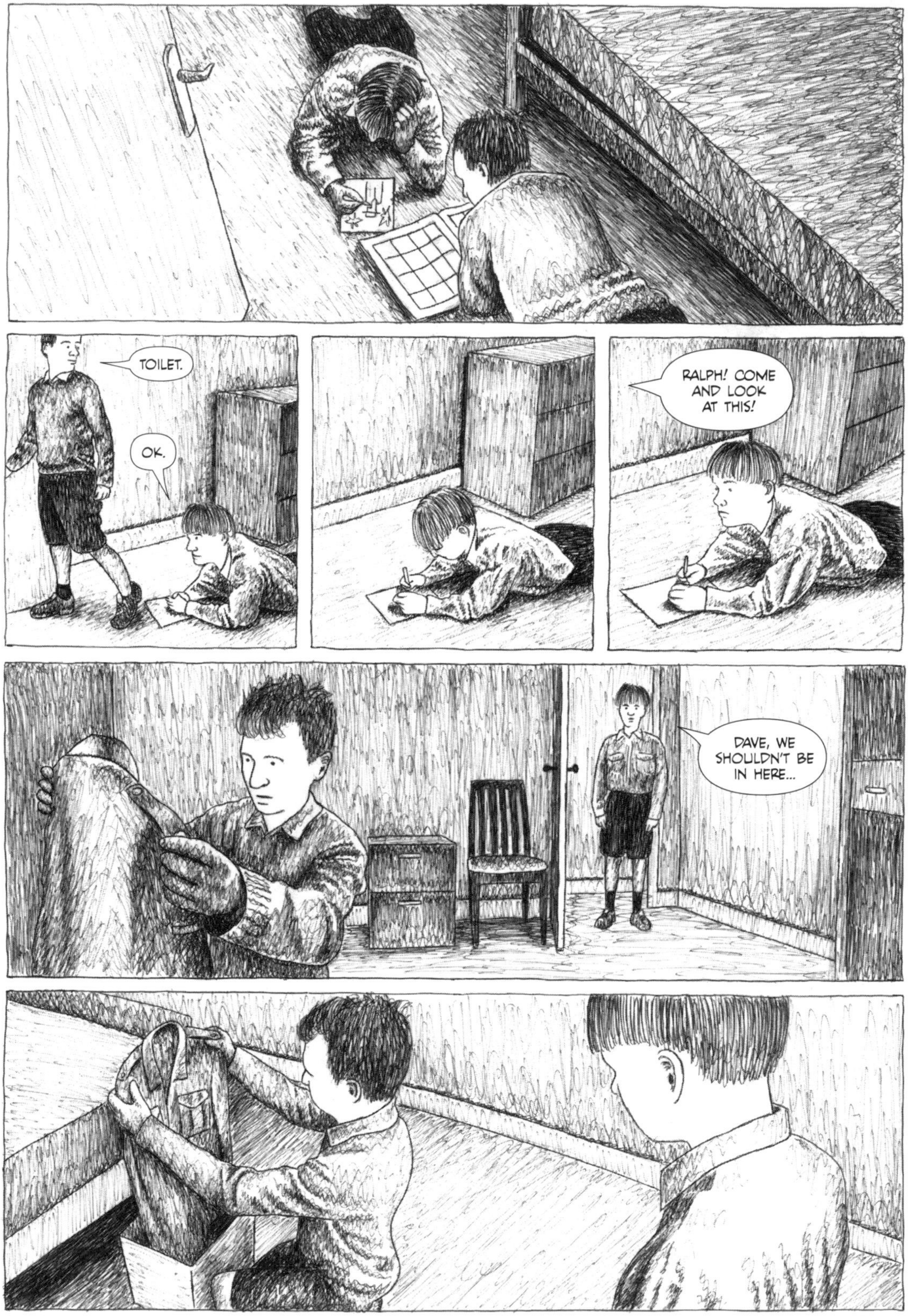
TOILET.
OK.
RALPH! COME AND LOOK AT THIS!
DAVE, WE SHOULDN'T BE IN HERE...

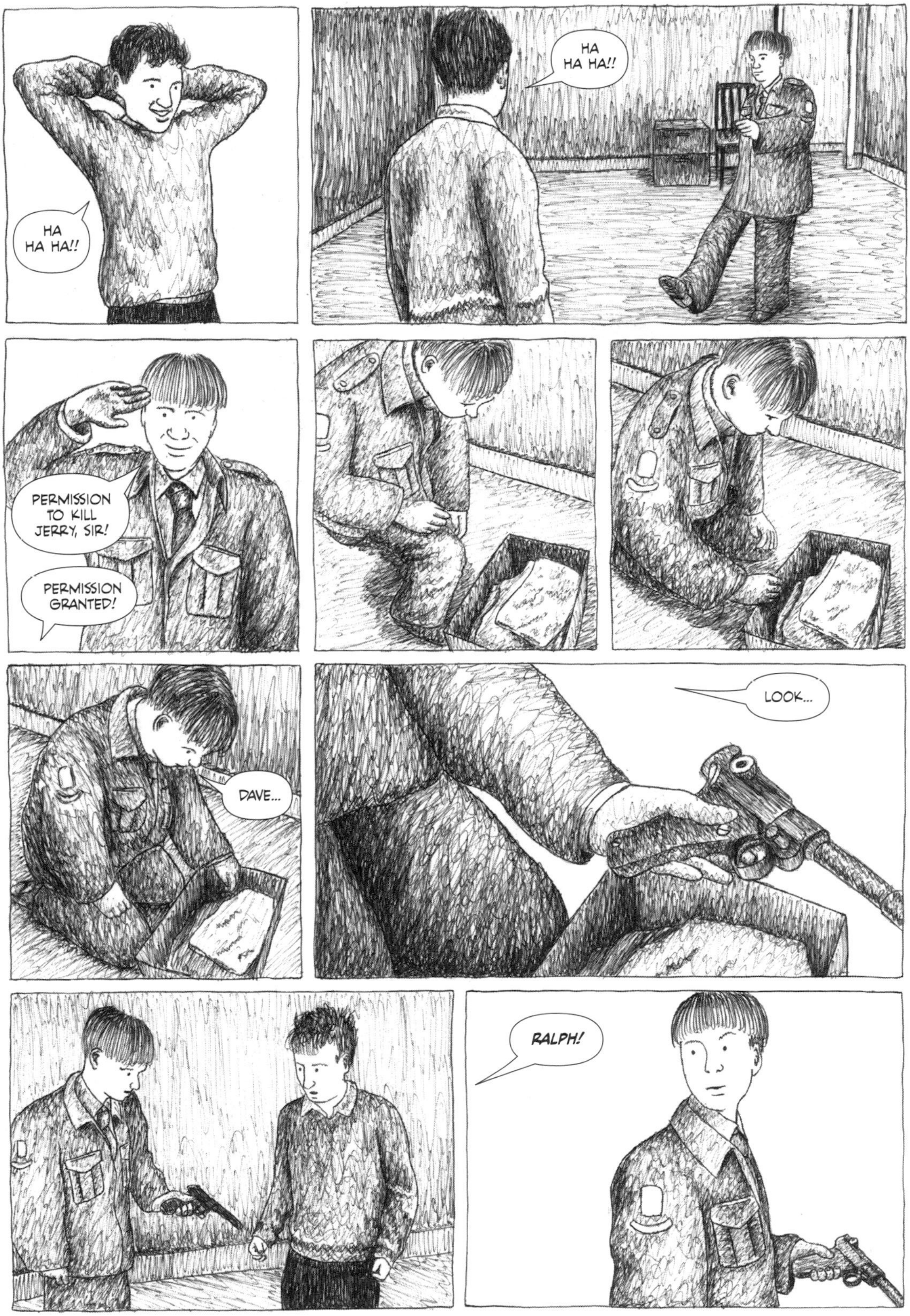
HA HA HA!!
HA HA HA!!
PERMISSION TO KILL JERRY, SIR!
PERMISSION GRANTED!
DAVE...
LOOK...
RALPH!

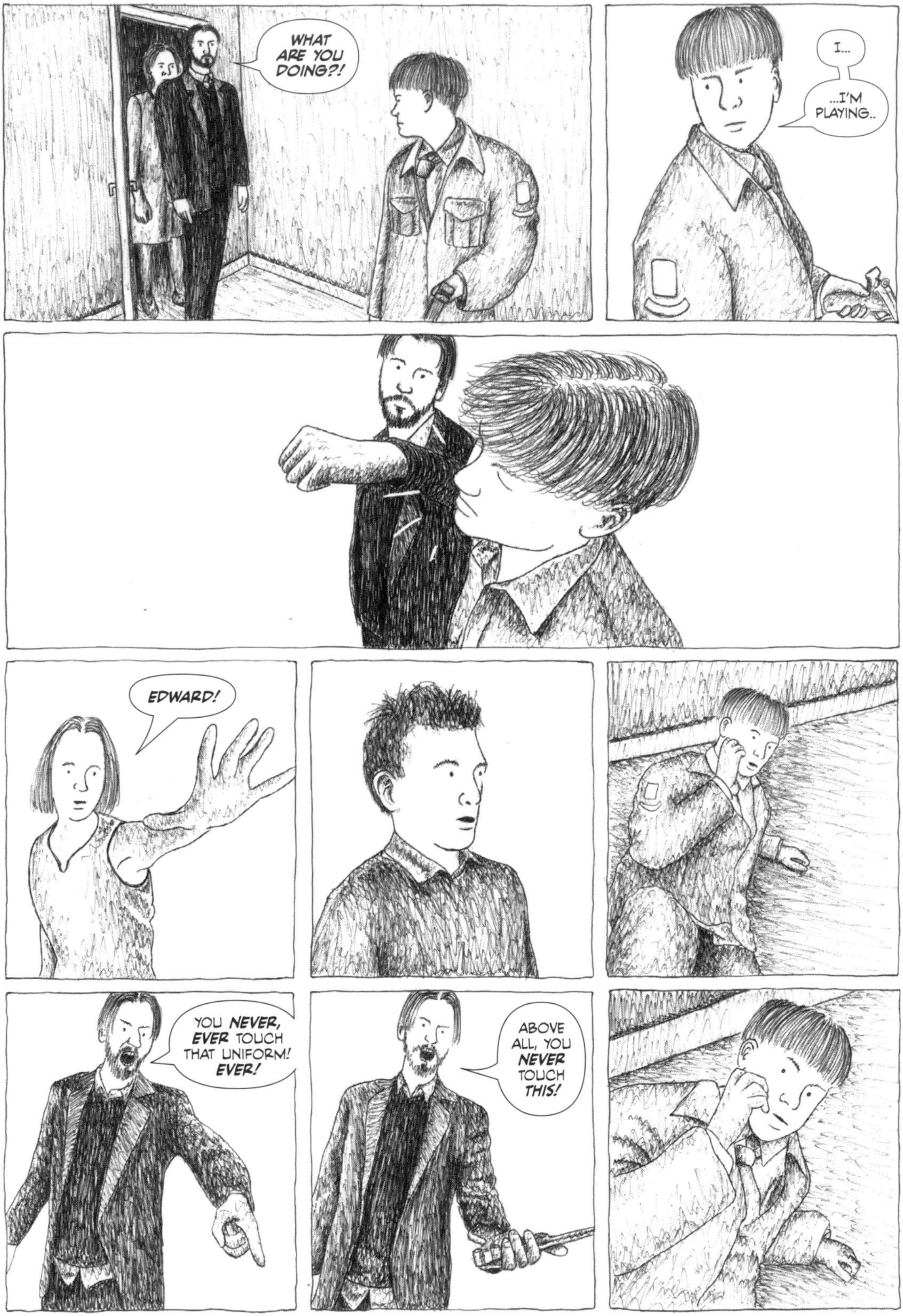
WHAT ARE YOU DOING?!
I...
...I'M PLAYING..
EDWARD!
YOU NEVER, EVER TOUCH THAT UNIFORM! EVER!
ABOVE ALL, YOU NEVER TOUCH THIS!

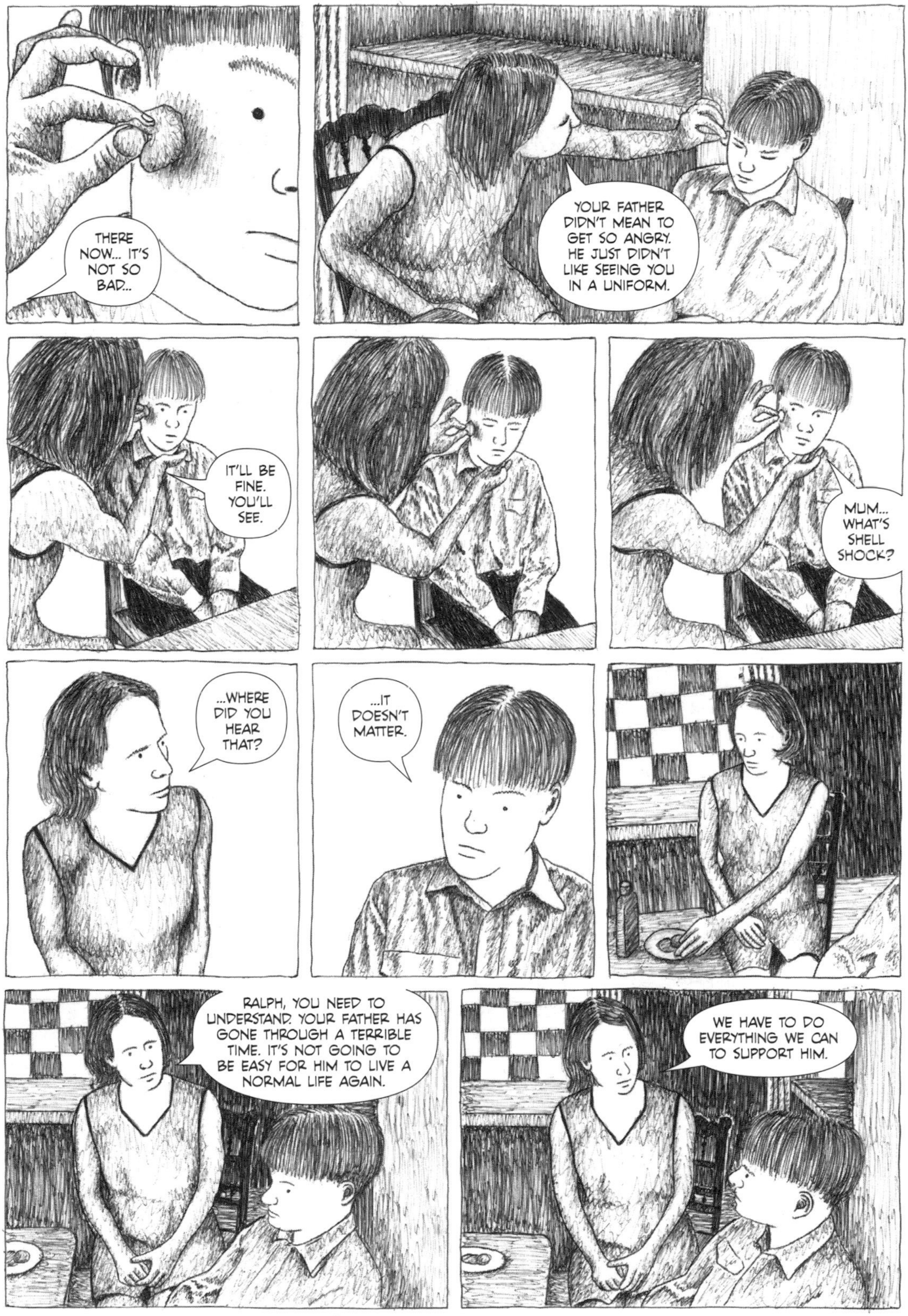
THERE NOW... IT'S NOT SO BAD...
YOUR FATHER DIDN'T MEAN TO GET SO ANGRY. HE JUST DIDN'T LIKE SEEING YOU IN A UNIFORM.
IT'LL BE FINE. YOU'LL SEE.
MUM... WHAT'S SHELL SHOCK?
...WHERE DID YOU HEAR THAT?
...IT DOESN'T MATTER.
RALPH, YOU NEED TO UNDERSTAND. YOUR FATHER HAS GONE THROUGH A TERRIBLE TIME. IT'S NOT GOING TO BE EASY FOR HIM TO LIVE A NORMAL LIFE AGAIN.
WE HAVE TO DO EVERYTHING WE CAN TO SUPPORT HIM.

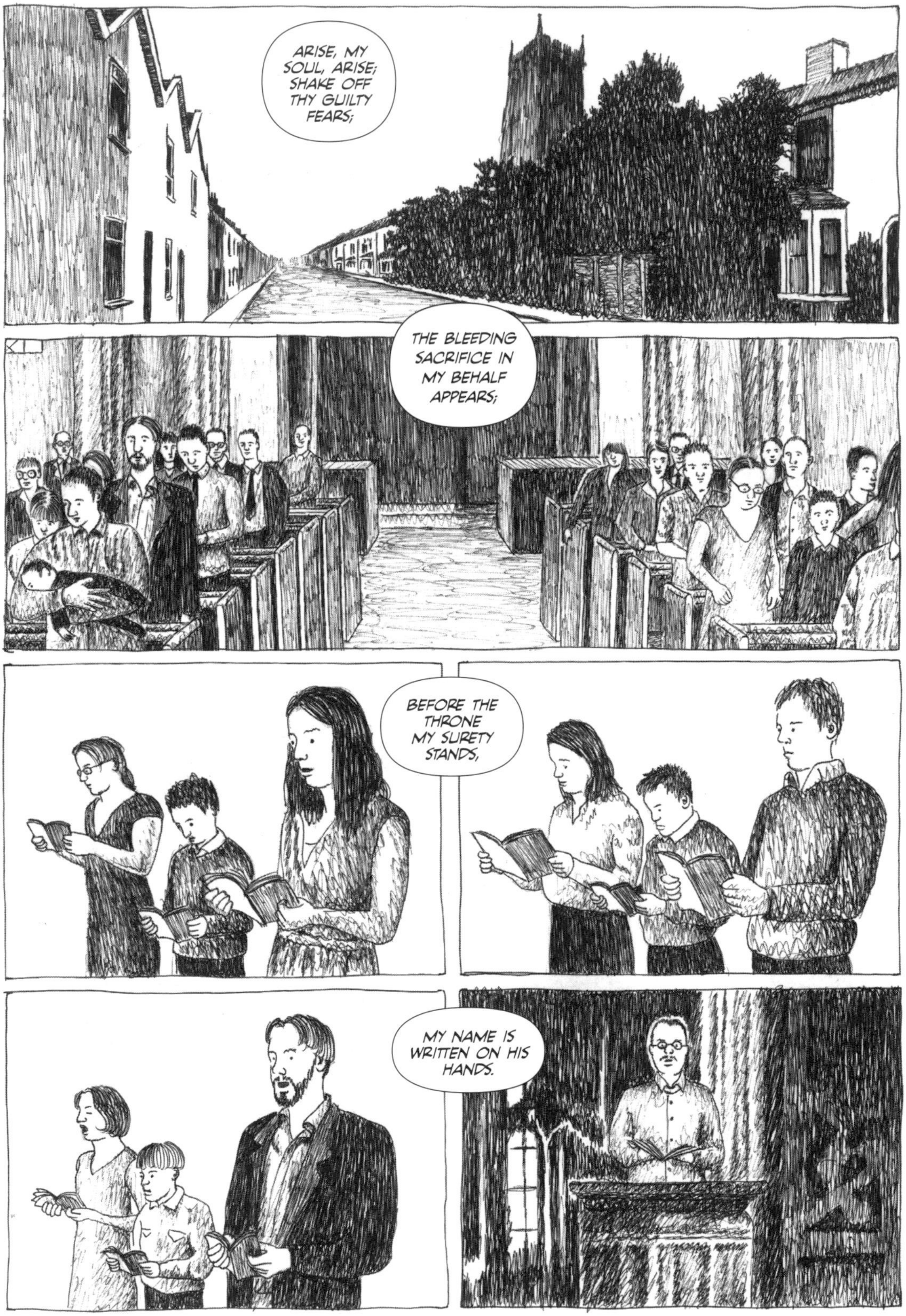
ARISE, MY SOUL, ARISE; SHAKE OFF THY GUILTY FEARS;
THE BLEEDING SACRIFICE IN MY BEHALF APPEARS;
BEFORE THE THRONE MY SURETY STANDS,
MY NAME IS WRITTEN ON HIS HANDS.

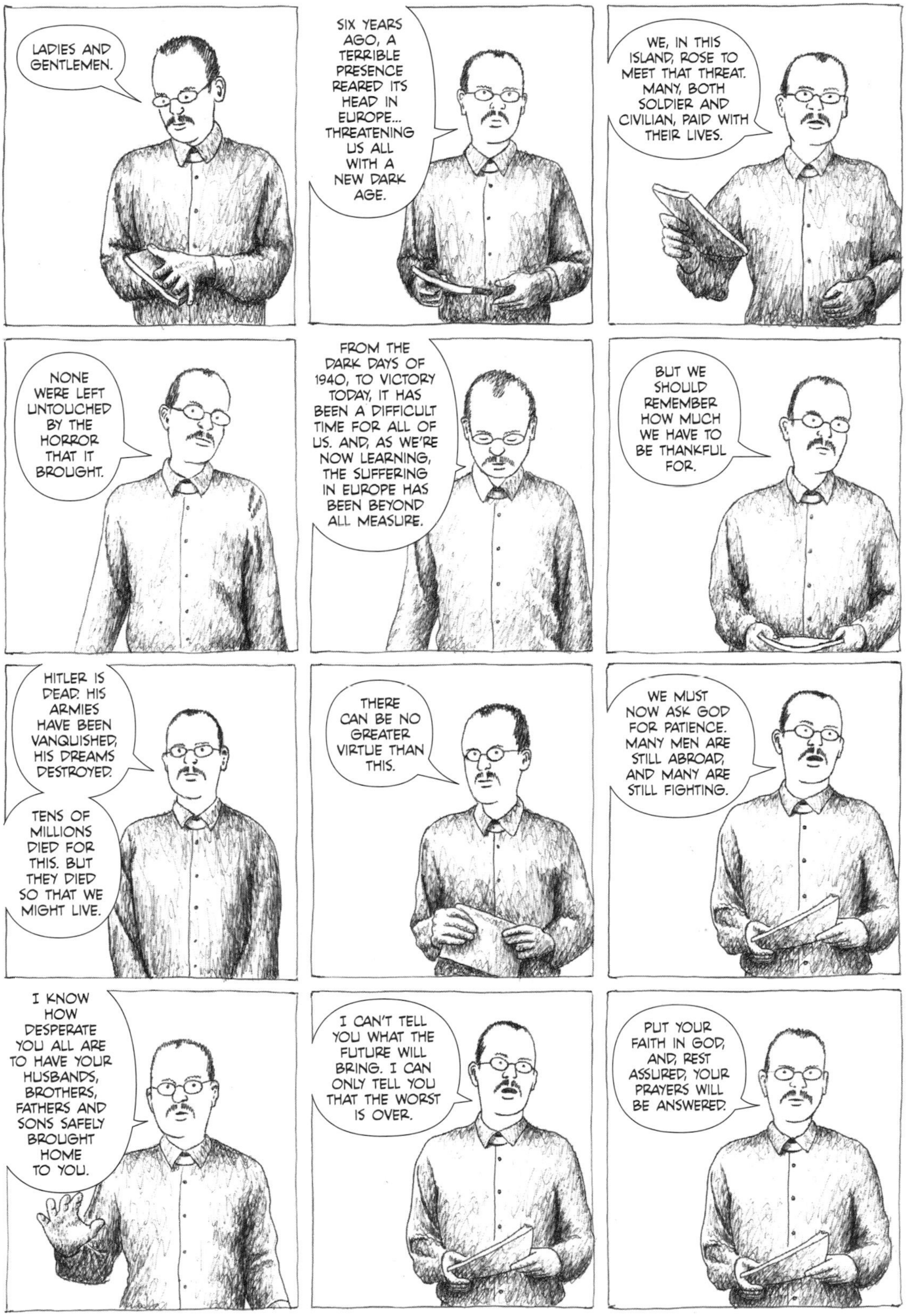
LADIES AND GENTLEMEN.
SIX YEARS AGO, A TERRIBLE PRESENCE REARED ITS HEAD IN EUROPE... THREATENING US ALL WITH A NEW DARK AGE.
WE, IN THIS ISLAND, ROSE TO MEET THAT THREAT. MANY, BOTH SOLDIER AND CIVILIAN, PAID WITH THEIR LIVES.
NONE WERE LEFT UNTOUCHED BY THE HORROR THAT IT BROUGHT.
FROM THE DARK DAYS OF 1940, TO VICTORY TODAY, IT HAS BEEN A DIFFICULT TIME FOR ALL OF US. AND, AS WE'RE NOW LEARNING, THE SUFFERING IN EUROPE HAS BEEN BEYOND ALL MEASURE.
BUT WE SHOULD REMEMBER HOW MUCH WE HAVE TO BE THANKFUL FOR.
HITLER IS DEAD. HIS ARMIES HAVE BEEN VANQUISHED, HIS DREAMS DESTROYED.
TENS OF MILLIONS DIED FOR THIS. BUT THEY DIED SO THAT WE MIGHT LIVE.
THERE CAN BE NO GREATER VIRTUE THAN THIS.
WE MUST NOW ASK GOD FOR PATIENCE. MANY MEN ARE STILL ABROAD, AND MANY ARE STILL FIGHTING.
I KNOW HOW DESPERATE YOU ALL ARE TO HAVE YOUR HUSBANDS, BROTHERS, FATHERS AND SONS SAFELY BROUGHT HOME TO YOU.
I CAN'T TELL YOU WHAT THE FUTURE WILL BRING. I CAN ONLY TELL YOU THAT THE WORST IS OVER.
PUT YOUR FAITH IN GOD, AND, REST ASSURED, YOUR PRAYERS WILL BE ANSWERED.

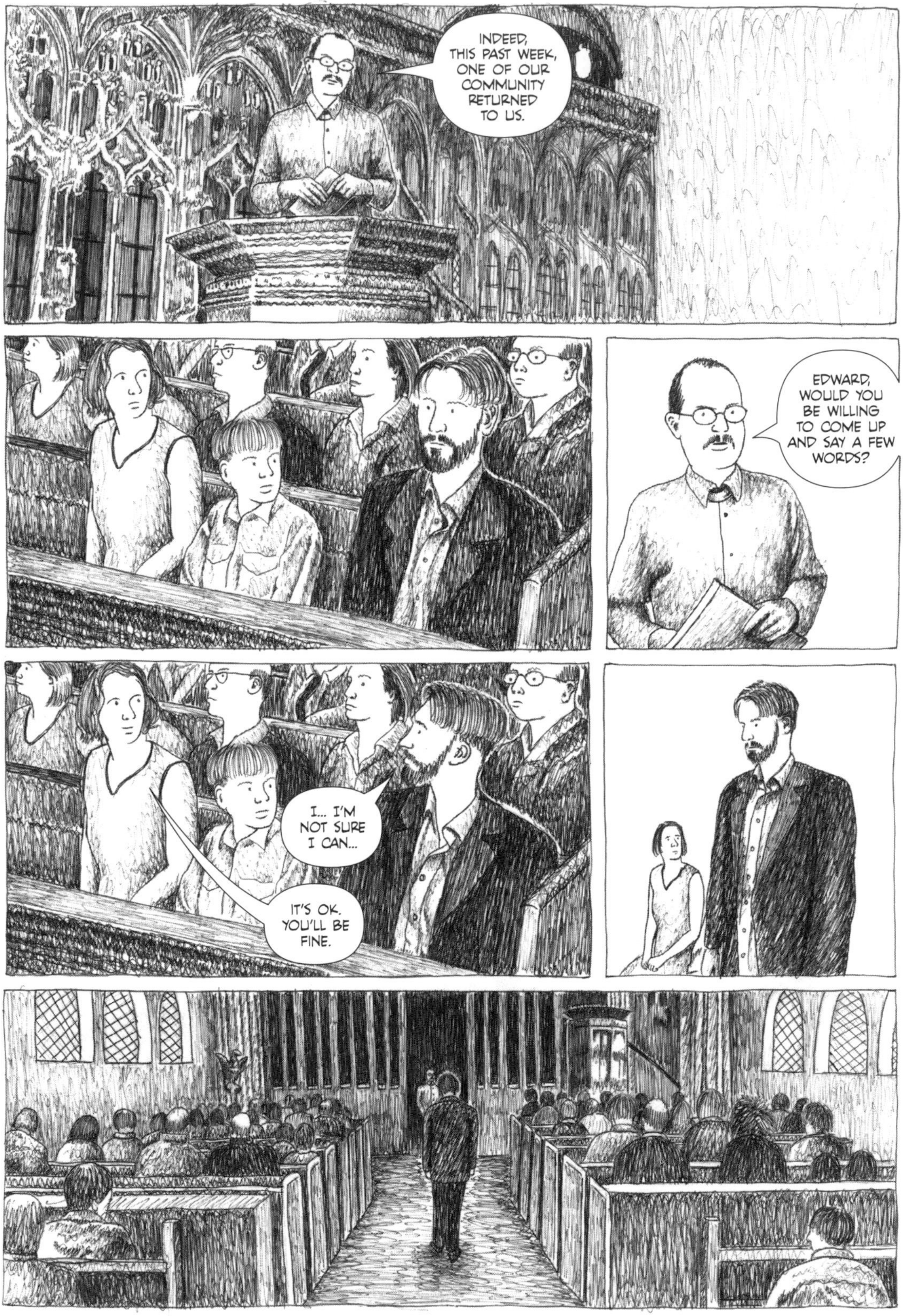
INDEED, THIS PAST WEEK, ONE OF OUR COMMUNITY RETURNED TO US.
EDWARD, WOULD YOU BE WILLING TO COME UP AND SAY A FEW WORDS?
I... I'M NOT SURE I CAN...
IT'S OK. YOU'LL BE FINE.

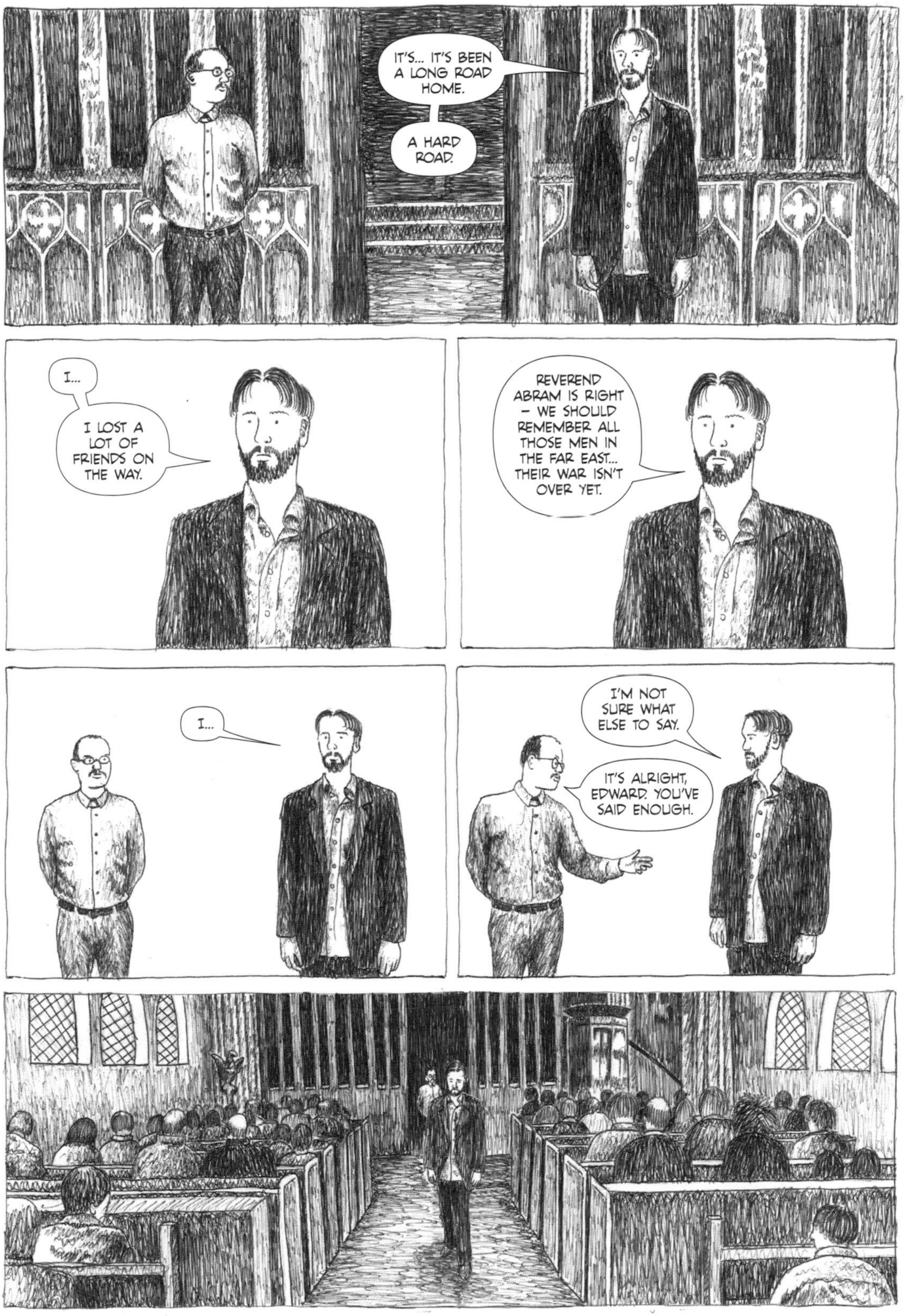
IT'S... IT'S BEEN A LONG ROAD HOME.
A HARD ROAD.
I...
I LOST A LOT OF FRIENDS ON THE WAY.
REVEREND ABRAM IS RIGHT – WE SHOULD REMEMBER ALL THOSE MEN IN THE FAR EAST... THEIR WAR ISN'T OVER YET.
I...
I'M NOT SURE WHAT ELSE TO SAY.
IT'S ALRIGHT, EDWARD. YOU'VE SAID ENOUGH.

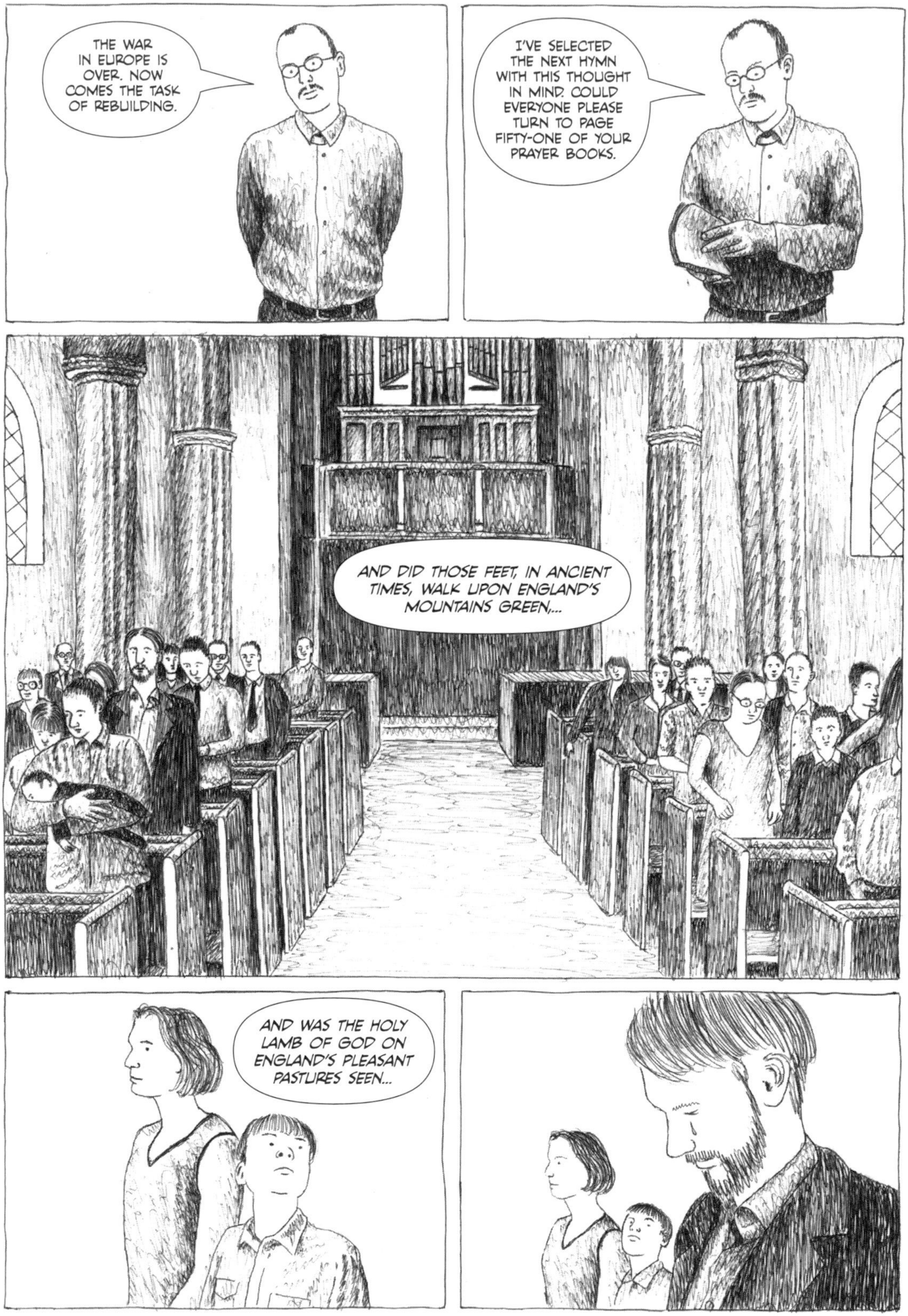
THE WAR IN EUROPE IS OVER. NOW COMES THE TASK OF REBUILDING.
I'VE SELECTED THE NEXT HYMN WITH THIS THOUGHT IN MIND. COULD EVERYONE PLEASE TURN TO PAGE FIFTY-ONE OF YOUR PRAYER BOOKS.
AND DID THOSE FEET, IN ANCIENT TIMES, WALK UPON ENGLAND'S MOUNTAINS GREEN,...
AND WAS THE HOLY LAMB OF GOD ON ENGLAND'S PLEASANT PASTURES SEEN...

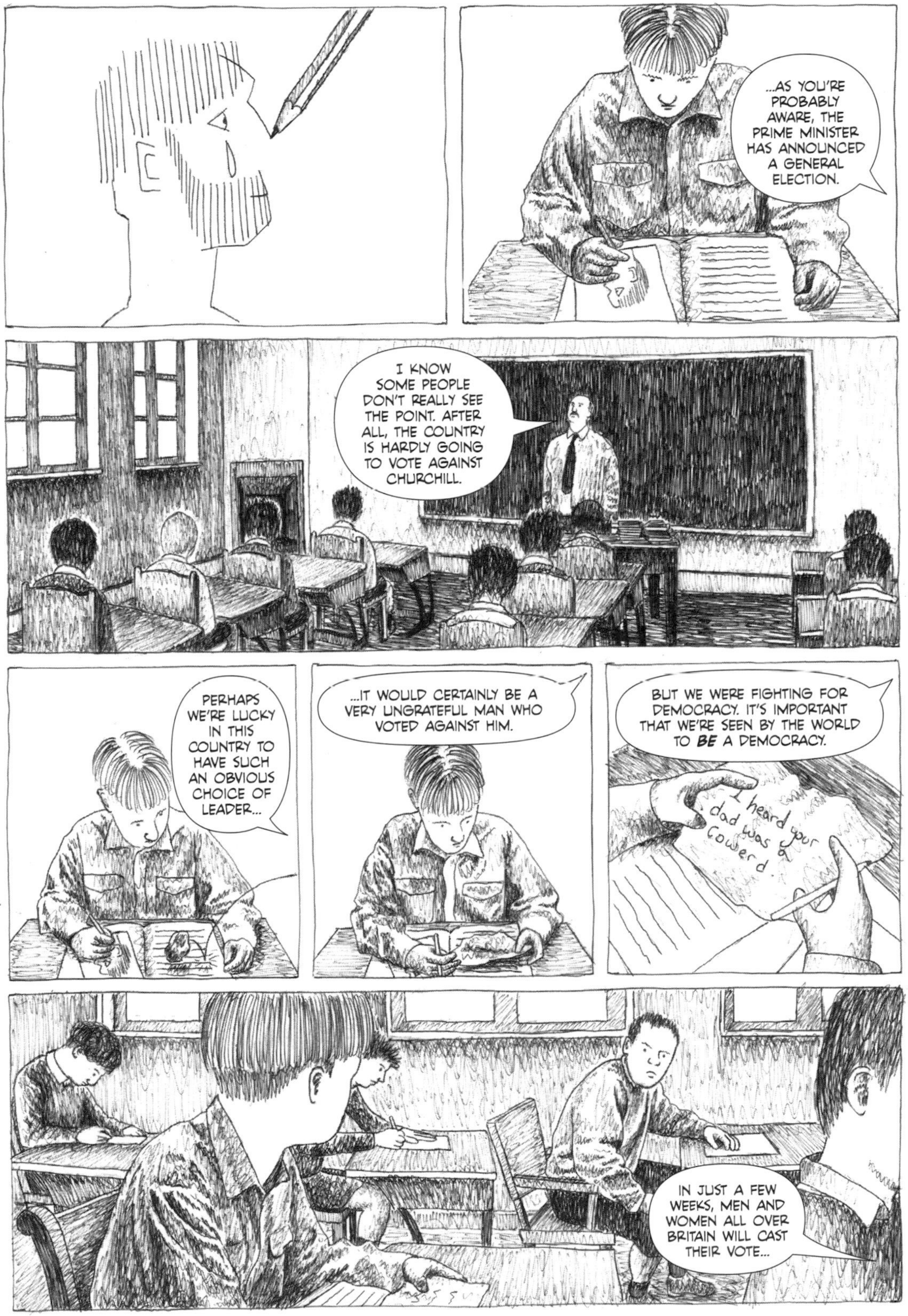
...AS YOU'RE PROBABLY AWARE, THE PRIME MINISTER HAS ANNOUNCED A GENERAL ELECTION.
I KNOW SOME PEOPLE DON'T REALLY SEE THE POINT. AFTER ALL, THE COUNTRY IS HARDLY GOING TO VOTE AGAINST CHURCHILL.
PERHAPS WE'RE LUCKY IN THIS COUNTRY TO HAVE SUCH AN OBVIOUS CHOICE OF LEADER...
...IT WOULD CERTAINLY BE A VERY UNGRATEFUL MAN WHO VOTED AGAINST HIM.
BUT WE WERE FIGHTING FOR DEMOCRACY. IT'S IMPORTANT THAT WE'RE SEEN BY THE WORLD TO **BE** A DEMOCRACY.
I heard your dad was a cowerd.
IN JUST A FEW WEEKS, MEN AND WOMEN ALL OVER BRITAIN WILL CAST THEIR VOTE...

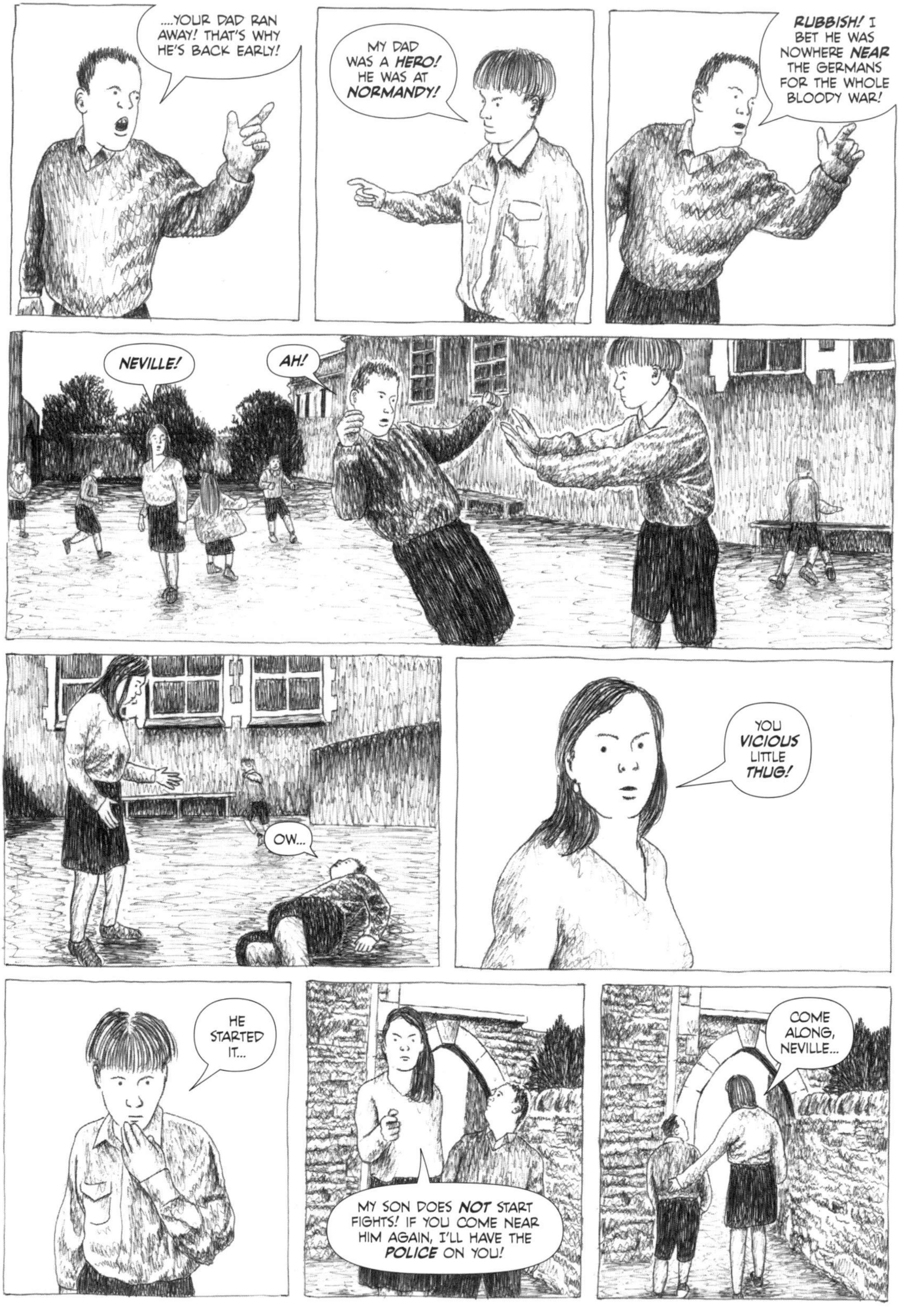
....YOUR DAD RAN AWAY! THAT'S WHY HE'S BACK EARLY!
MY DAD WAS A HERO! HE WAS AT NORMANDY!
RUBBISH! I BET HE WAS NOWHERE NEAR THE GERMANS FOR THE WHOLE BLOODY WAR!
NEVILLE!
AH!
OW...
YOU VICIOUS LITTLE THUG!
HE STARTED IT...
MY SON DOES NOT START FIGHTS! IF YOU COME NEAR HIM AGAIN, I'LL HAVE THE POLICE ON YOU!
COME ALONG, NEVILLE...

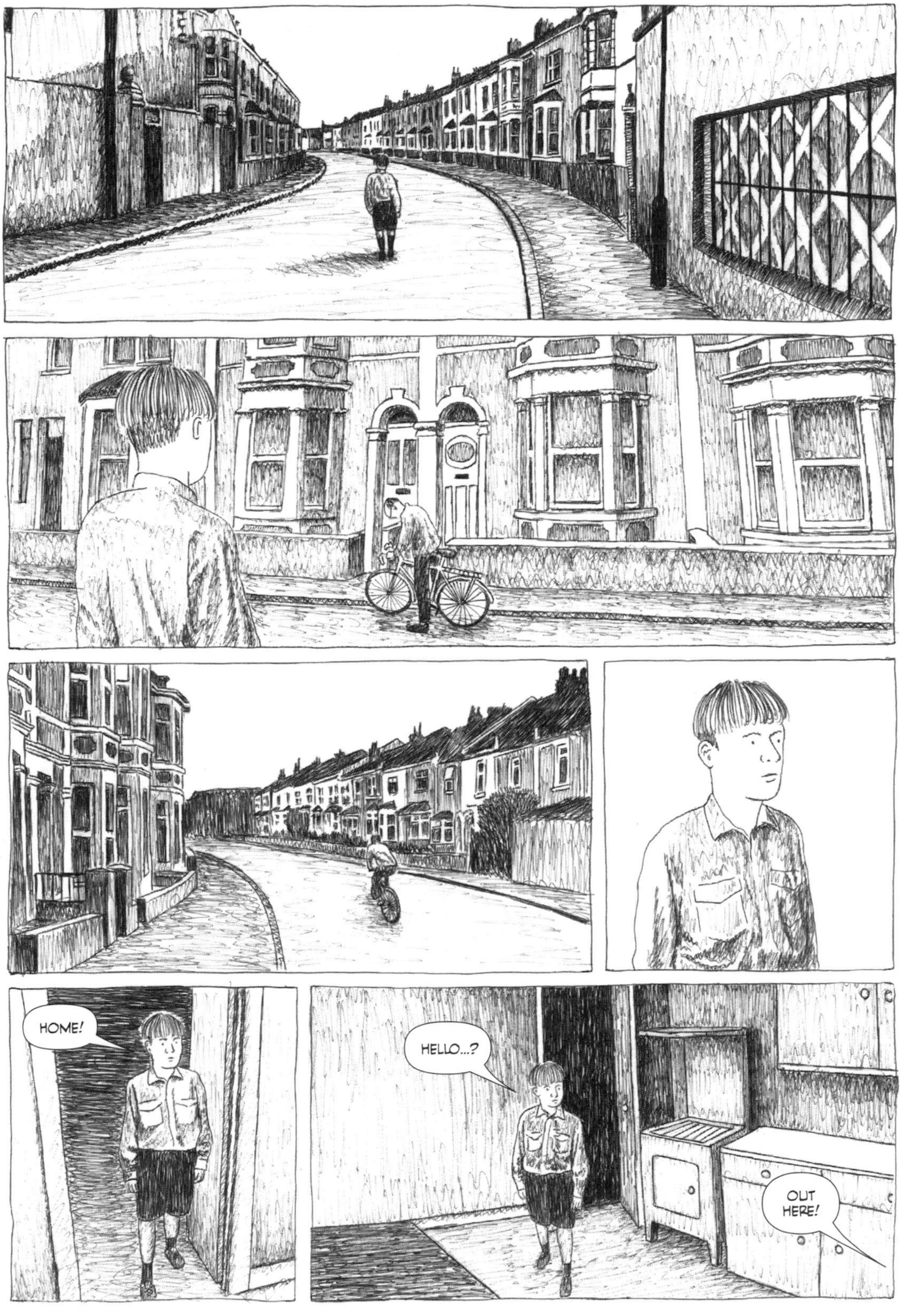
HOME!
HELLO...?
OUT HERE!

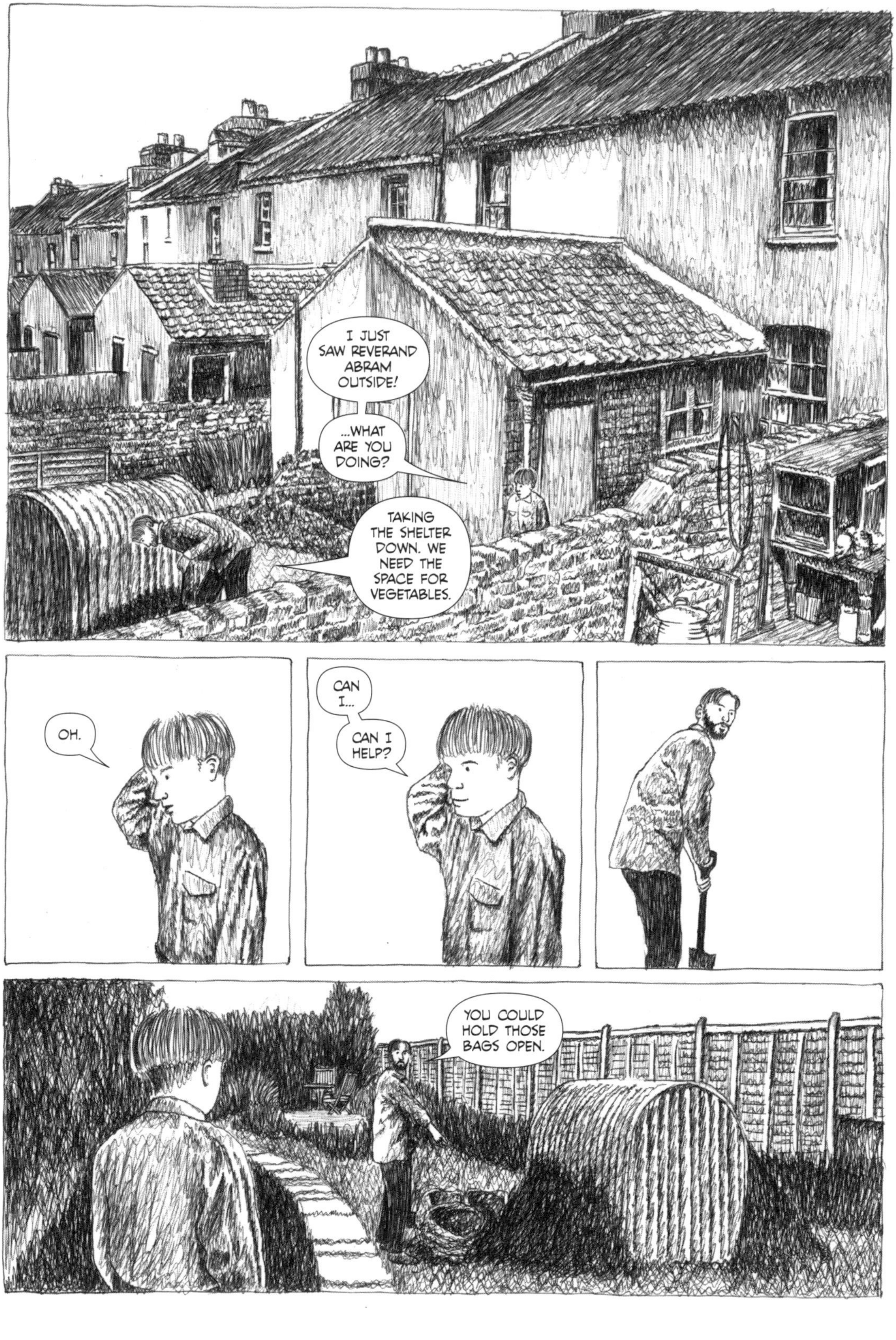
I JUST SAW REVEREND ABRAM OUTSIDE!
...WHAT ARE YOU DOING?
TAKING THE SHELTER DOWN. WE NEED THE SPACE FOR VEGETABLES.
OH.
CAN I...
CAN I HELP?
YOU COULD HOLD THOSE BAGS OPEN.

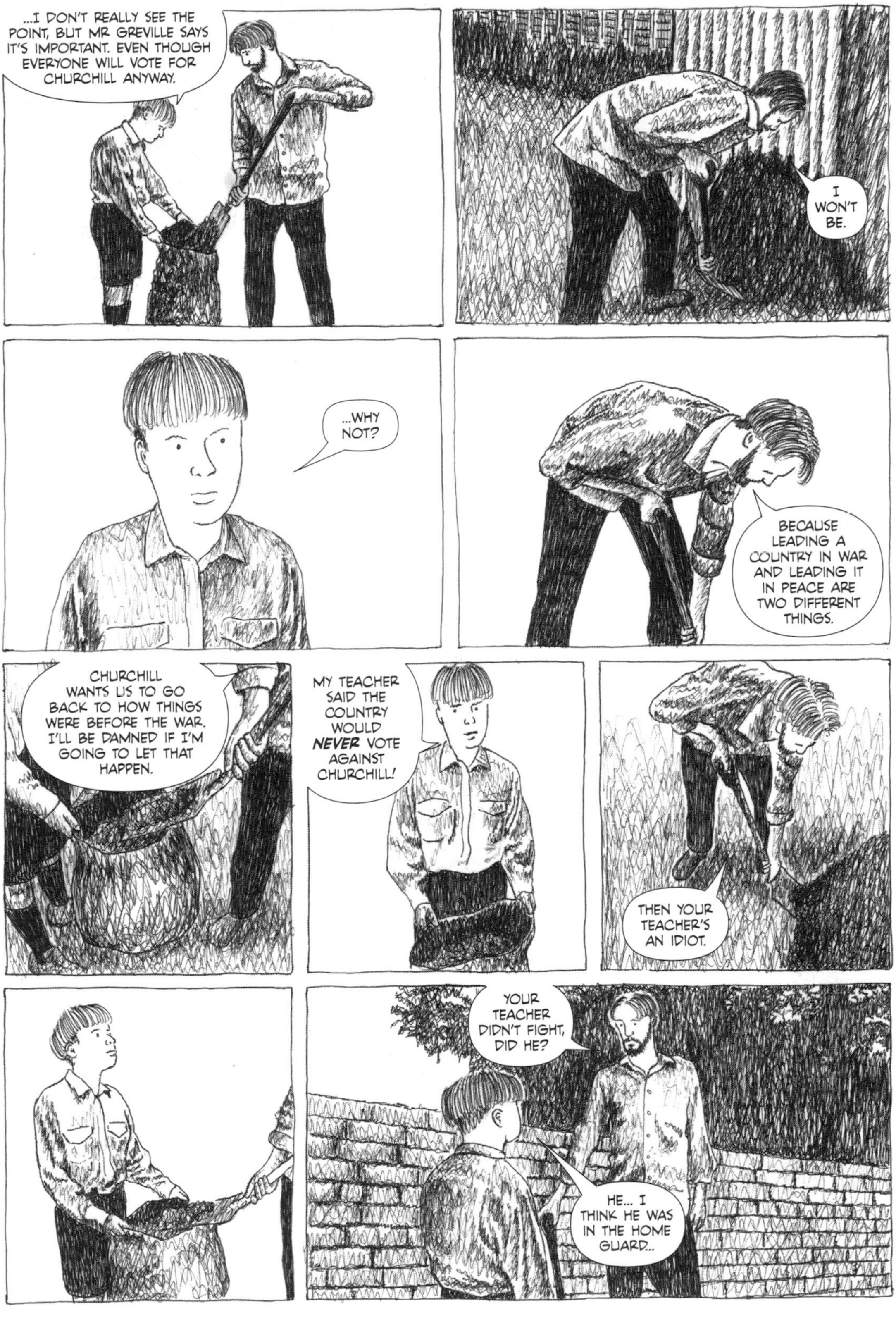
...I DON'T REALLY SEE THE POINT, BUT MR GREVILLE SAYS IT'S IMPORTANT. EVEN THOUGH EVERYONE WILL VOTE FOR CHURCHILL ANYWAY.
I WON'T BE.
...WHY NOT?
BECAUSE LEADING A COUNTRY IN WAR AND LEADING IT IN PEACE ARE TWO DIFFERENT THINGS.
CHURCHILL WANTS US TO GO BACK TO HOW THINGS WERE BEFORE THE WAR. I'LL BE DAMNED IF I'M GOING TO LET THAT HAPPEN.
MY TEACHER SAID THE COUNTRY WOULD ***NEVER*** VOTE AGAINST CHURCHILL!
THEN YOUR TEACHER'S AN IDIOT.
YOUR TEACHER DIDN'T FIGHT, DID HE?
HE... I THINK HE WAS IN THE HOME GUARD...

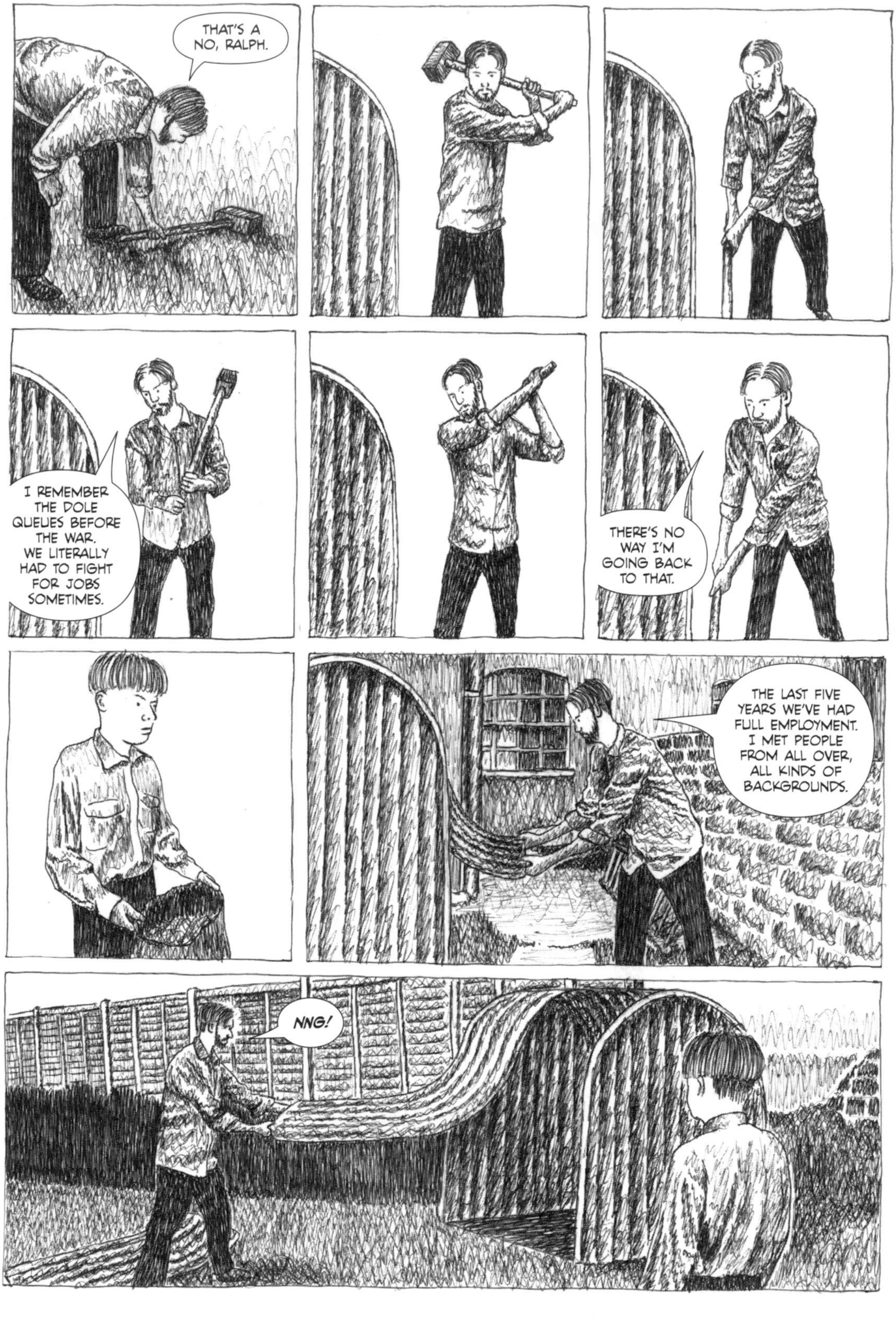
THAT'S A NO, RALPH.
I REMEMBER THE DOLE QUEUES BEFORE THE WAR. WE LITERALLY HAD TO FIGHT FOR JOBS SOMETIMES.
THERE'S NO WAY I'M GOING BACK TO THAT.
THE LAST FIVE YEARS WE'VE HAD FULL EMPLOYMENT. I MET PEOPLE FROM ALL OVER, ALL KINDS OF BACKGROUNDS.
NNG!

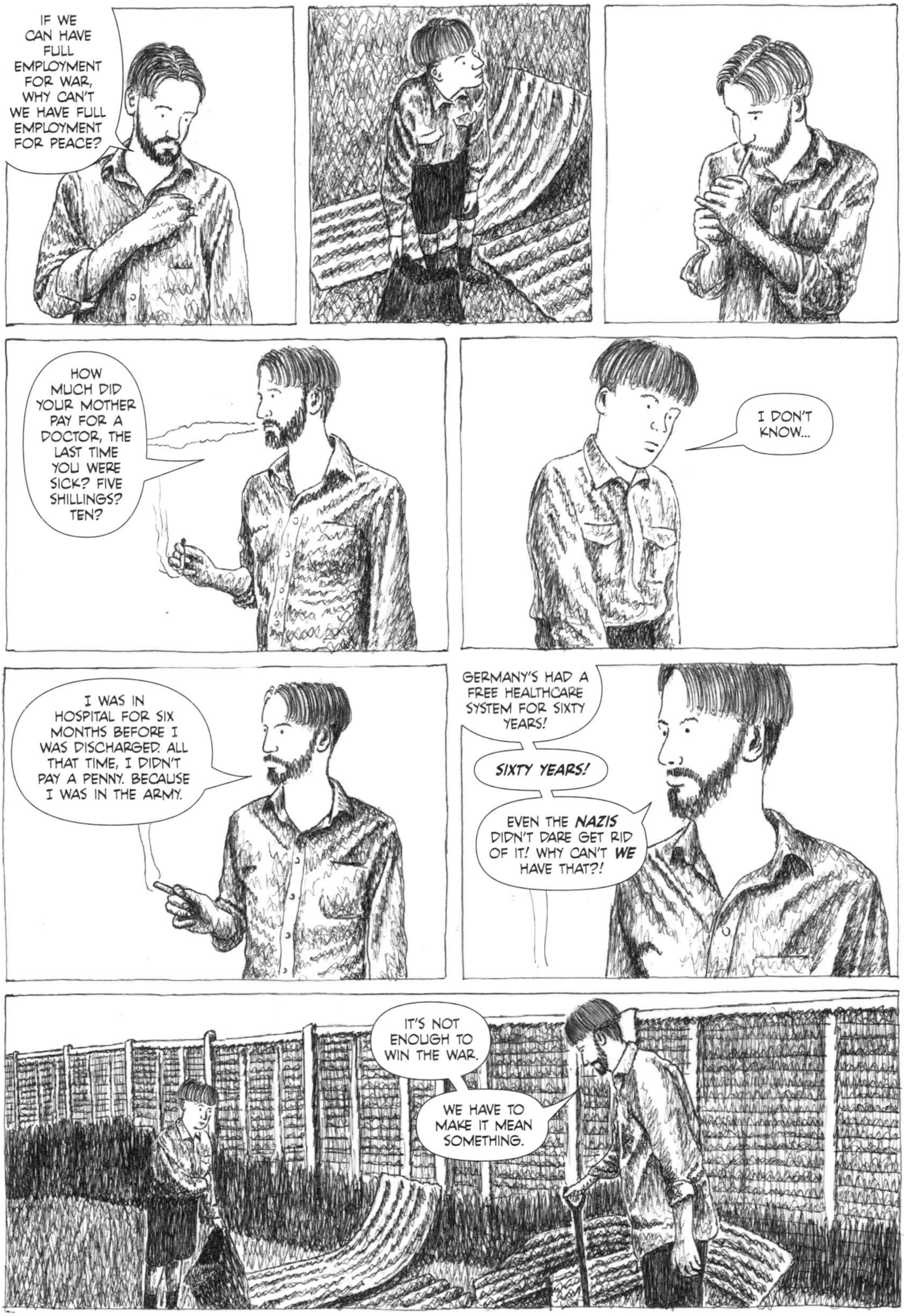
IF WE CAN HAVE FULL EMPLOYMENT FOR WAR, WHY CAN'T WE HAVE FULL EMPLOYMENT FOR PEACE?
HOW MUCH DID YOUR MOTHER PAY FOR A DOCTOR, THE LAST TIME YOU WERE SICK? FIVE SHILLINGS? TEN?
I DON'T KNOW...
I WAS IN HOSPITAL FOR SIX MONTHS BEFORE I WAS DISCHARGED. ALL THAT TIME, I DIDN'T PAY A PENNY. BECAUSE I WAS IN THE ARMY.
GERMANY'S HAD A FREE HEALTHCARE SYSTEM FOR SIXTY YEARS!
SIXTY YEARS!
EVEN THE ***NAZIS*** DIDN'T DARE GET RID OF IT! WHY CAN'T ***WE*** HAVE THAT?!
IT'S NOT ENOUGH TO WIN THE WAR.
WE HAVE TO MAKE IT MEAN SOMETHING.

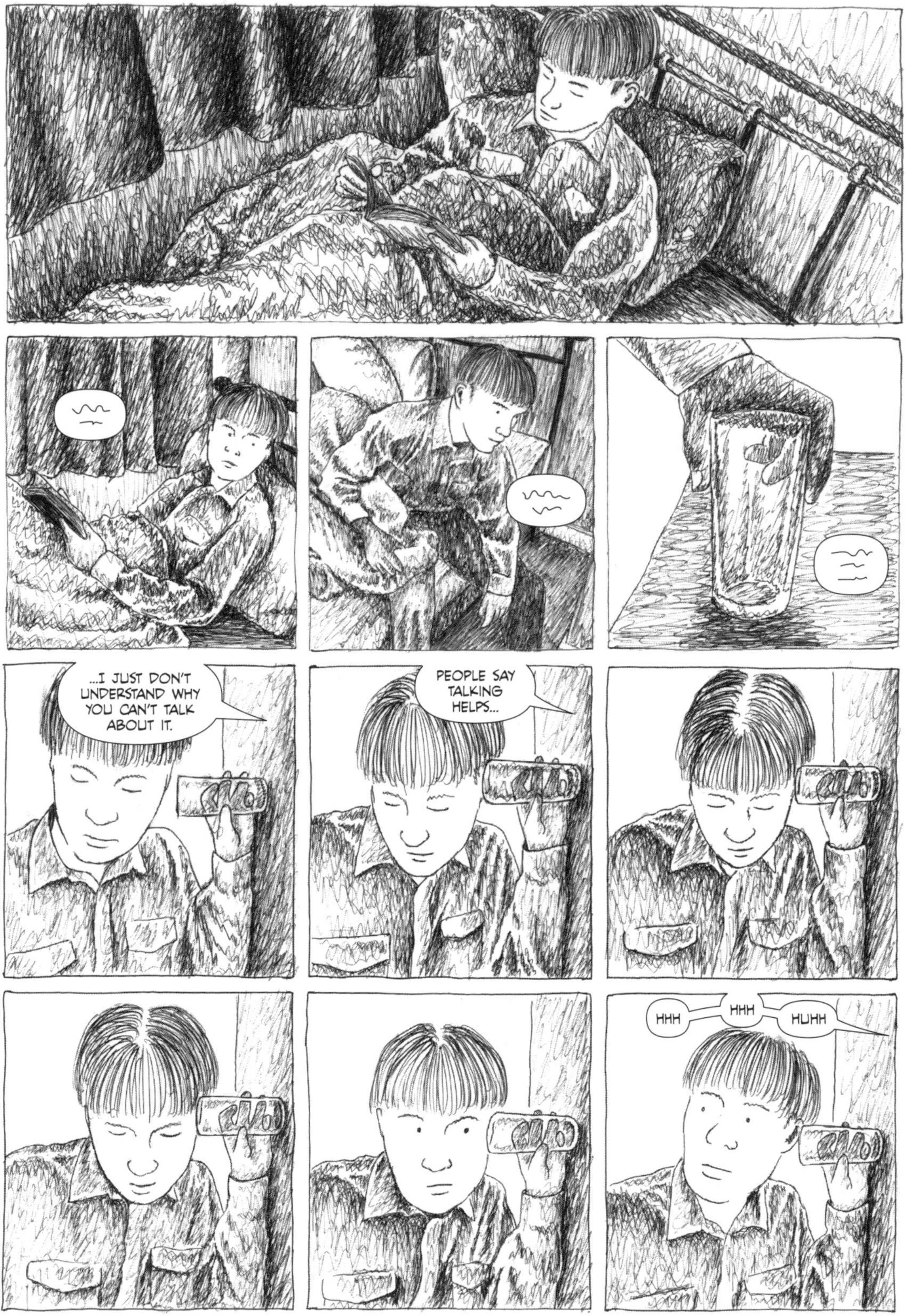
...I JUST DON'T UNDERSTAND WHY YOU CAN'T TALK ABOUT IT.
PEOPLE SAY TALKING HELPS...
HHH
HHH
HUHH

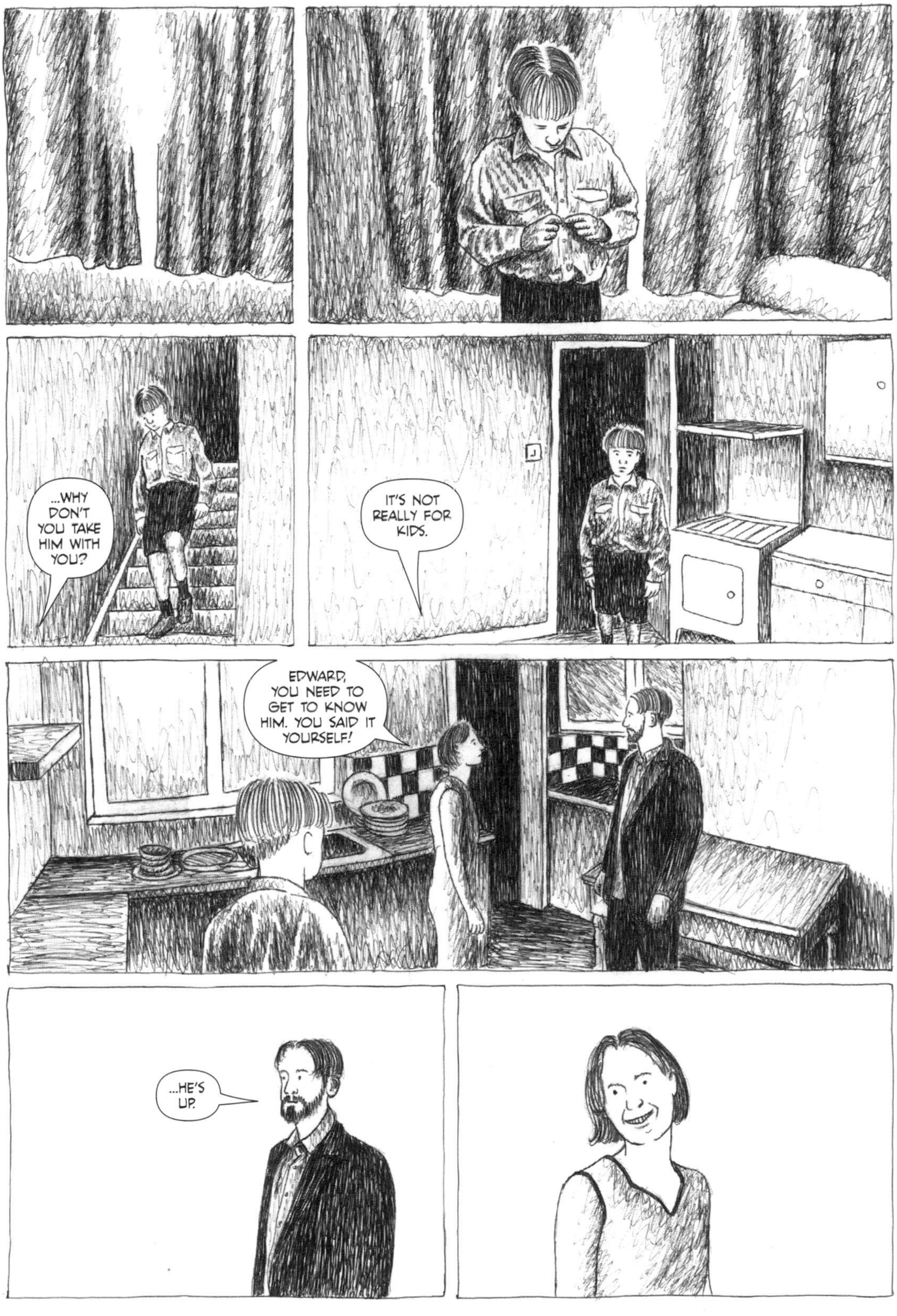
...WHY DON'T YOU TAKE HIM WITH YOU?
IT'S NOT REALLY FOR KIDS.
EDWARD, YOU NEED TO GET TO KNOW HIM. YOU SAID IT YOURSELF!
...HE'S UP.

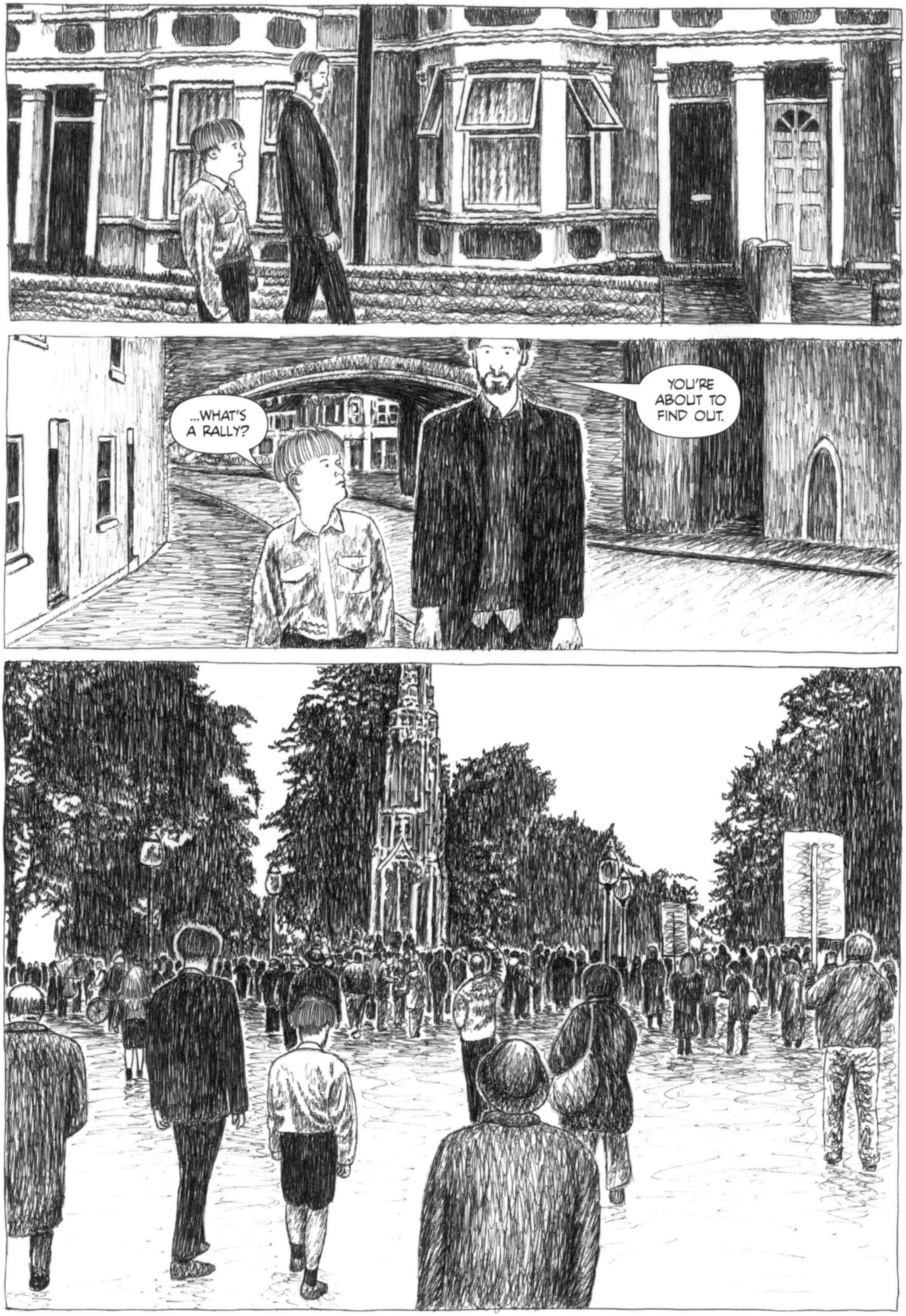
...WHAT'S A RALLY?
YOU'RE ABOUT TO FIND OUT.

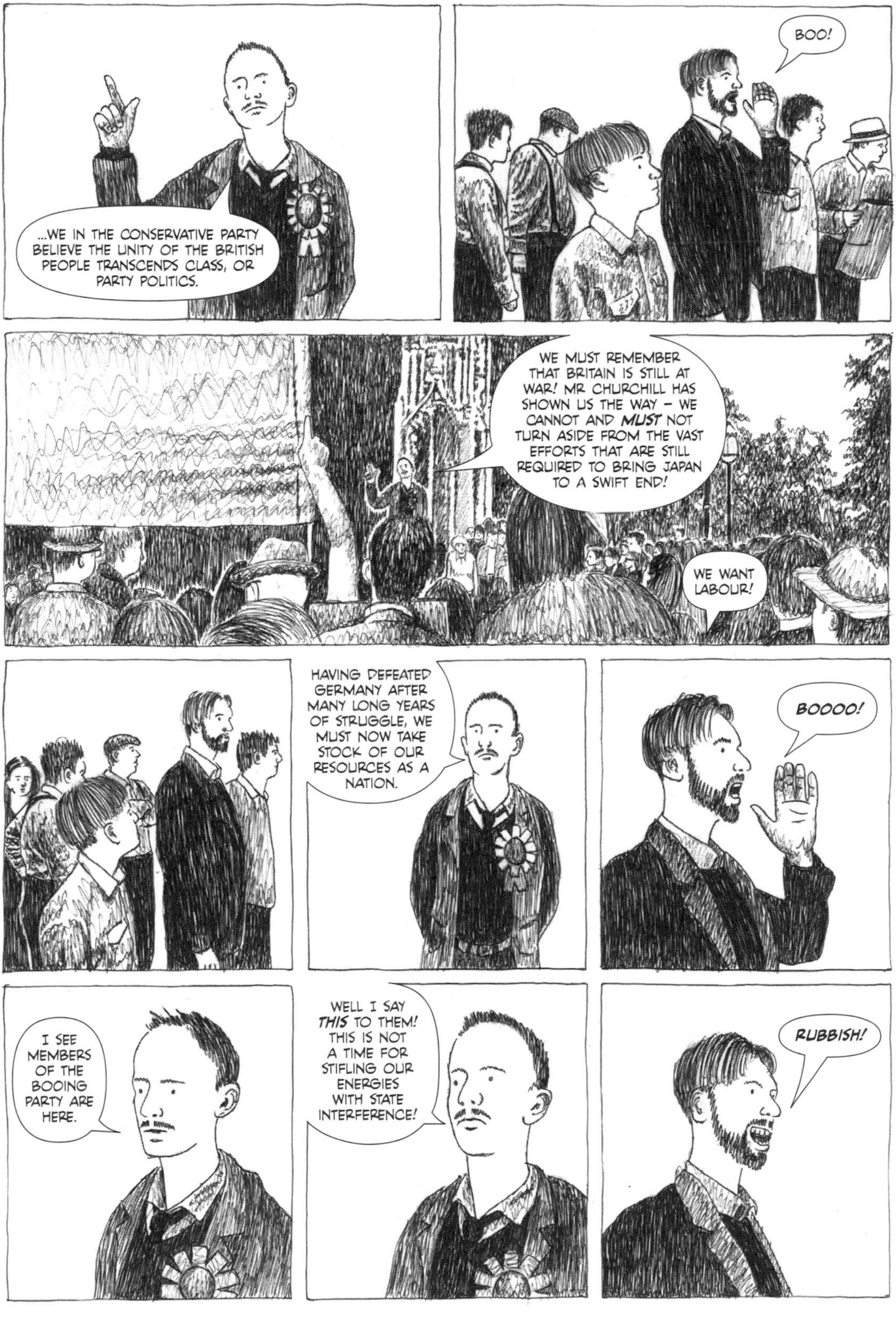
...WE IN THE CONSERVATIVE PARTY BELIEVE THE UNITY OF THE BRITISH PEOPLE TRANSCENDS CLASS, OR PARTY POLITICS.
BOO!
WE MUST REMEMBER THAT BRITAIN IS STILL AT WAR! MR CHURCHILL HAS SHOWN US THE WAY – WE CANNOT AND MUST NOT TURN ASIDE FROM THE VAST EFFORTS THAT ARE STILL REQUIRED TO BRING JAPAN TO A SWIFT END!
WE WANT LABOUR!
HAVING DEFEATED GERMANY AFTER MANY LONG YEARS OF STRUGGLE, WE MUST NOW TAKE STOCK OF OUR RESOURCES AS A NATION.
BOOOO!
I SEE MEMBERS OF THE BOOING PARTY ARE HERE.
WELL I SAY THIS TO THEM! THIS IS NOT A TIME FOR STIFLING OUR ENERGIES WITH STATE INTERFERENCE!
RUBBISH!

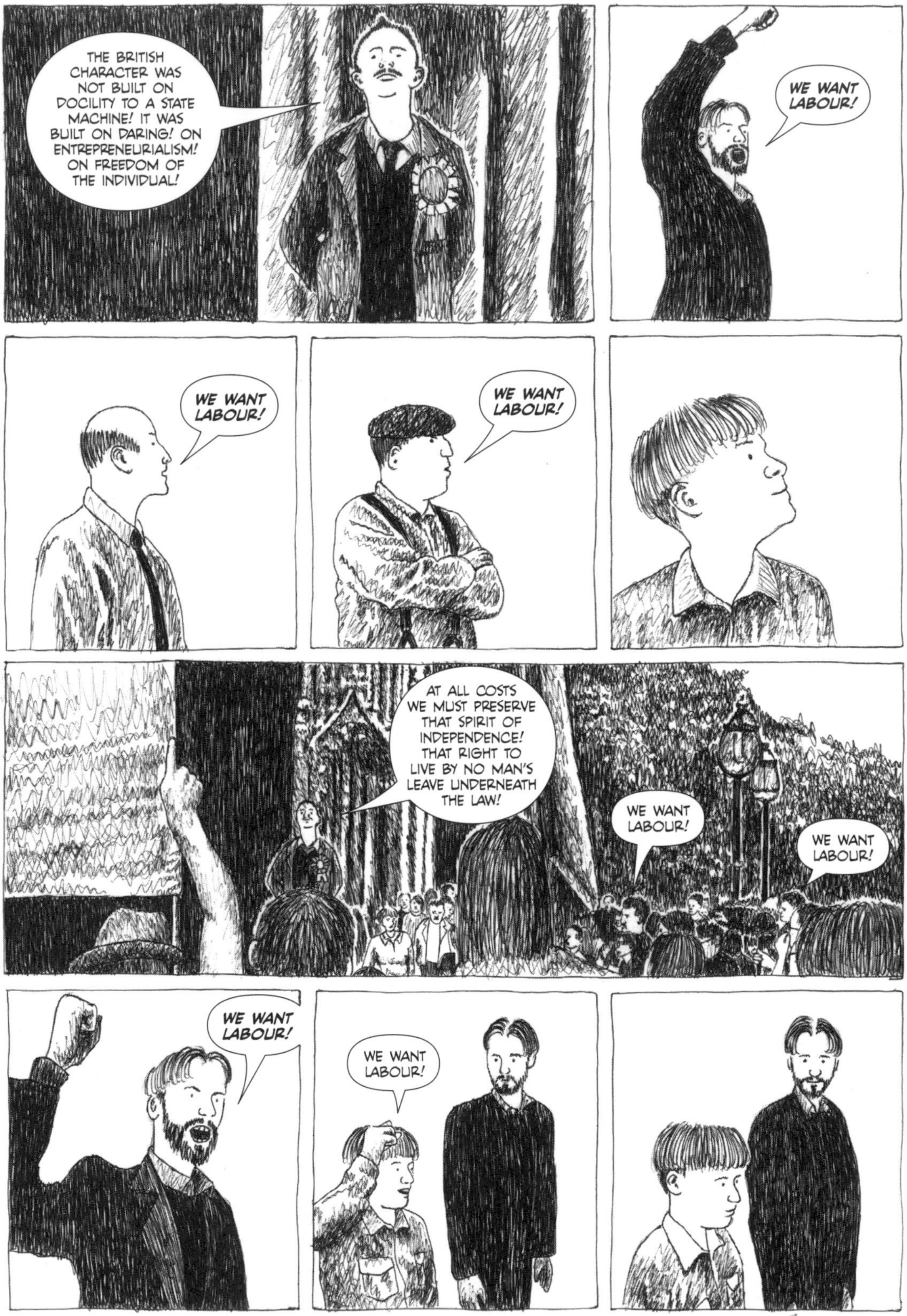
THE BRITISH CHARACTER WAS NOT BUILT ON DOCILITY TO A STATE MACHINE! IT WAS BUILT ON DARING! ON ENTREPRENEURIALISM! ON FREEDOM OF THE INDIVIDUAL!
WE WANT LABOUR!
WE WANT LABOUR!
WE WANT LABOUR!
AT ALL COSTS WE MUST PRESERVE THAT SPIRIT OF INDEPENDENCE! THAT RIGHT TO LIVE BY NO MAN'S LEAVE UNDERNEATH THE LAW!
WE WANT LABOUR!
WE WANT LABOUR!
WE WANT LABOUR!
WE WANT LABOUR!

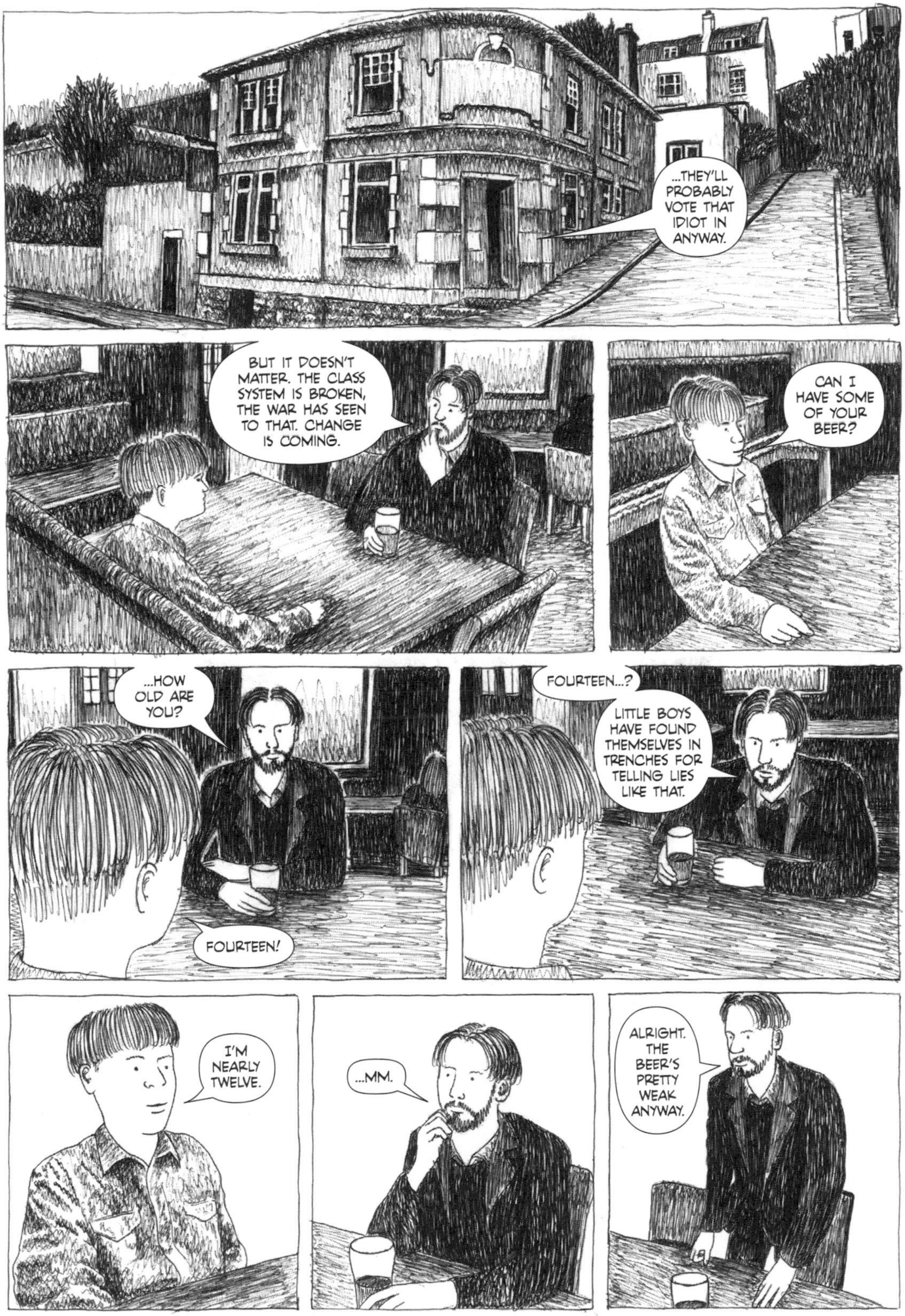
...THEY'LL PROBABLY VOTE THAT IDIOT IN ANYWAY.
BUT IT DOESN'T MATTER. THE CLASS SYSTEM IS BROKEN, THE WAR HAS SEEN TO THAT. CHANGE IS COMING.
CAN I HAVE SOME OF YOUR BEER?
...HOW OLD ARE YOU?
FOURTEEN!
FOURTEEN...?
LITTLE BOYS HAVE FOUND THEMSELVES IN TRENCHES FOR TELLING LIES LIKE THAT.
I'M NEARLY TWELVE.
...MM.
ALRIGHT. THE BEER'S PRETTY WEAK ANYWAY.

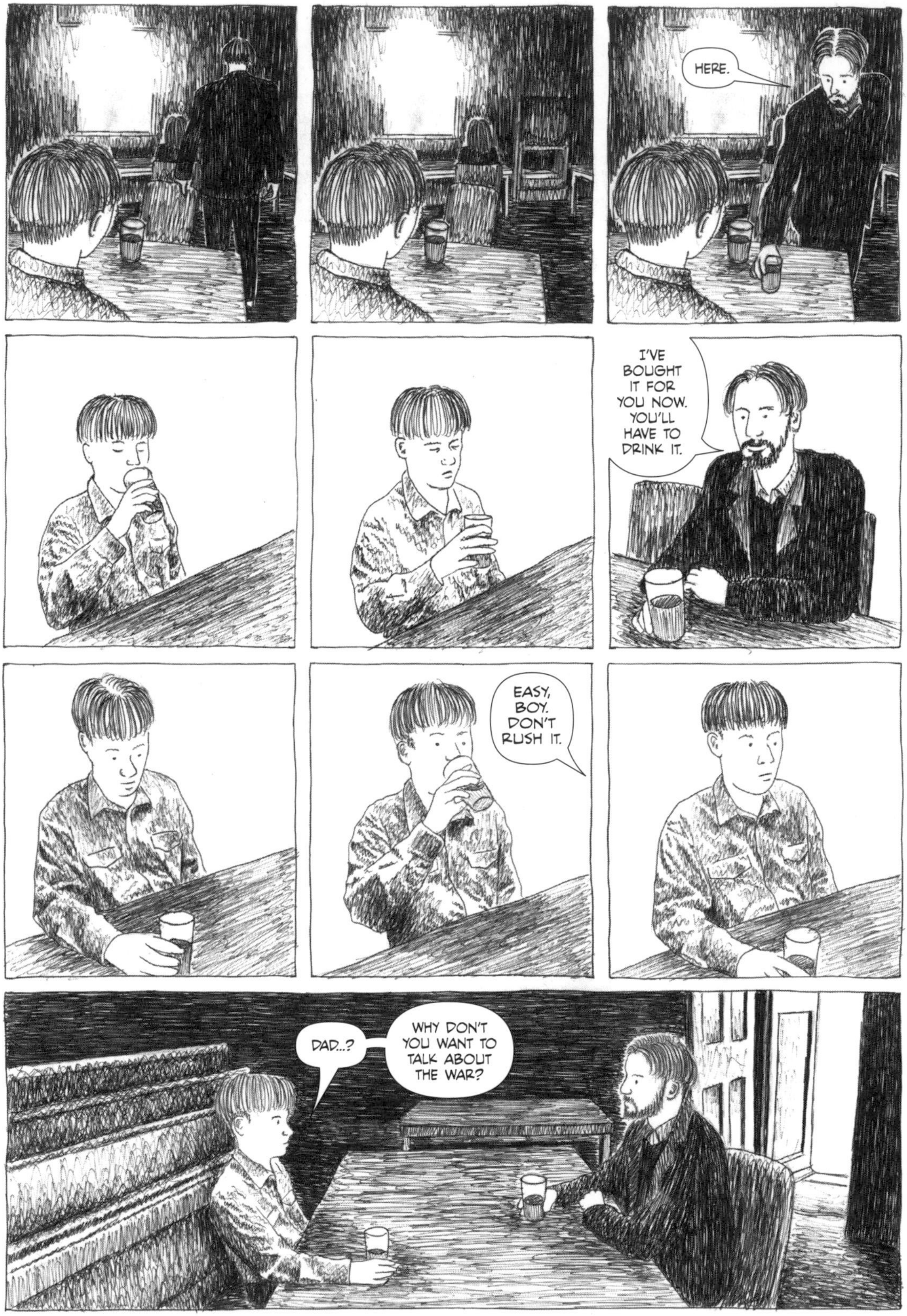
HERE.
I'VE BOUGHT IT FOR YOU NOW. YOU'LL HAVE TO DRINK IT.
EASY, BOY. DON'T RUSH IT.
DAD...?
WHY DON'T YOU WANT TO TALK ABOUT THE WAR?

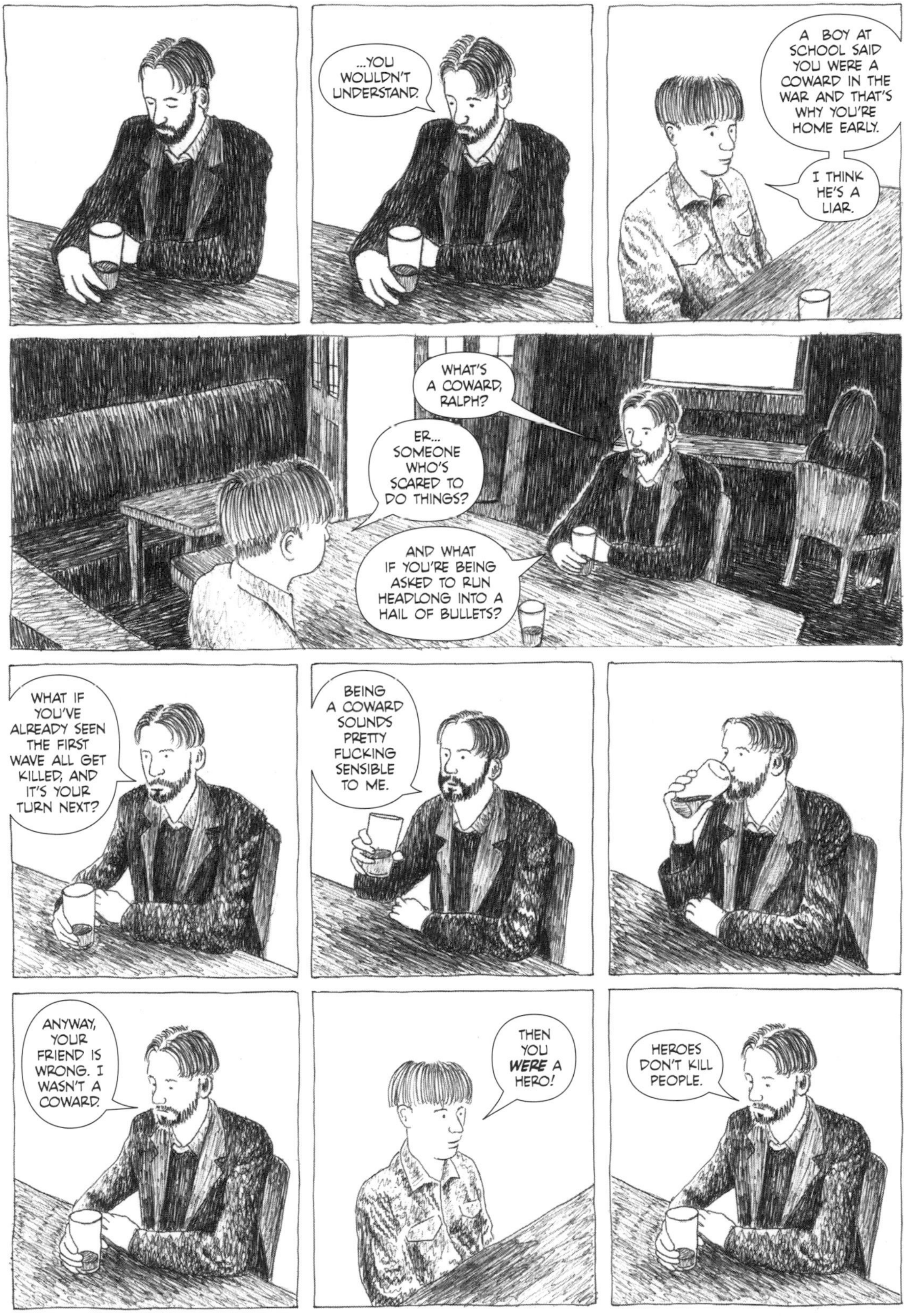
...YOU WOULDN'T UNDERSTAND.
A BOY AT SCHOOL SAID YOU WERE A COWARD IN THE WAR AND THAT'S WHY YOU'RE HOME EARLY.
I THINK HE'S A LIAR.
WHAT'S A COWARD, RALPH?
ER... SOMEONE WHO'S SCARED TO DO THINGS?
AND WHAT IF YOU'RE BEING ASKED TO RUN HEADLONG INTO A HAIL OF BULLETS?
WHAT IF YOU'VE ALREADY SEEN THE FIRST WAVE ALL GET KILLED, AND IT'S YOUR TURN NEXT?
BEING A COWARD SOUNDS PRETTY FUCKING SENSIBLE TO ME.
ANYWAY, YOUR FRIEND IS WRONG. I WASN'T A COWARD.
THEN YOU *WERE* A HERO!
HEROES DON'T KILL PEOPLE.

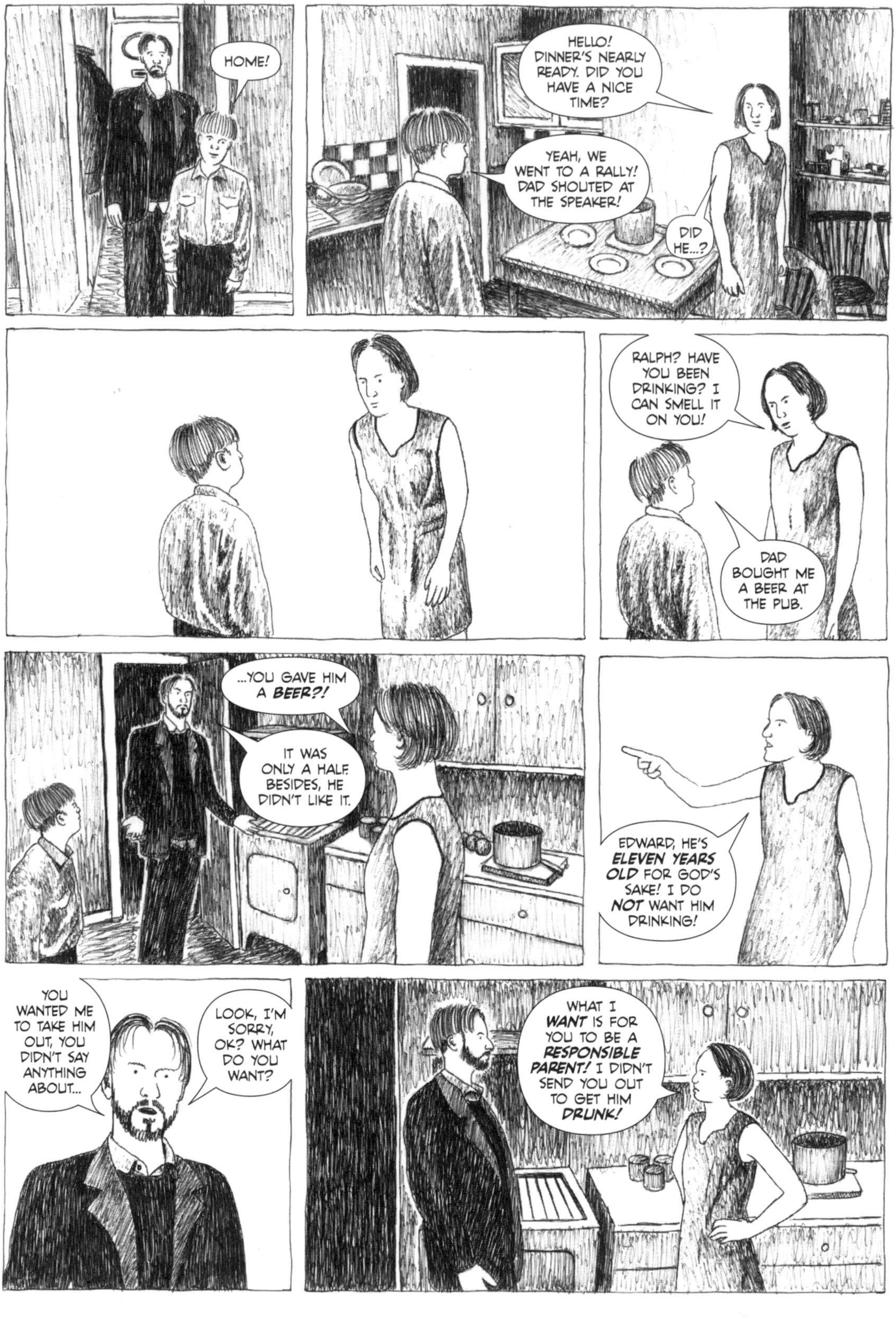

HOME!
HELLO! DINNER'S NEARLY READY. DID YOU HAVE A NICE TIME?
YEAH, WE WENT TO A RALLY! DAD SHOUTED AT THE SPEAKER!
DID HE...?
RALPH? HAVE YOU BEEN DRINKING? I CAN SMELL IT ON YOU!
DAD BOUGHT ME A BEER AT THE PUB.
...YOU GAVE HIM A BEER?!
IT WAS ONLY A HALF. BESIDES, HE DIDN'T LIKE IT.
EDWARD, HE'S ELEVEN YEARS OLD FOR GOD'S SAKE! I DO NOT WANT HIM DRINKING!
YOU WANTED ME TO TAKE HIM OUT, YOU DIDN'T SAY ANYTHING ABOUT...
LOOK, I'M SORRY, OK? WHAT DO YOU WANT?
WHAT I WANT IS FOR YOU TO BE A RESPONSIBLE PARENT! I DIDN'T SEND YOU OUT TO GET HIM DRUNK!

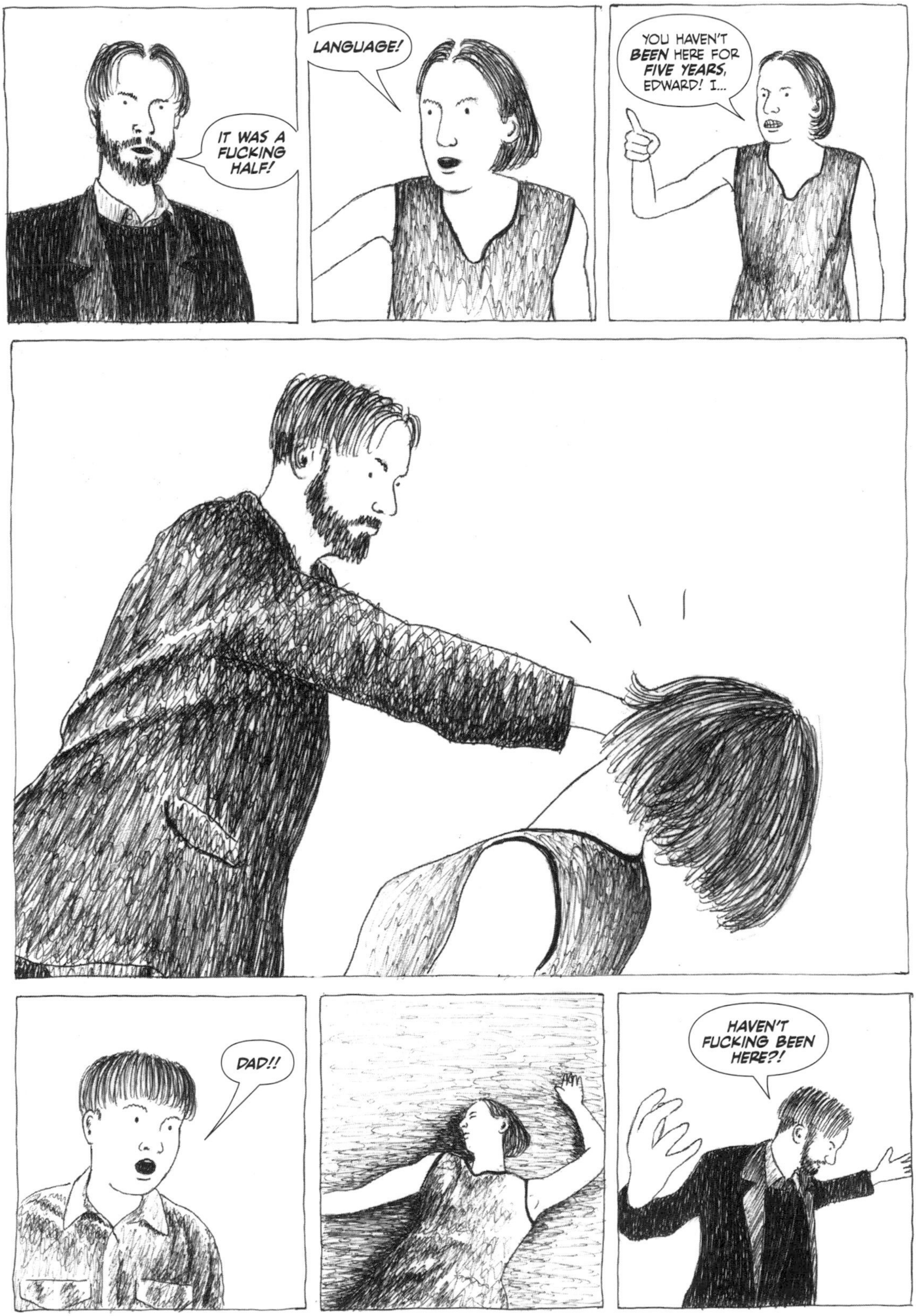
IT WAS A FUCKING HALF!
LANGUAGE!
YOU HAVEN'T BEEN HERE FOR FIVE YEARS, EDWARD! I...
DAD!!
HAVEN'T FUCKING BEEN HERE?!

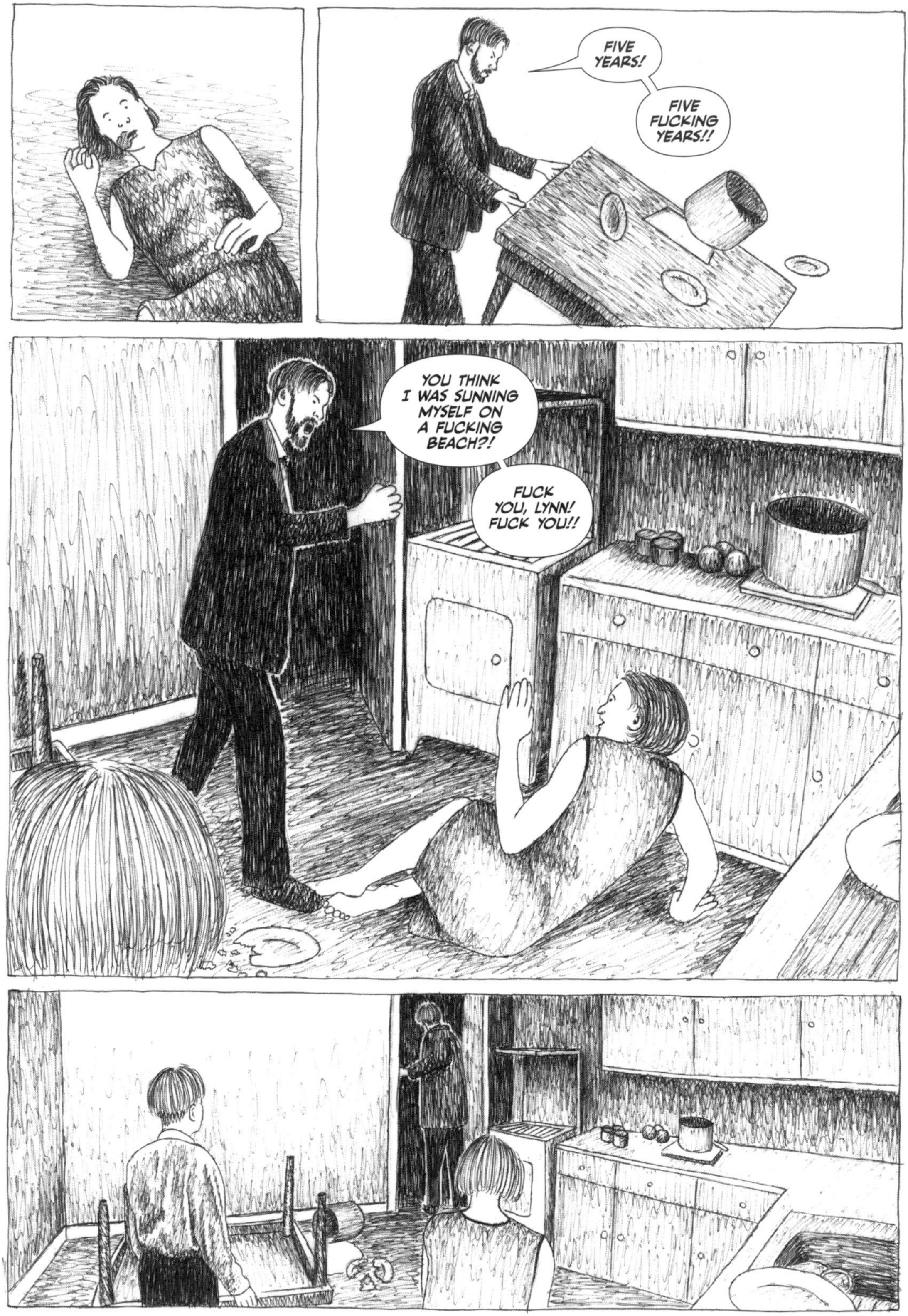
FIVE YEARS!
FIVE FUCKING YEARS!!
YOU THINK I WAS SUNNING MYSELF ON A FUCKING BEACH?!
FUCK YOU, LYNN! FUCK YOU!!

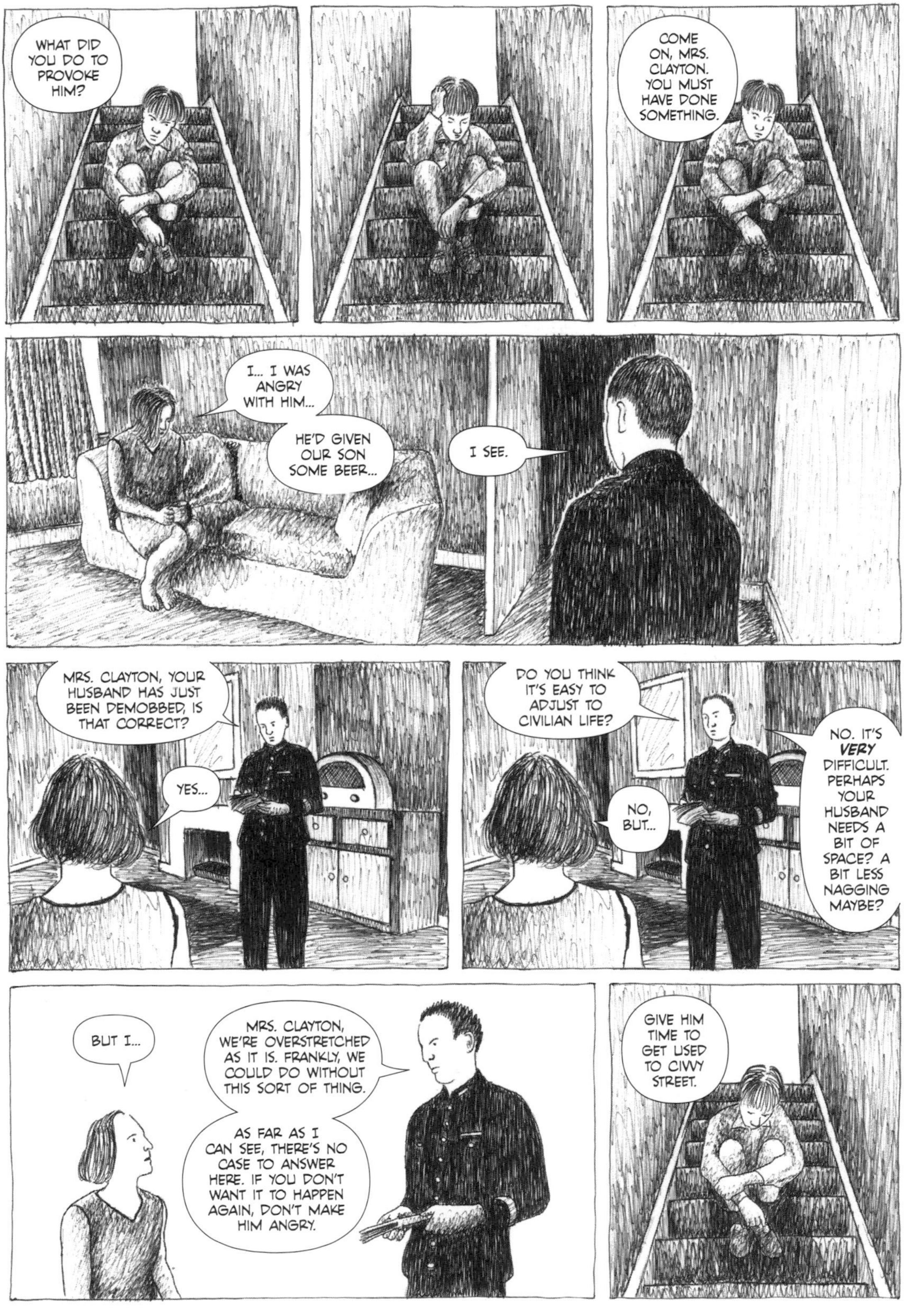
WHAT DID YOU DO TO PROVOKE HIM?
COME ON, MRS. CLAYTON. YOU MUST HAVE DONE SOMETHING.
I... I WAS ANGRY WITH HIM...
HE'D GIVEN OUR SON SOME BEER...
I SEE.
MRS. CLAYTON, YOUR HUSBAND HAS JUST BEEN DEMOBBED, IS THAT CORRECT?
YES...
DO YOU THINK IT'S EASY TO ADJUST TO CIVILIAN LIFE?
NO, BUT...
NO. IT'S *VERY* DIFFICULT. PERHAPS YOUR HUSBAND NEEDS A BIT OF SPACE? A BIT LESS NAGGING MAYBE?
BUT I...
MRS. CLAYTON, WE'RE OVERSTRETCHED AS IT IS. FRANKLY, WE COULD DO WITHOUT THIS SORT OF THING.
AS FAR AS I CAN SEE, THERE'S NO CASE TO ANSWER HERE. IF YOU DON'T WANT IT TO HAPPEN AGAIN, DON'T MAKE HIM ANGRY.
GIVE HIM TIME TO GET USED TO CIVVY STREET.

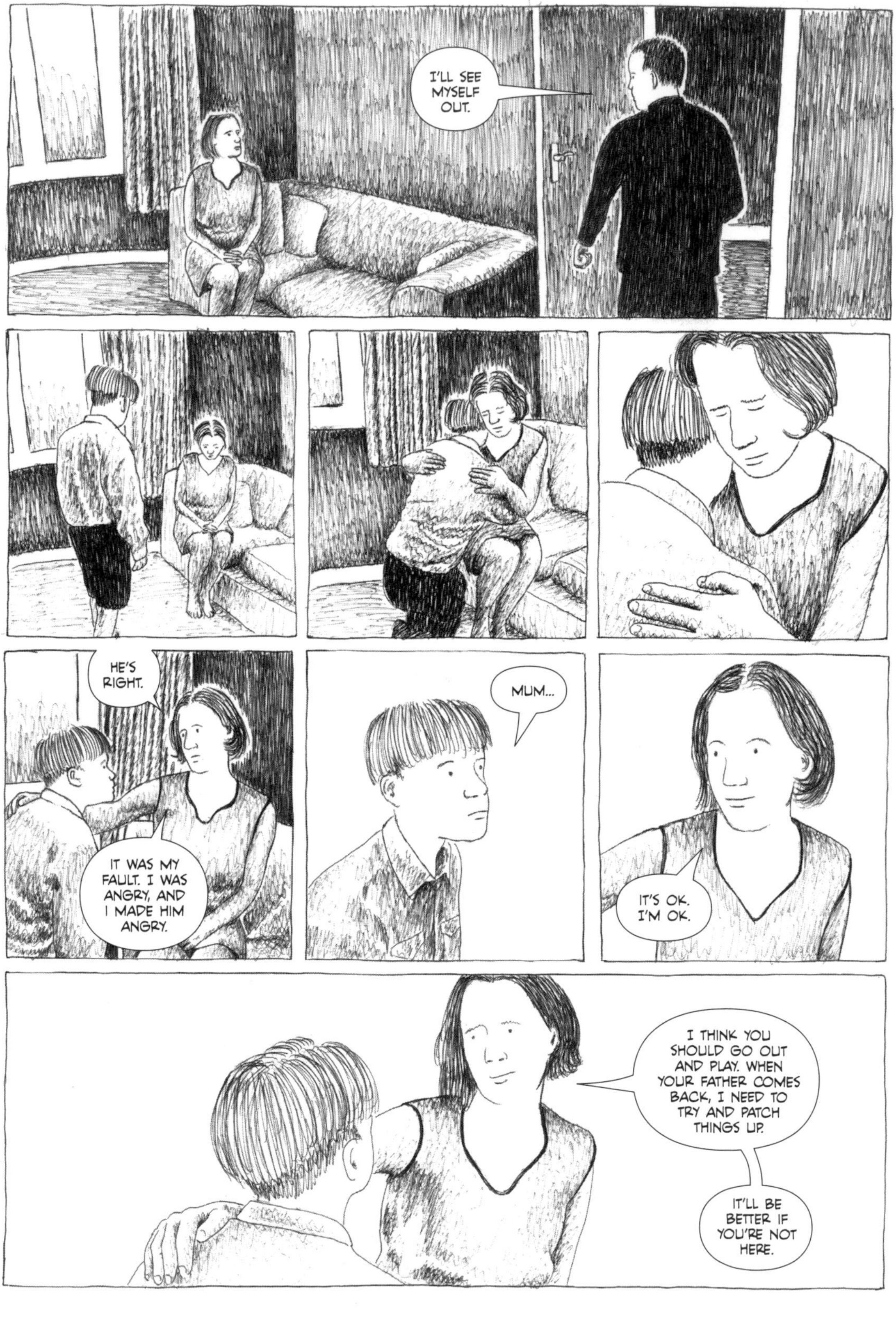
I'LL SEE MYSELF OUT.
HE'S RIGHT.
IT WAS MY FAULT. I WAS ANGRY, AND I MADE HIM ANGRY.
MUM...
IT'S OK. I'M OK.
I THINK YOU SHOULD GO OUT AND PLAY. WHEN YOUR FATHER COMES BACK, I NEED TO TRY AND PATCH THINGS UP.
IT'LL BE BETTER IF YOU'RE NOT HERE.

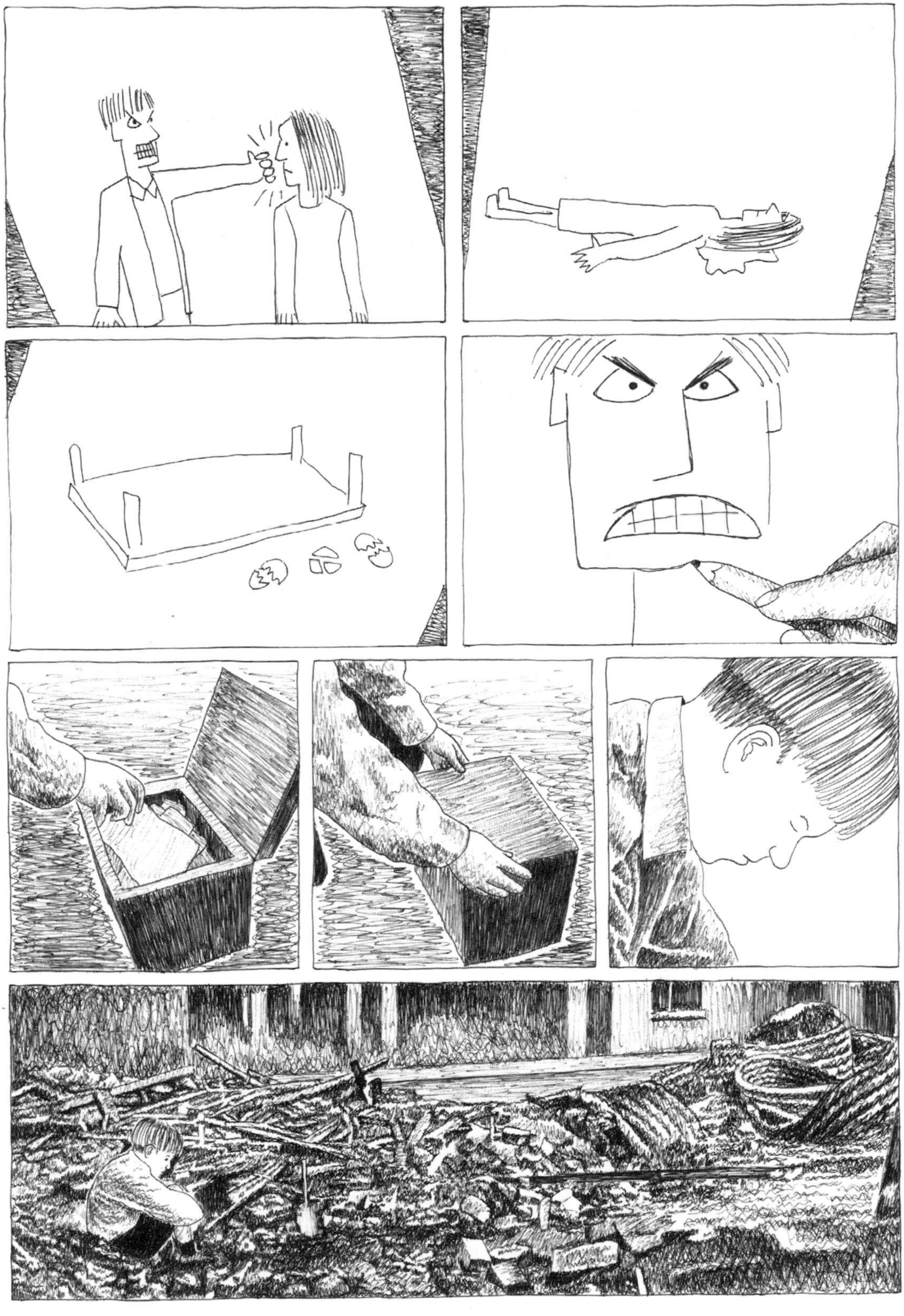

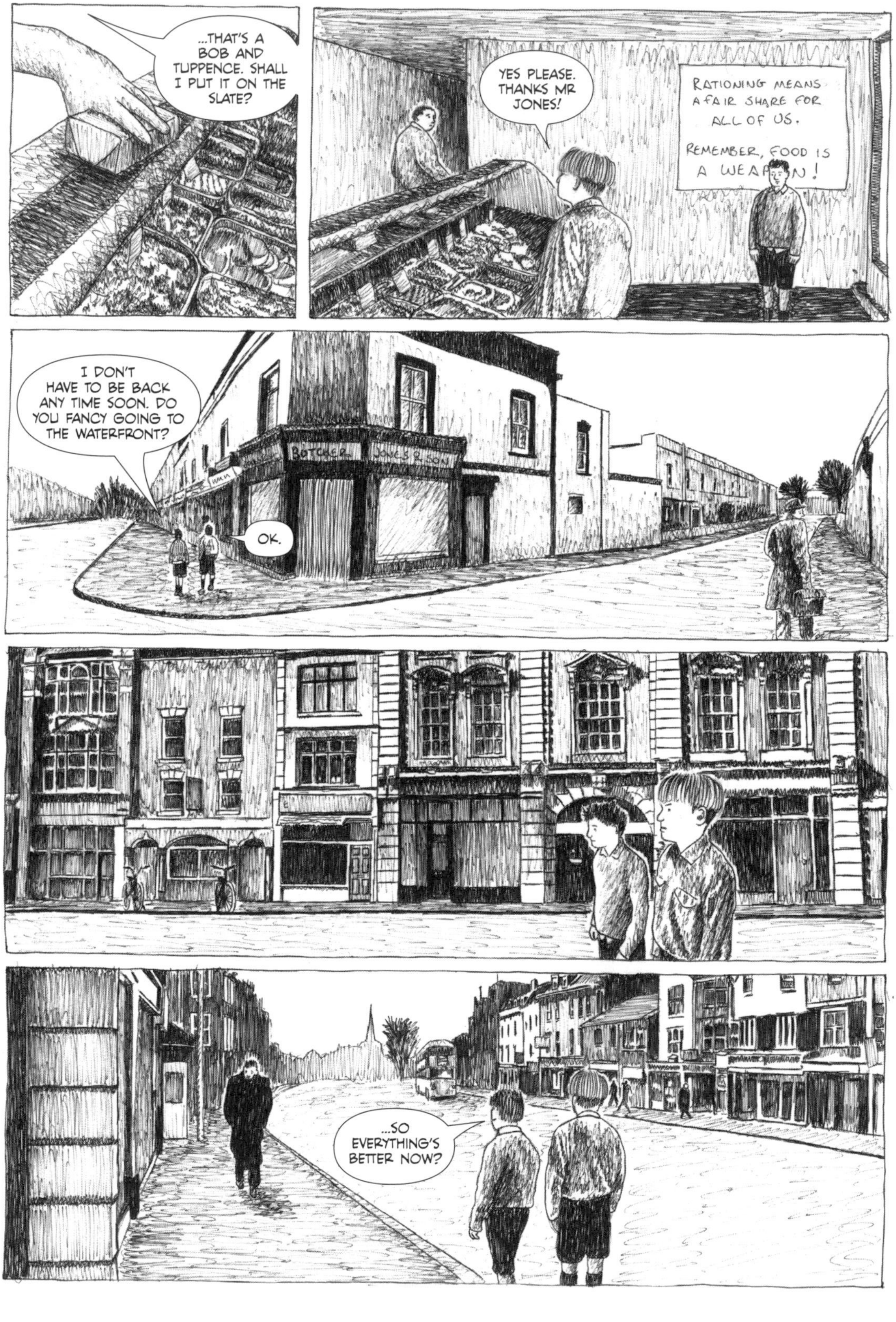
...THAT'S A BOB AND TUPPENCE. SHALL I PUT IT ON THE SLATE?
YES PLEASE. THANKS MR JONES!
RATIONING MEANS A FAIR SHARE FOR ALL OF US.
REMEMBER, FOOD IS A WEAP N!
I DON'T HAVE TO BE BACK ANY TIME SOON. DO YOU FANCY GOING TO THE WATERFRONT?
BUTCHER
JONES & SON
OK.
...SO EVERYTHING'S BETTER NOW?

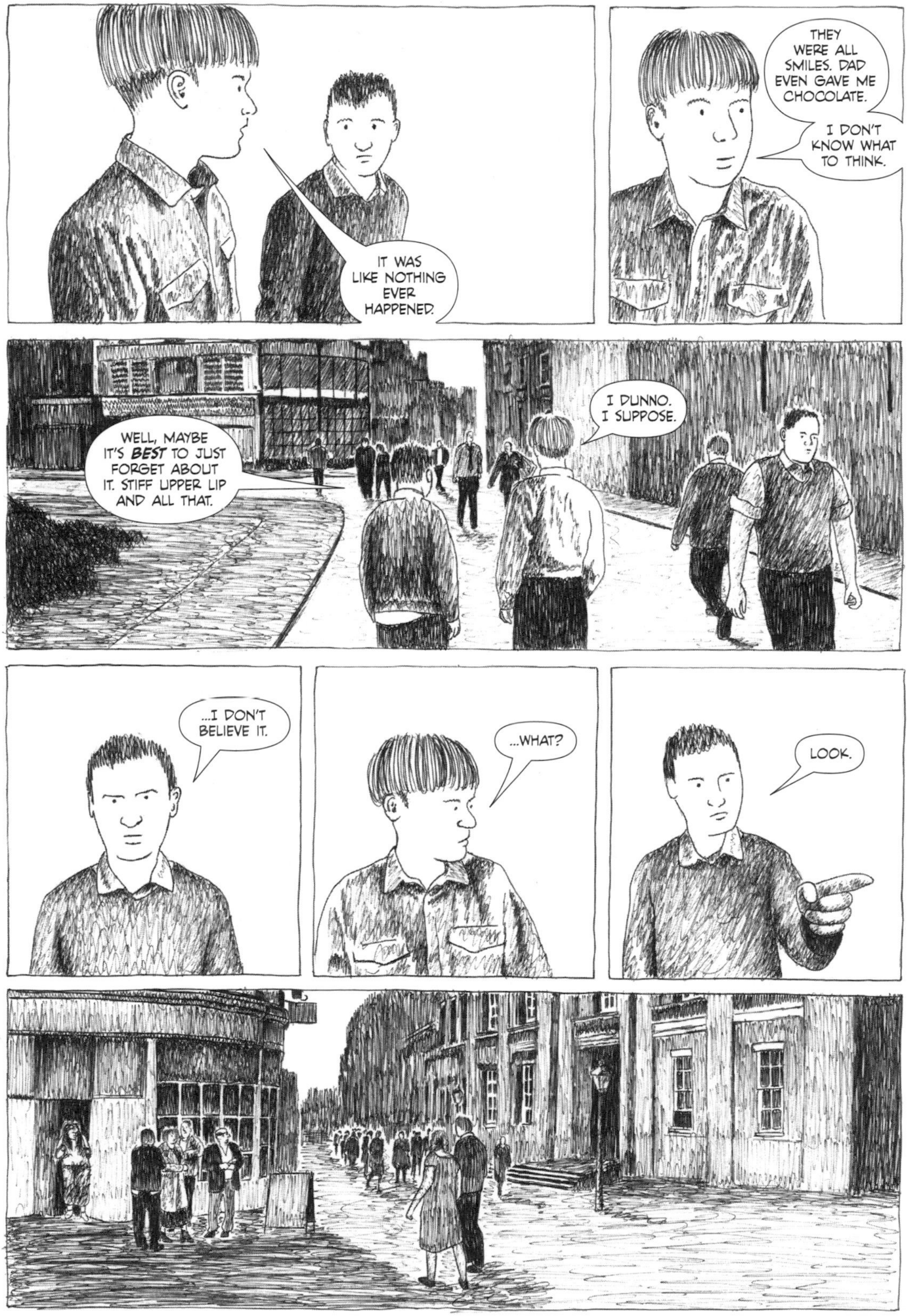
IT WAS LIKE NOTHING EVER HAPPENED.
THEY WERE ALL SMILES. DAD EVEN GAVE ME CHOCOLATE.
I DON'T KNOW WHAT TO THINK.
WELL, MAYBE IT'S BEST TO JUST FORGET ABOUT IT. STIFF UPPER LIP AND ALL THAT.
I DUNNO. I SUPPOSE.
...I DON'T BELIEVE IT.
...WHAT?
LOOK.

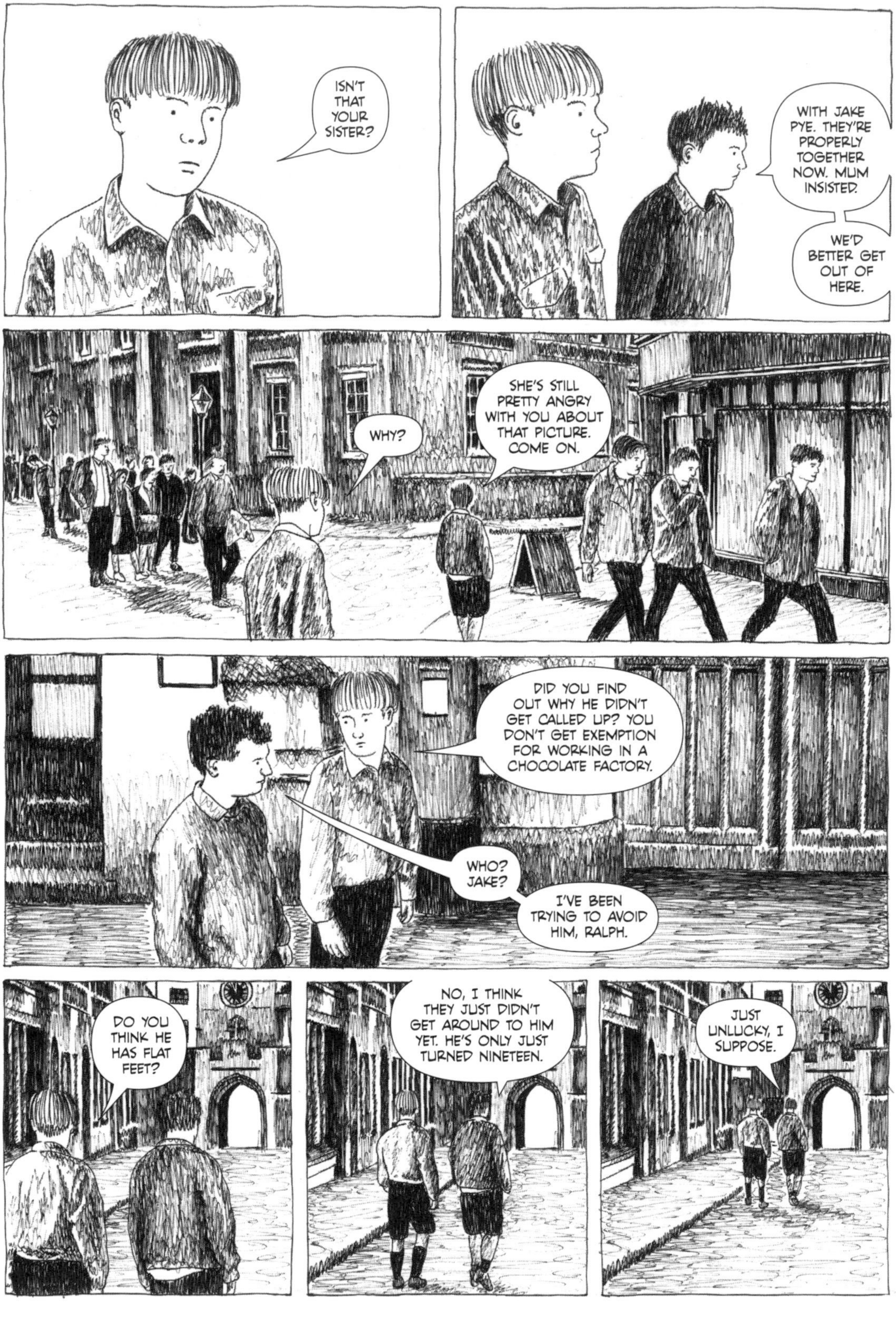
ISN'T THAT YOUR SISTER?
WITH JAKE PYE. THEY'RE PROPERLY TOGETHER NOW. MUM INSISTED.
WE'D BETTER GET OUT OF HERE.
WHY?
SHE'S STILL PRETTY ANGRY WITH YOU ABOUT THAT PICTURE. COME ON.
DID YOU FIND OUT WHY HE DIDN'T GET CALLED UP? YOU DON'T GET EXEMPTION FOR WORKING IN A CHOCOLATE FACTORY.
WHO? JAKE?
I'VE BEEN TRYING TO AVOID HIM, RALPH.
DO YOU THINK HE HAS FLAT FEET?
NO, I THINK THEY JUST DIDN'T GET AROUND TO HIM YET. HE'S ONLY JUST TURNED NINETEEN.
JUST UNLUCKY, I SUPPOSE.

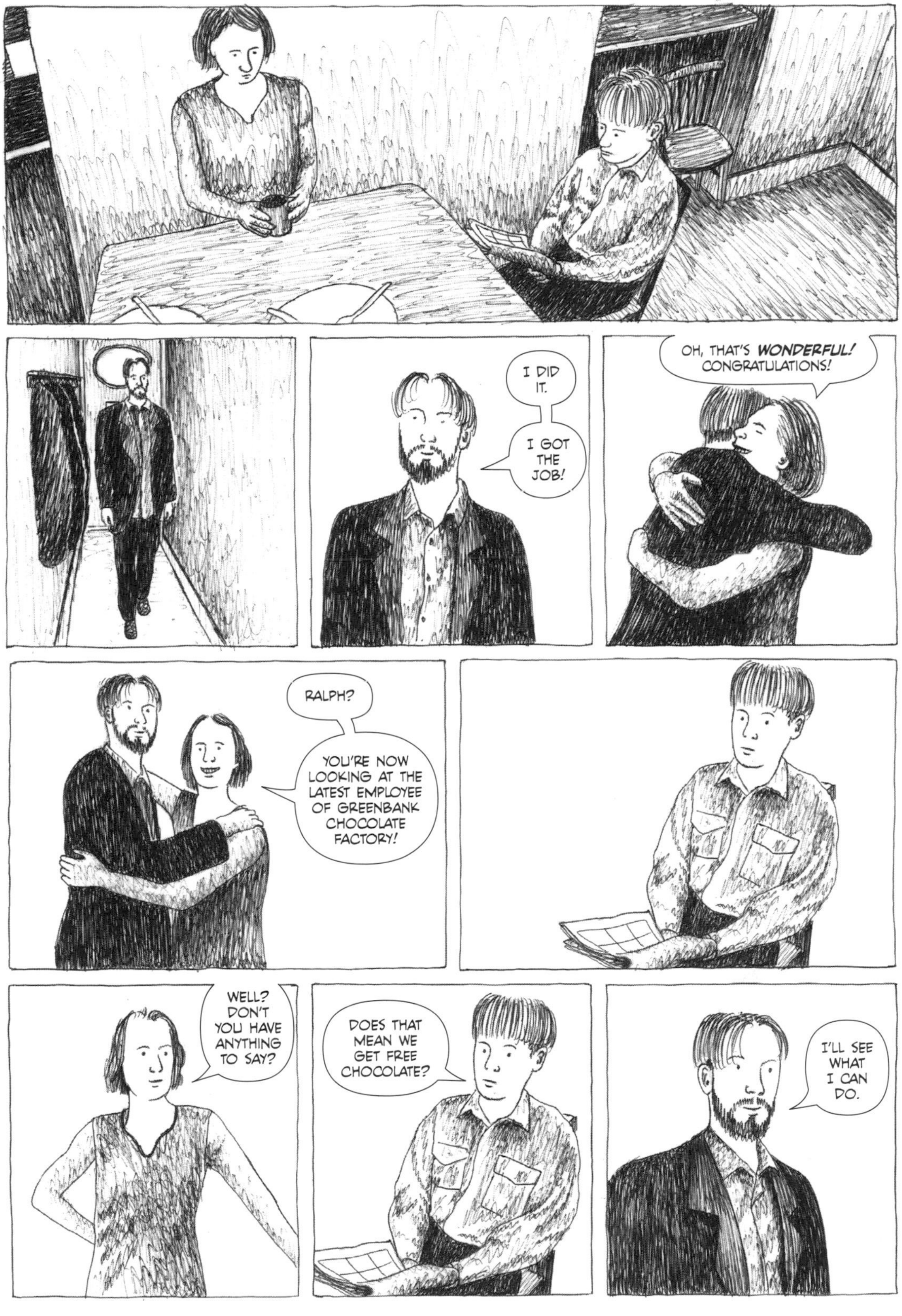
I DID IT.
I GOT THE JOB!
OH, THAT'S **WONDERFUL!** CONGRATULATIONS!
RALPH?
YOU'RE NOW LOOKING AT THE LATEST EMPLOYEE OF GREENBANK CHOCOLATE FACTORY!
WELL? DON'T YOU HAVE ANYTHING TO SAY?
DOES THAT MEAN WE GET FREE CHOCOLATE?
I'LL SEE WHAT I CAN DO.

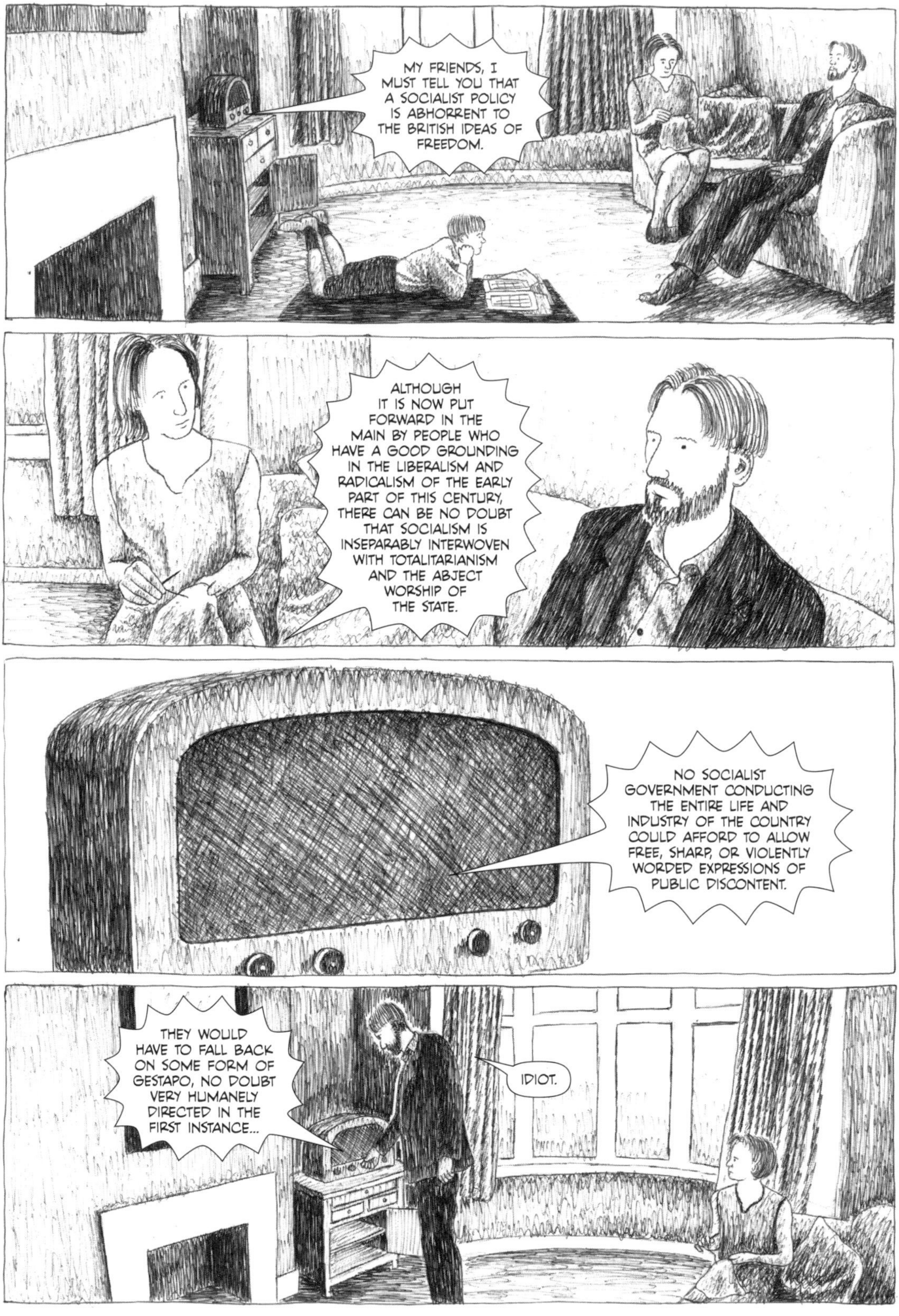
MY FRIENDS, I MUST TELL YOU THAT A SOCIALIST POLICY IS ABHORRENT TO THE BRITISH IDEAS OF FREEDOM.
ALTHOUGH IT IS NOW PUT FORWARD IN THE MAIN BY PEOPLE WHO HAVE A GOOD GROUNDING IN THE LIBERALISM AND RADICALISM OF THE EARLY PART OF THIS CENTURY, THERE CAN BE NO DOUBT THAT SOCIALISM IS INSEPARABLY INTERWOVEN WITH TOTALITARIANISM AND THE ABJECT WORSHIP OF THE STATE.
NO SOCIALIST GOVERNMENT CONDUCTING THE ENTIRE LIFE AND INDUSTRY OF THE COUNTRY COULD AFFORD TO ALLOW FREE, SHARP, OR VIOLENTLY WORDED EXPRESSIONS OF PUBLIC DISCONTENT.
THEY WOULD HAVE TO FALL BACK ON SOME FORM OF GESTAPO, NO DOUBT VERY HUMANELY DIRECTED IN THE FIRST INSTANCE...
IDIOT.

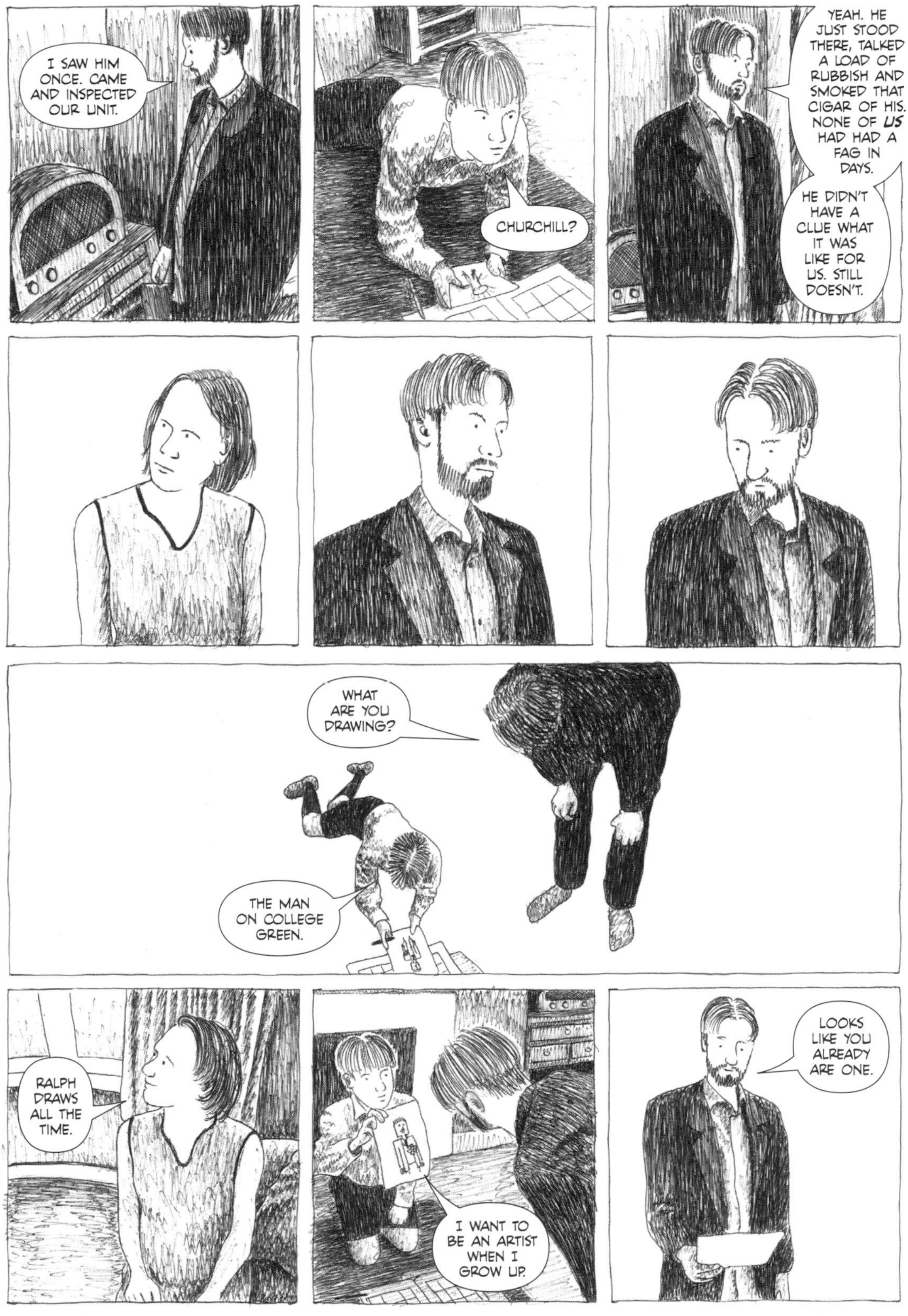
I SAW HIM ONCE. CAME AND INSPECTED OUR UNIT.
CHURCHILL?
YEAH. HE JUST STOOD THERE, TALKED A LOAD OF RUBBISH AND SMOKED THAT CIGAR OF HIS. NONE OF *US* HAD HAD A FAG IN DAYS.
HE DIDN'T HAVE A CLUE WHAT IT WAS LIKE FOR US. STILL DOESN'T.
WHAT ARE YOU DRAWING?
THE MAN ON COLLEGE GREEN.
RALPH DRAWS ALL THE TIME.
I WANT TO BE AN ARTIST WHEN I GROW UP.
LOOKS LIKE YOU ALREADY ARE ONE.

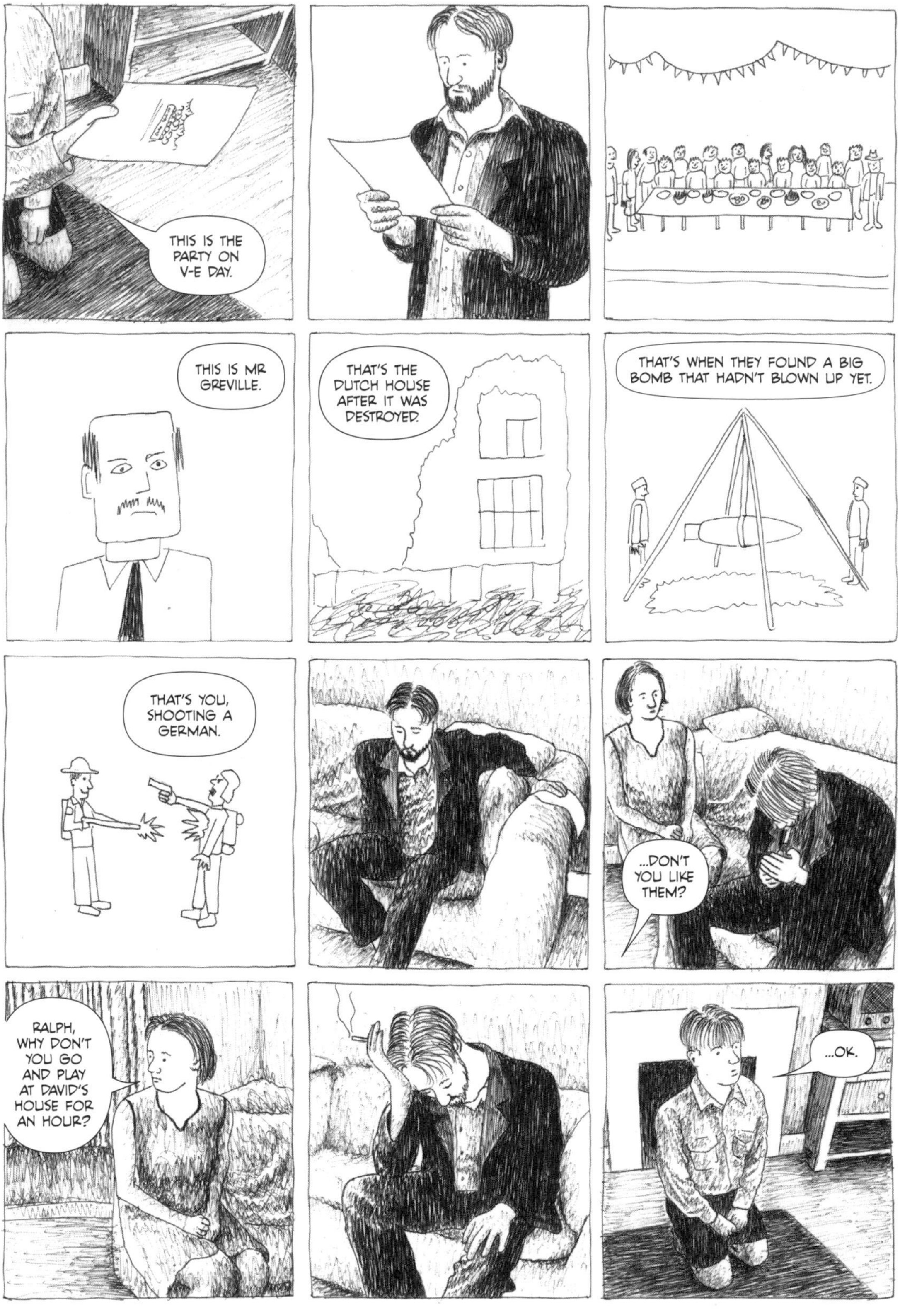
THIS IS THE PARTY ON V-E DAY.
THIS IS MR GREVILLE.
THAT'S THE DUTCH HOUSE AFTER IT WAS DESTROYED.
THAT'S WHEN THEY FOUND A BIG BOMB THAT HADN'T BLOWN UP YET.
THAT'S YOU, SHOOTING A GERMAN.
...DON'T YOU LIKE THEM?
RALPH, WHY DON'T YOU GO AND PLAY AT DAVID'S HOUSE FOR AN HOUR?
...OK.

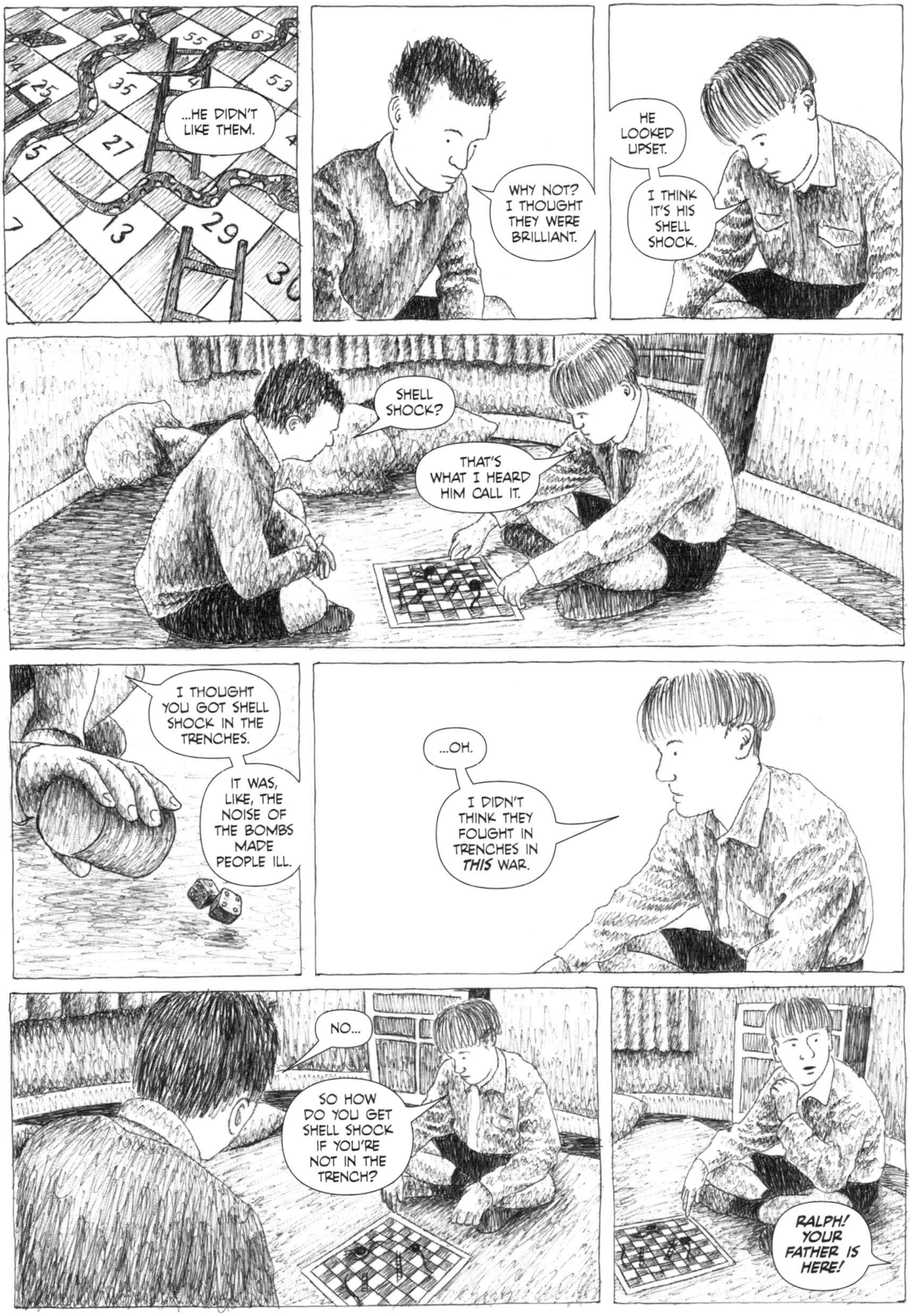

...HE DIDN'T LIKE THEM.
WHY NOT? I THOUGHT THEY WERE BRILLIANT.
HE LOOKED UPSET.
I THINK IT'S HIS SHELL SHOCK.
SHELL SHOCK?
THAT'S WHAT I HEARD HIM CALL IT.
I THOUGHT YOU GOT SHELL SHOCK IN THE TRENCHES.
IT WAS, LIKE, THE NOISE OF THE BOMBS MADE PEOPLE ILL.
...OH.
I DIDN'T THINK THEY FOUGHT IN TRENCHES IN *THIS* WAR.
NO...
SO HOW DO YOU GET SHELL SHOCK IF YOU'RE NOT IN THE TRENCH?
RALPH! YOUR FATHER IS HERE!

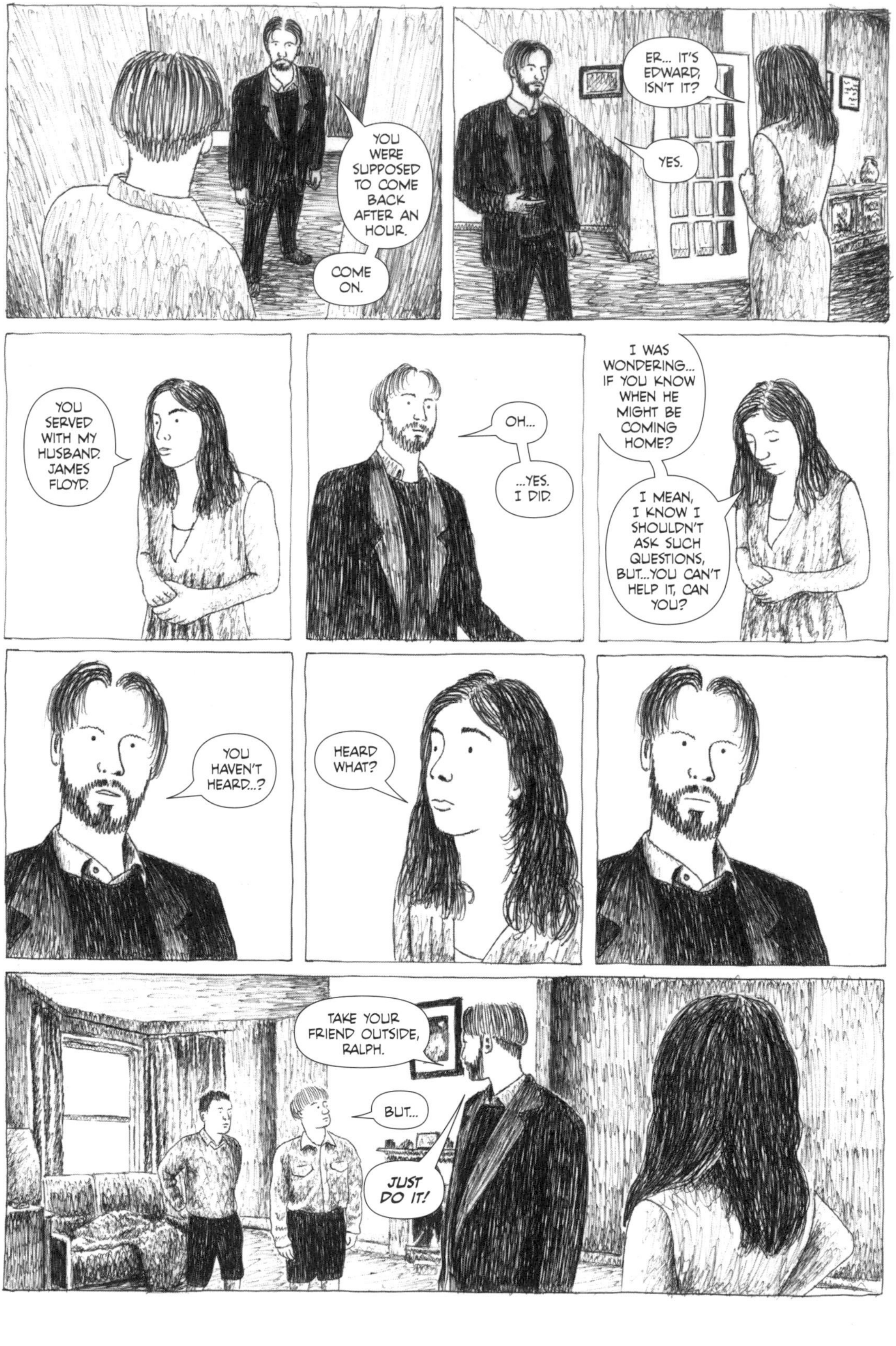
YOU WERE SUPPOSED TO COME BACK AFTER AN HOUR.
COME ON.
ER... IT'S EDWARD, ISN'T IT?
YES.
YOU SERVED WITH MY HUSBAND. JAMES FLOYD.
OH...
...YES. I DID.
I WAS WONDERING... IF YOU KNOW WHEN HE MIGHT BE COMING HOME?
I MEAN, I KNOW I SHOULDN'T ASK SUCH QUESTIONS, BUT...YOU CAN'T HELP IT, CAN YOU?
YOU HAVEN'T HEARD...?
HEARD WHAT?
TAKE YOUR FRIEND OUTSIDE, RALPH.
BUT...
JUST DO IT!

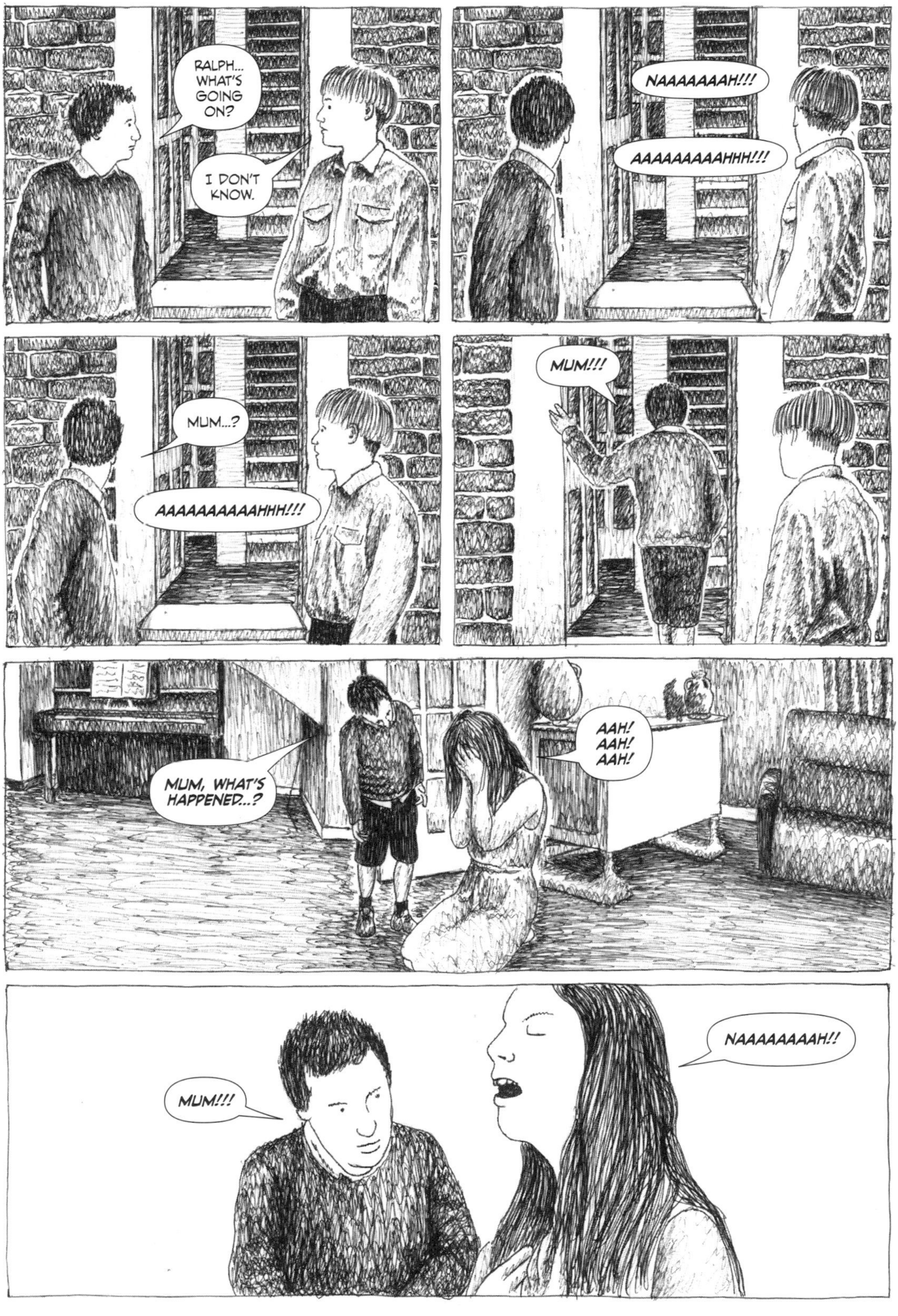
RALPH... WHAT'S GOING ON?
I DON'T KNOW.
NAAAAAAAH!!!
AAAAAAAAAHHH!!!
MUM...?
AAAAAAAAAAHHH!!!
MUM!!!
MUM, WHAT'S HAPPENED...?
AAH! AAH! AAH!
MUM!!!
NAAAAAAAAH!!

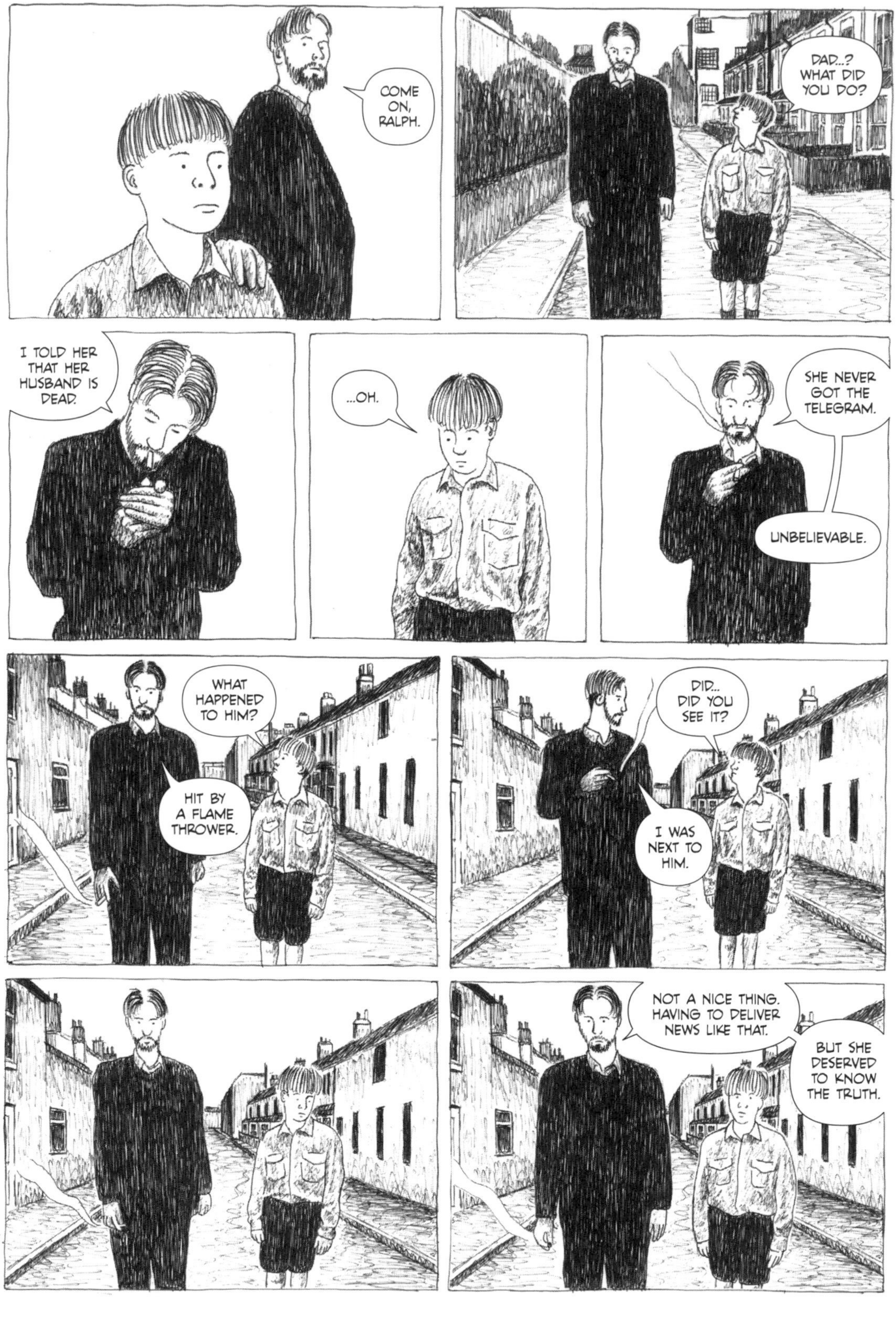
COME ON, RALPH.
DAD...? WHAT DID YOU DO?
I TOLD HER THAT HER HUSBAND IS DEAD.
...OH.
SHE NEVER GOT THE TELEGRAM.
UNBELIEVABLE.
WHAT HAPPENED TO HIM?
HIT BY A FLAME THROWER.
DID... DID YOU SEE IT?
I WAS NEXT TO HIM.
NOT A NICE THING. HAVING TO DELIVER NEWS LIKE THAT.
BUT SHE DESERVED TO KNOW THE TRUTH.

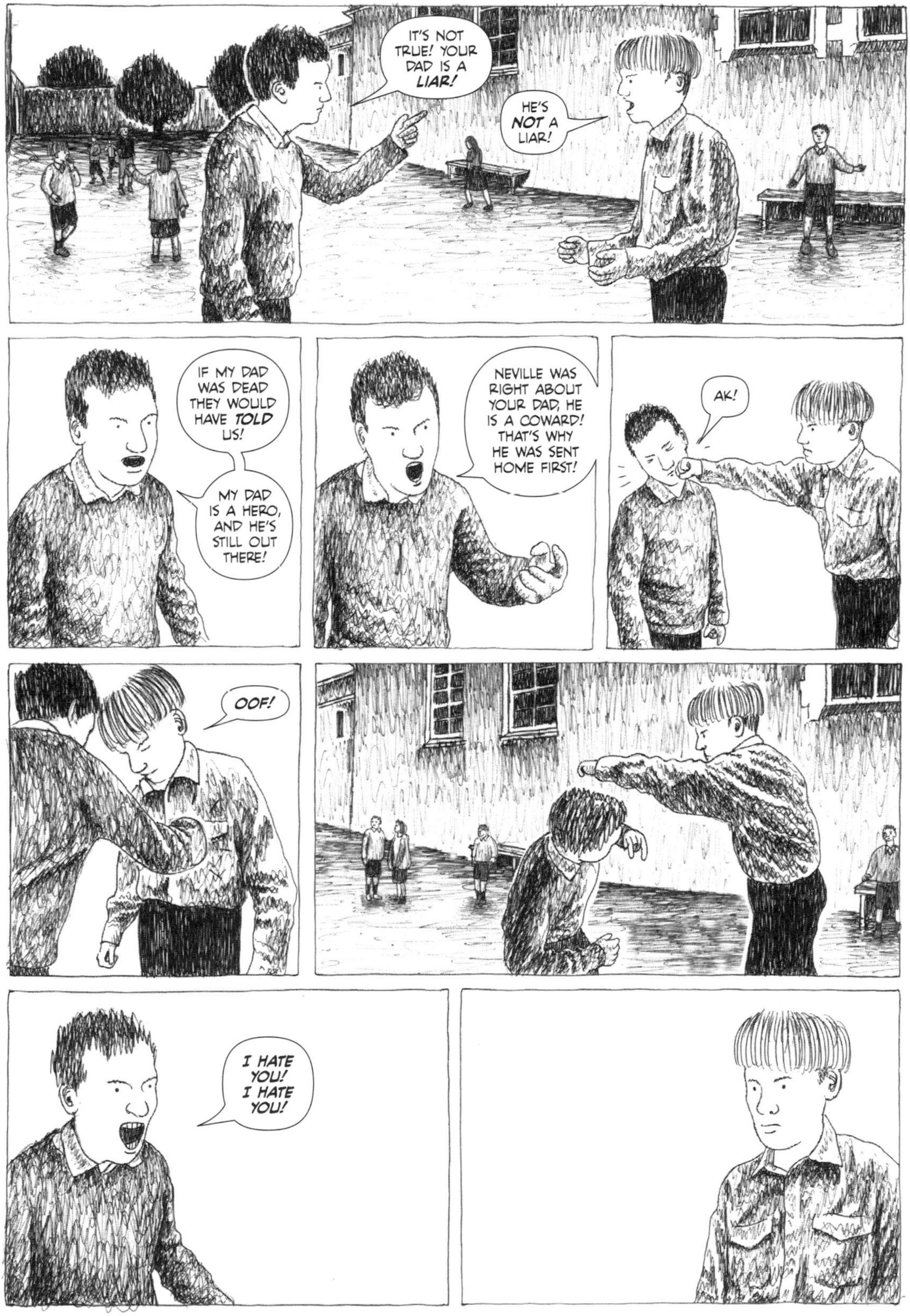
IT'S NOT TRUE! YOUR DAD IS A LIAR!
HE'S NOT A LIAR!
IF MY DAD WAS DEAD THEY WOULD HAVE TOLD US!
MY DAD IS A HERO, AND HE'S STILL OUT THERE!
NEVILLE WAS RIGHT ABOUT YOUR DAD, HE IS A COWARD! THAT'S WHY HE WAS SENT HOME FIRST!
AK!
OOF!
I HATE YOU! I HATE YOU!

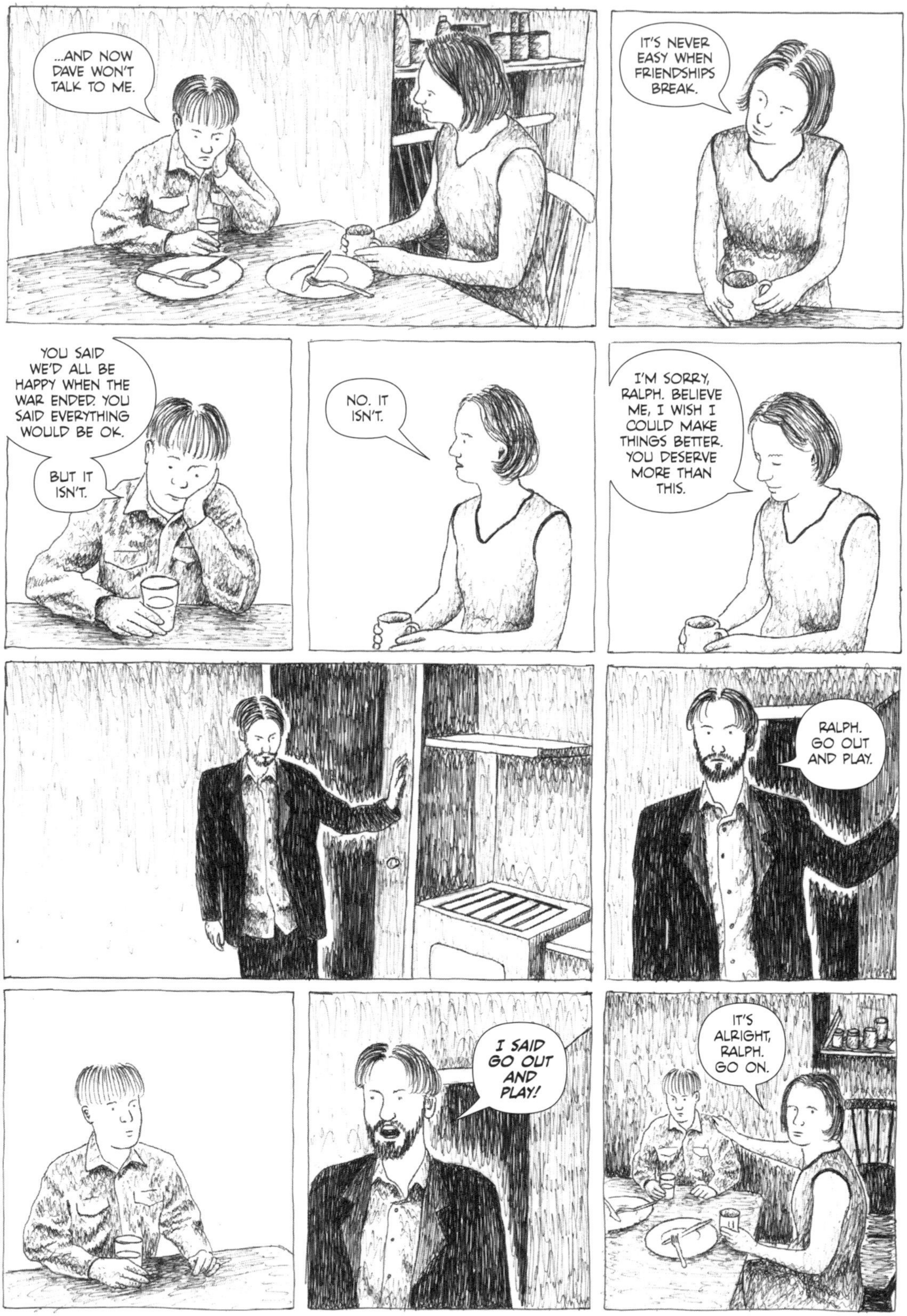
...AND NOW DAVE WON'T TALK TO ME.
IT'S NEVER EASY WHEN FRIENDSHIPS BREAK.
YOU SAID WE'D ALL BE HAPPY WHEN THE WAR ENDED. YOU SAID EVERYTHING WOULD BE OK.
BUT IT ISN'T.
NO. IT ISN'T.
I'M SORRY, RALPH. BELIEVE ME, I WISH I COULD MAKE THINGS BETTER. YOU DESERVE MORE THAN THIS.
RALPH. GO OUT AND PLAY.
I SAID GO OUT AND PLAY!
IT'S ALRIGHT, RALPH. GO ON.

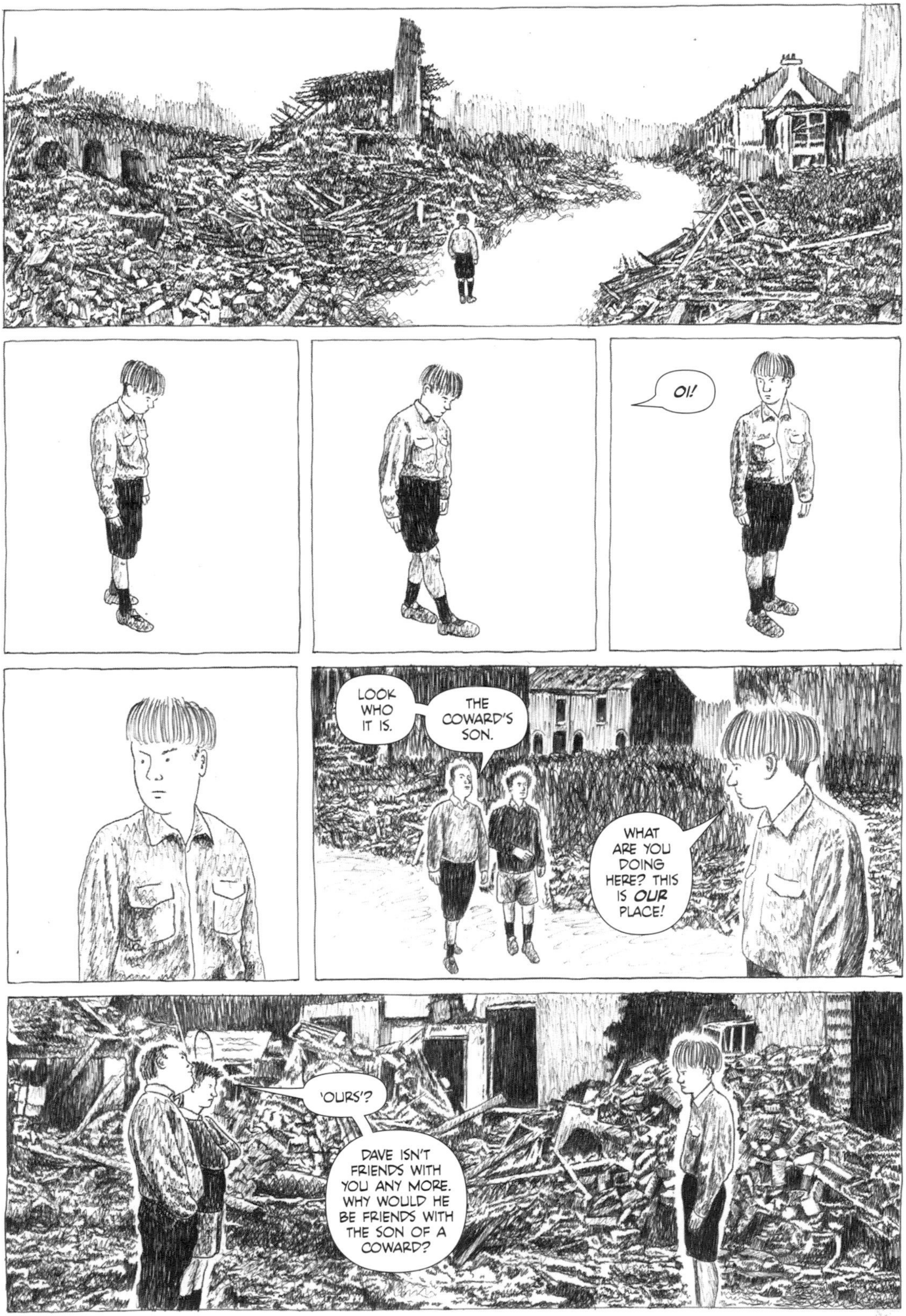
OI!
LOOK WHO IT IS.
THE COWARD'S SON.
WHAT ARE YOU DOING HERE? THIS IS OUR PLACE!
'OURS'?
DAVE ISN'T FRIENDS WITH YOU ANY MORE. WHY WOULD HE BE FRIENDS WITH THE SON OF A COWARD?

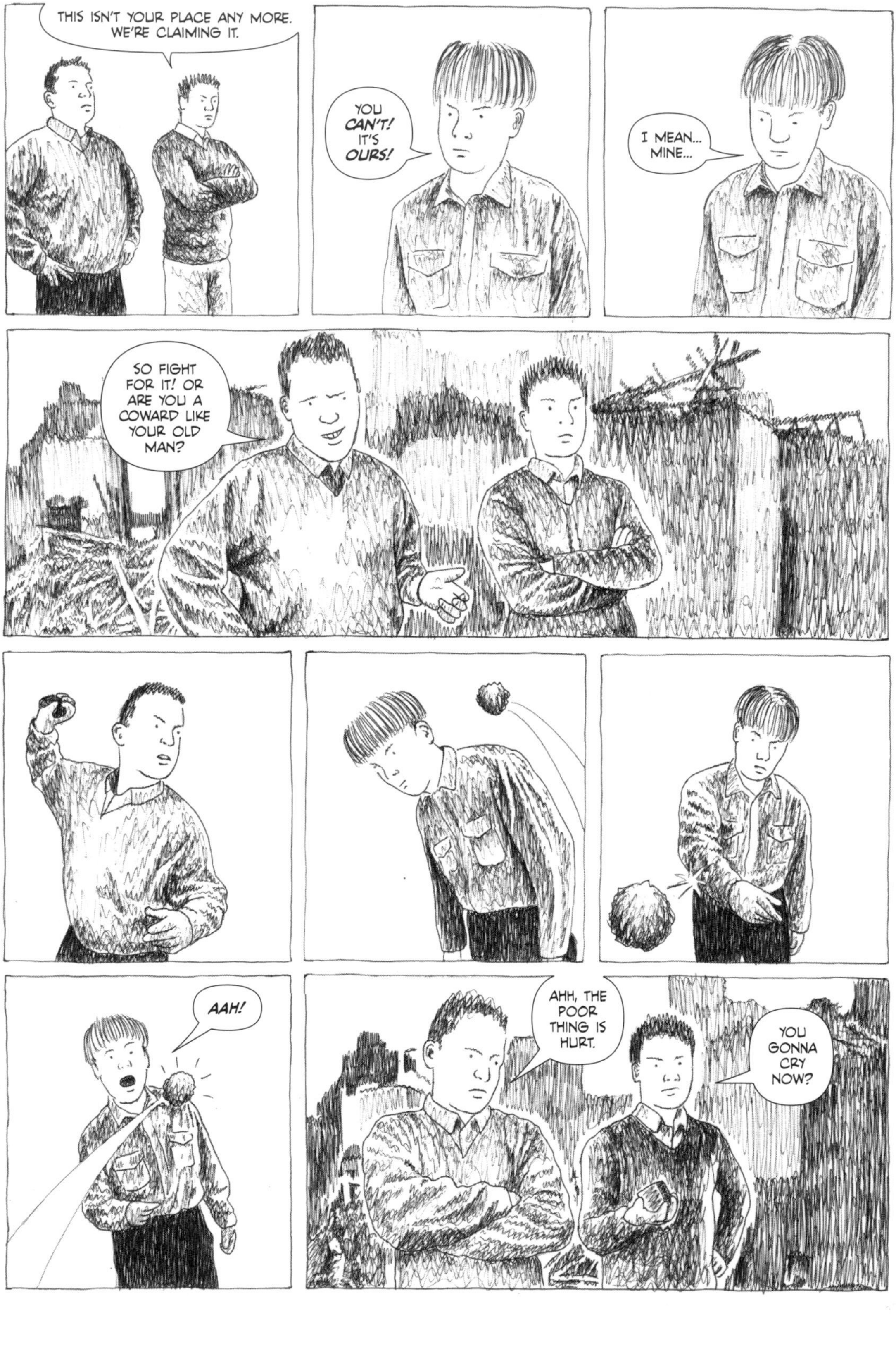
THIS ISN'T YOUR PLACE ANY MORE. WE'RE CLAIMING IT.
YOU CAN'T! IT'S OURS!
I MEAN... MINE...
SO FIGHT FOR IT! OR ARE YOU A COWARD LIKE YOUR OLD MAN?
AAH!
AHH, THE POOR THING IS HURT.
YOU GONNA CRY NOW?

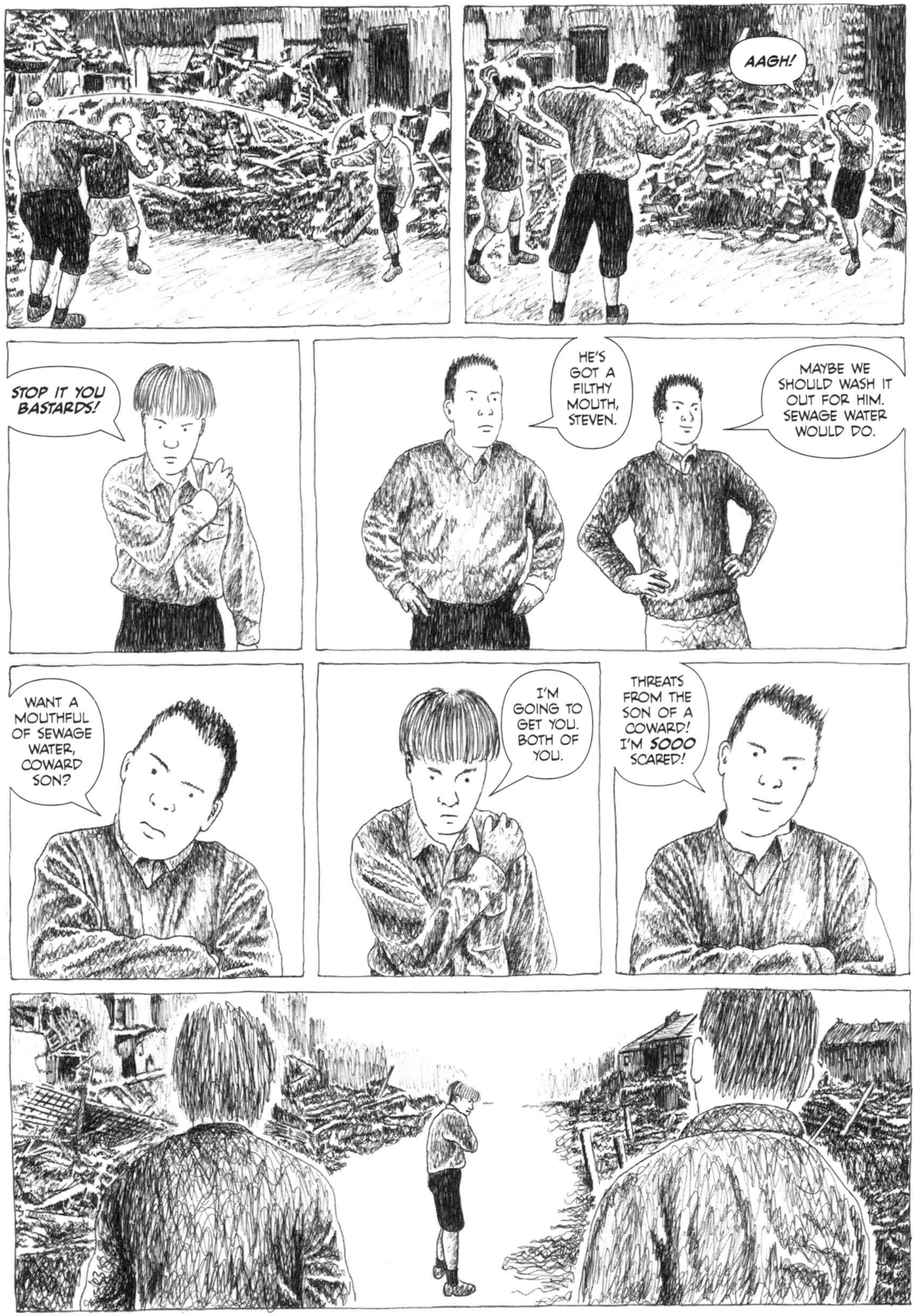
AAGH!
STOP IT YOU BASTARDS!
HE'S GOT A FILTHY MOUTH, STEVEN.
MAYBE WE SHOULD WASH IT OUT FOR HIM. SEWAGE WATER WOULD DO.
WANT A MOUTHFUL OF SEWAGE WATER, COWARD SON?
I'M GOING TO GET YOU. BOTH OF YOU.
THREATS FROM THE SON OF A COWARD! I'M SOOO SCARED!

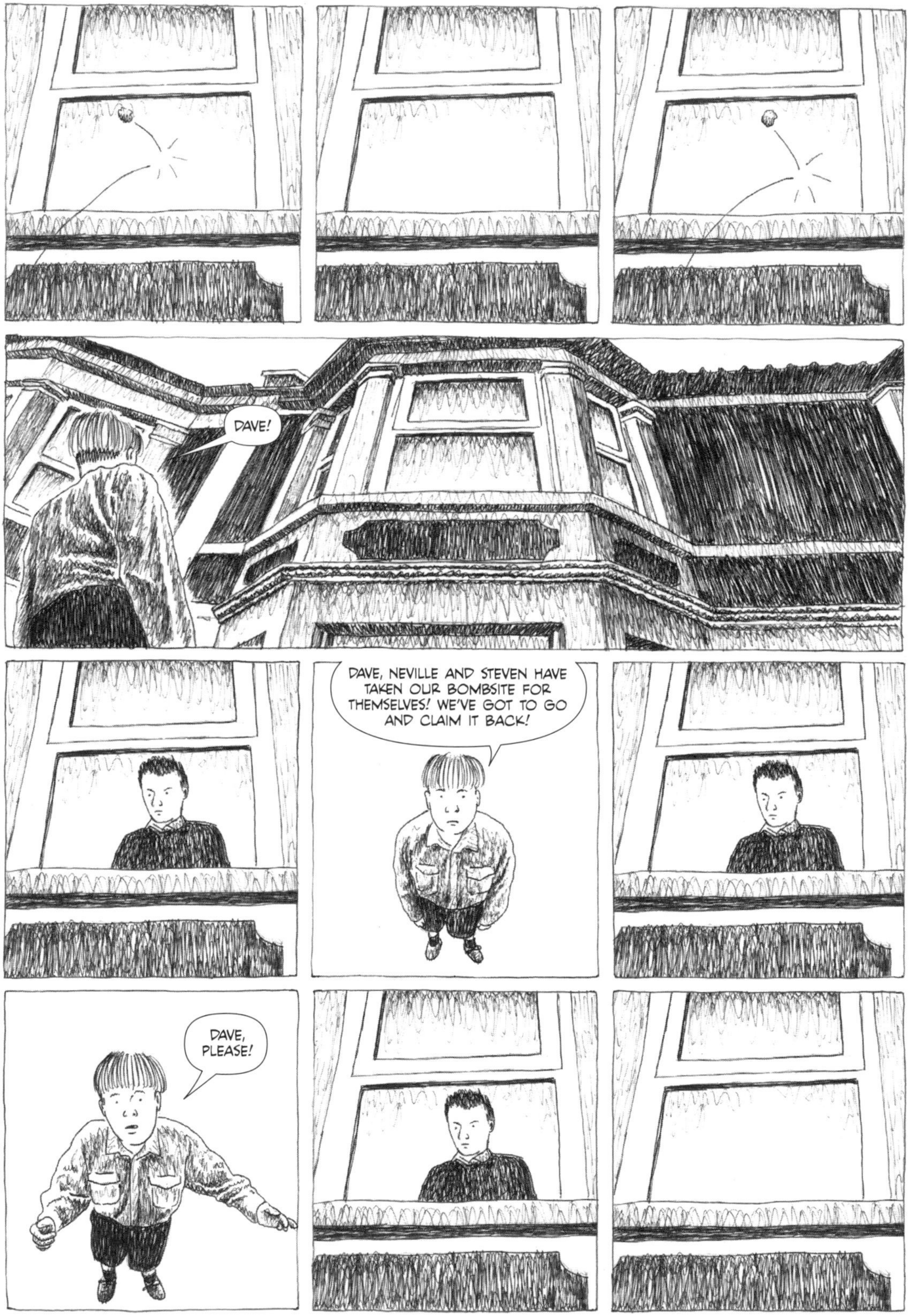
DAVE!
DAVE, NEVILLE AND STEVEN HAVE TAKEN OUR BOMBSITE FOR THEMSELVES! WE'VE GOT TO GO AND CLAIM IT BACK!
DAVE, PLEASE!

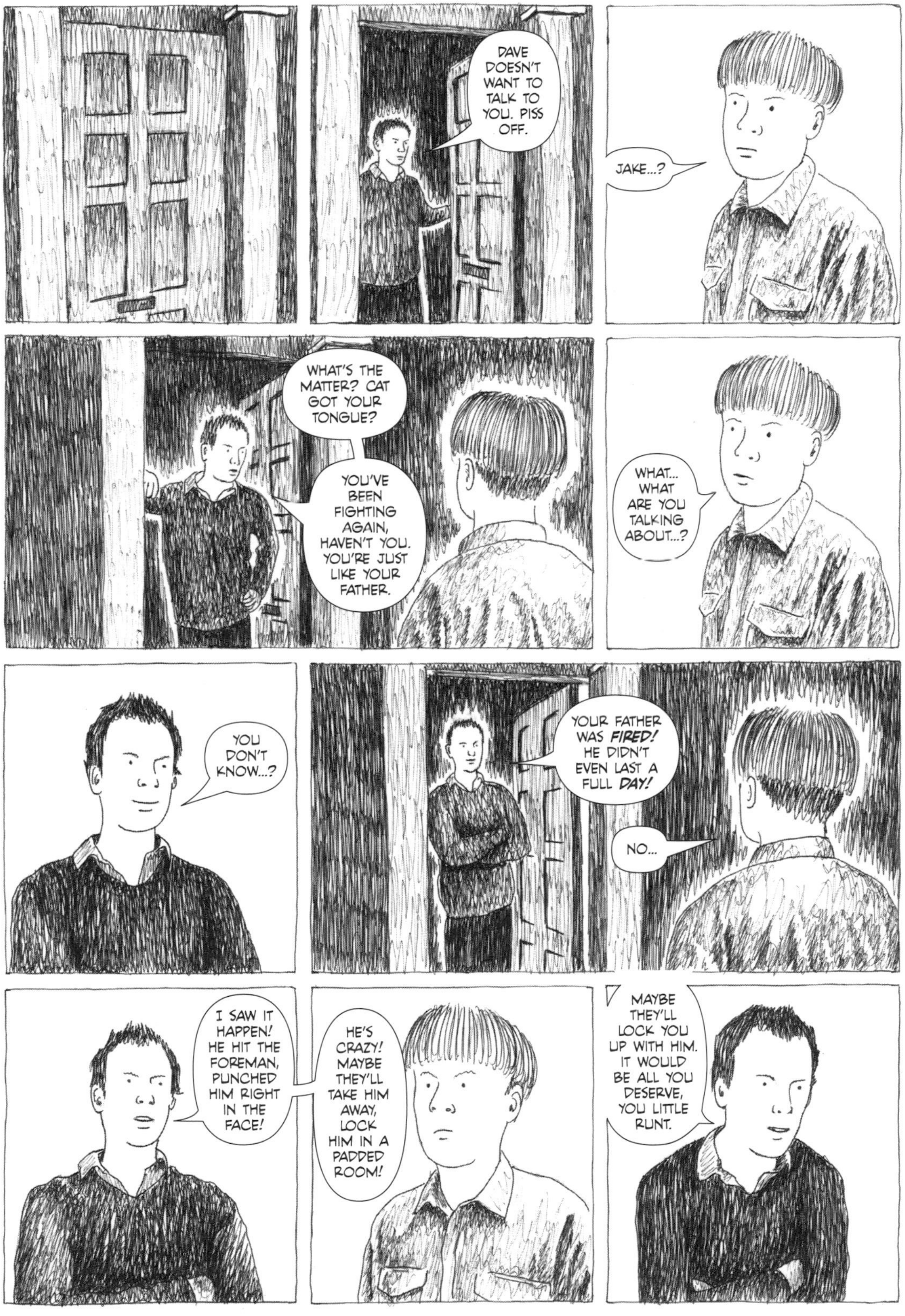

DAVE DOESN'T WANT TO TALK TO YOU. PISS OFF.
JAKE...?
WHAT'S THE MATTER? CAT GOT YOUR TONGUE?
YOU'VE BEEN FIGHTING AGAIN, HAVEN'T YOU. YOU'RE JUST LIKE YOUR FATHER.
WHAT... WHAT ARE YOU TALKING ABOUT...?
YOU DON'T KNOW...?
YOUR FATHER WAS *FIRED!* HE DIDN'T EVEN LAST A FULL *DAY!*
NO...
I SAW IT HAPPEN! HE HIT THE FOREMAN, PUNCHED HIM RIGHT IN THE FACE!
HE'S CRAZY! MAYBE THEY'LL TAKE HIM AWAY, LOCK HIM IN A PADDED ROOM!
MAYBE THEY'LL LOCK YOU UP WITH HIM. IT WOULD BE ALL YOU DESERVE, YOU LITTLE RUNT.

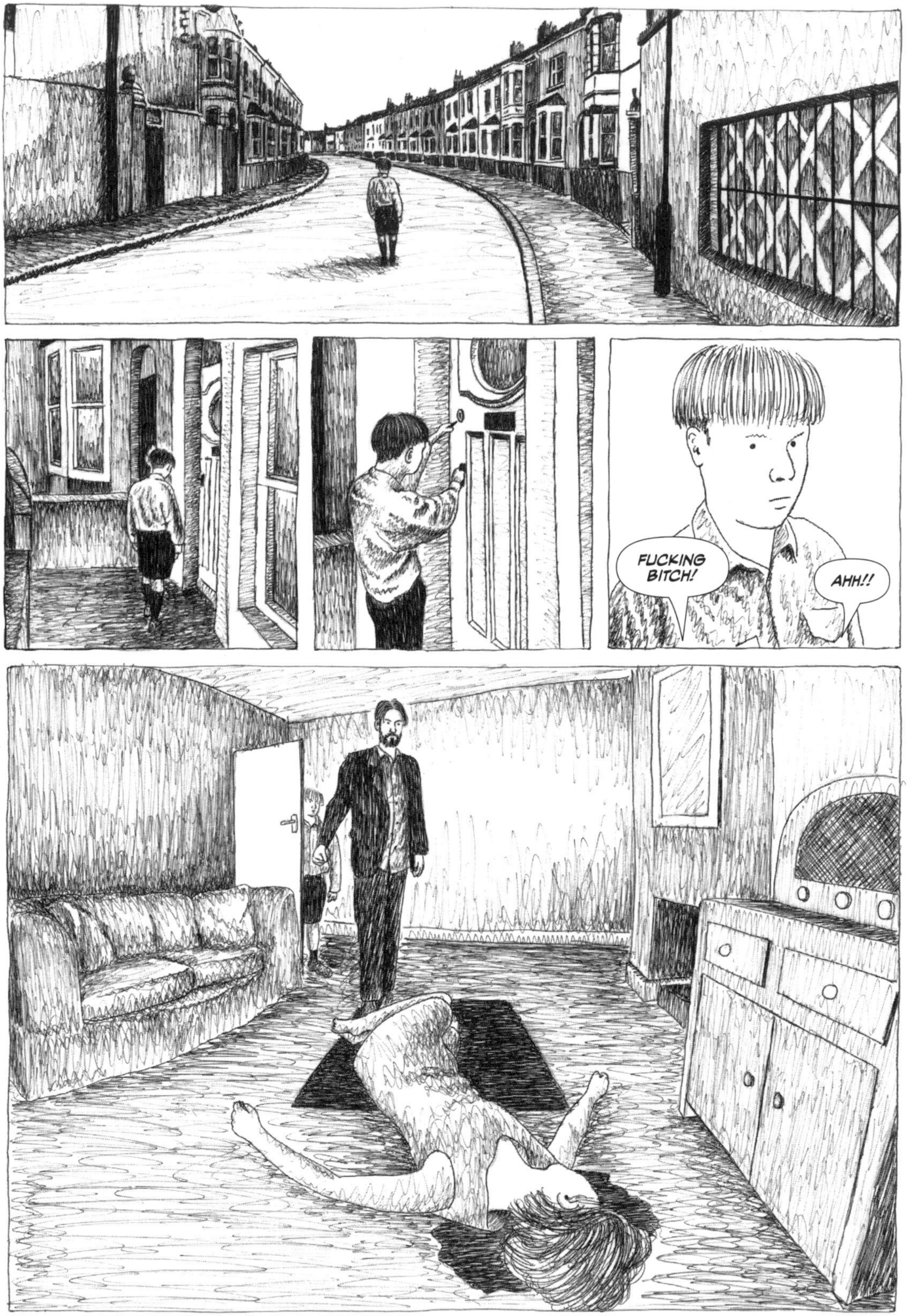
FUCKING BITCH!
AHH!!

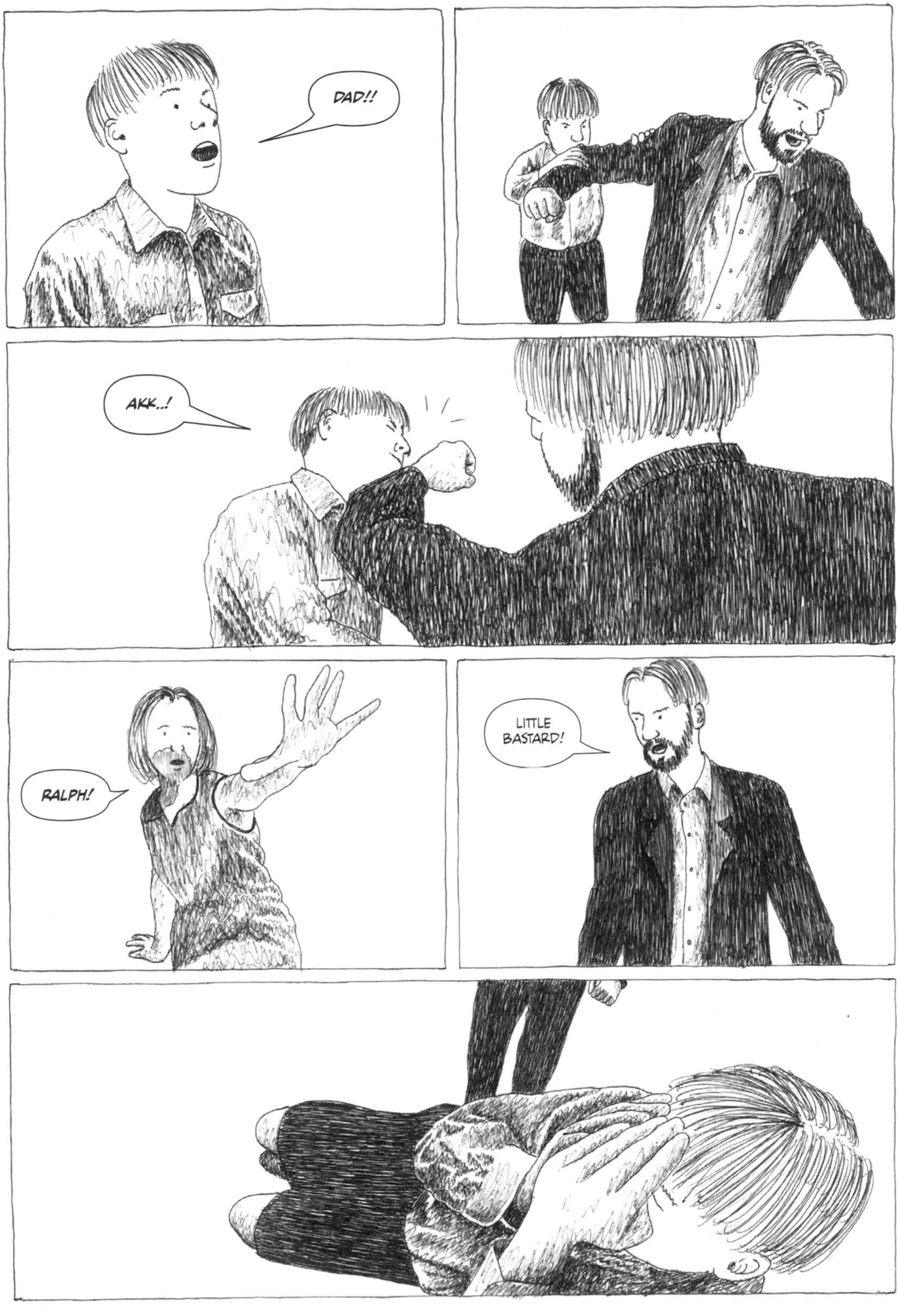
DAD!!
AKK..!
RALPH!
LITTLE BASTARD!

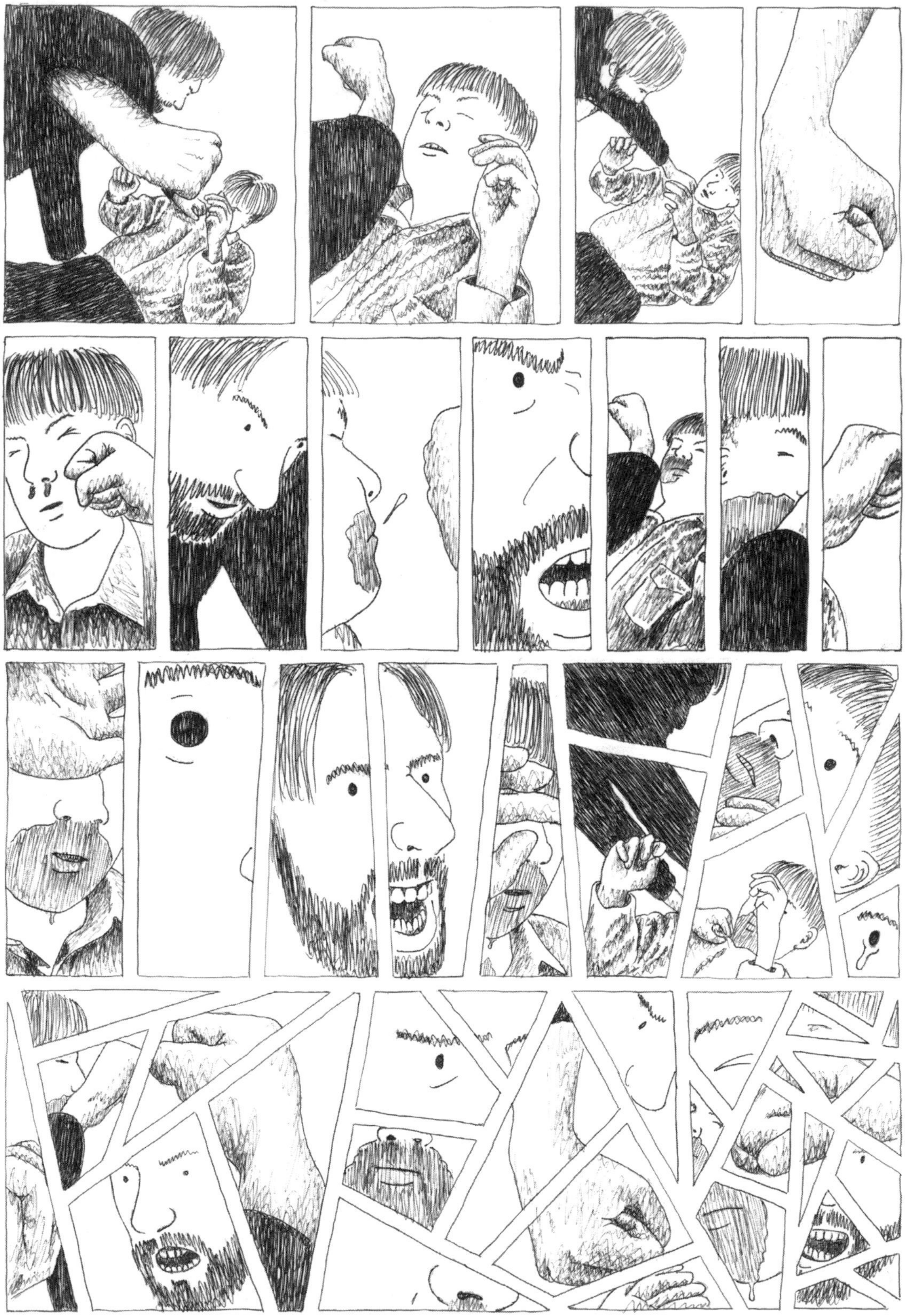

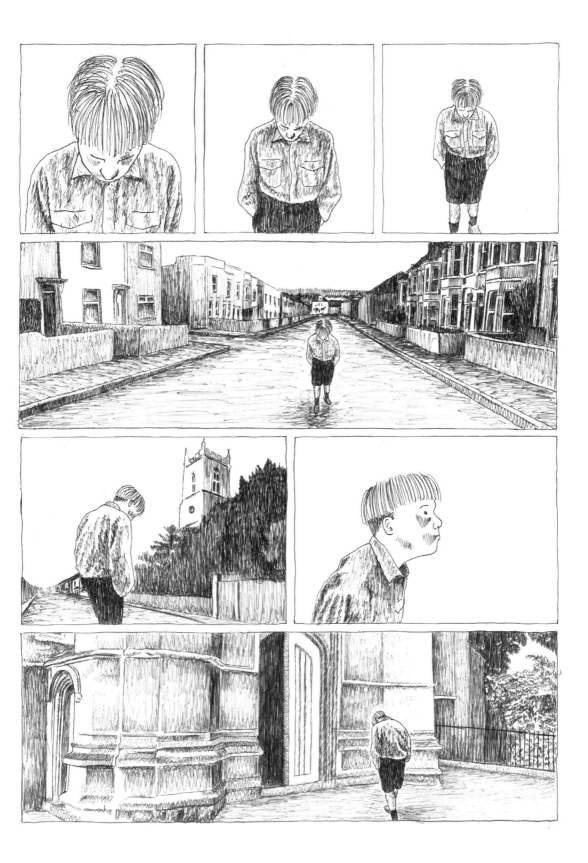

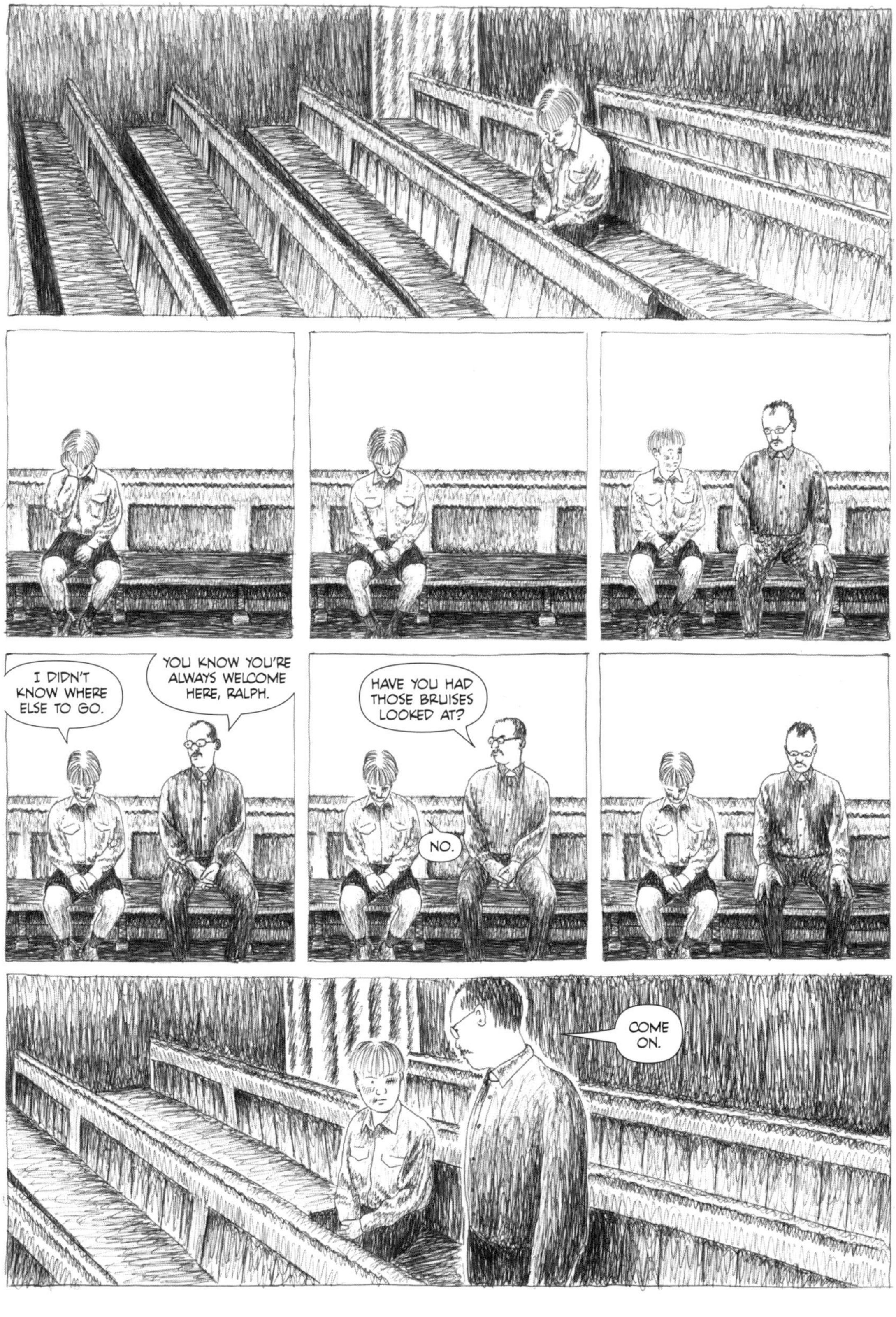
I DIDN'T KNOW WHERE ELSE TO GO.
YOU KNOW YOU'RE ALWAYS WELCOME HERE, RALPH.
HAVE YOU HAD THOSE BRUISES LOOKED AT?
NO.
COME ON.

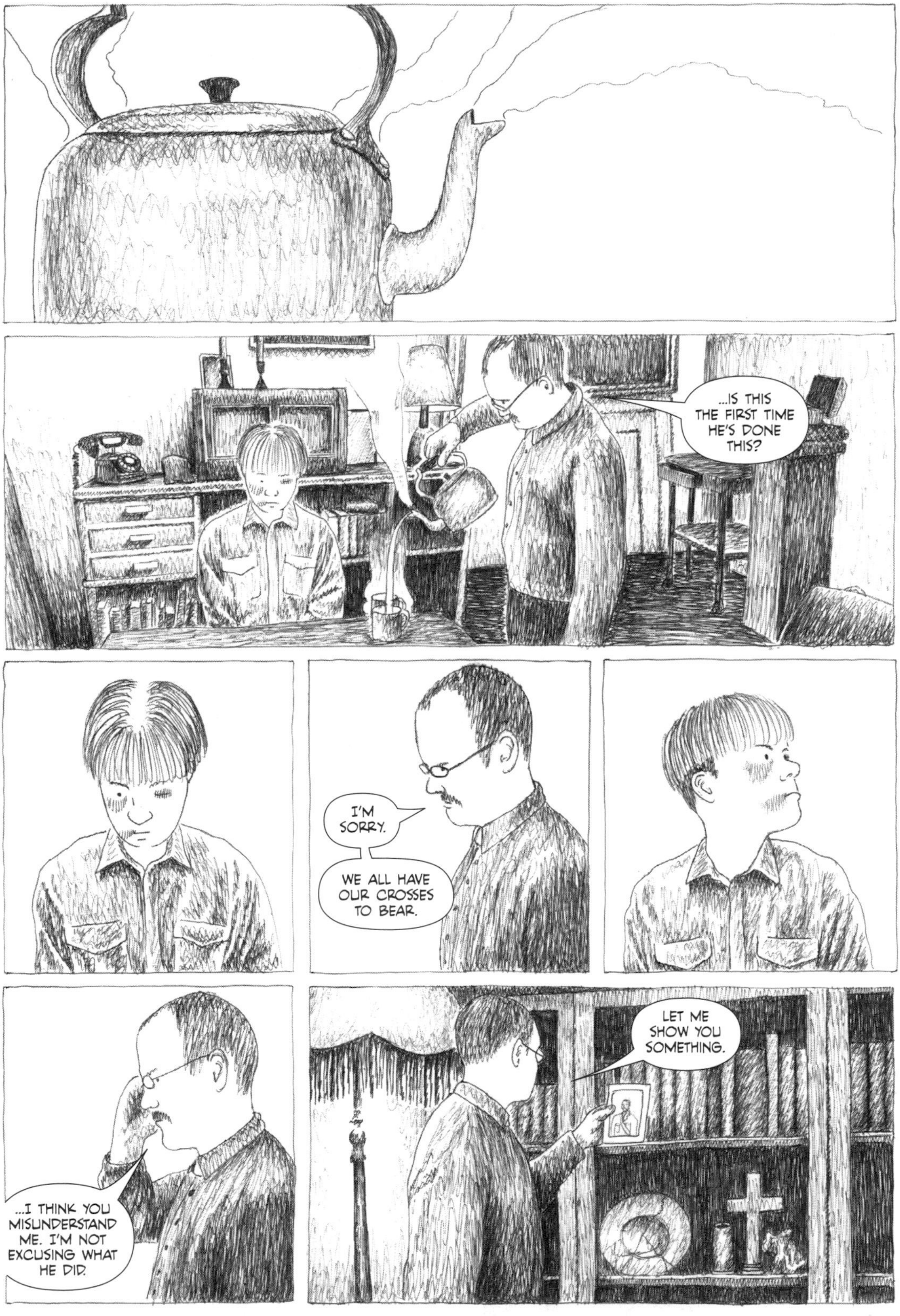
...IS THIS THE FIRST TIME HE'S DONE THIS?
I'M SORRY.
WE ALL HAVE OUR CROSSES TO BEAR.
...I THINK YOU MISUNDERSTAND ME. I'M NOT EXCUSING WHAT HE DID.
LET ME SHOW YOU SOMETHING.

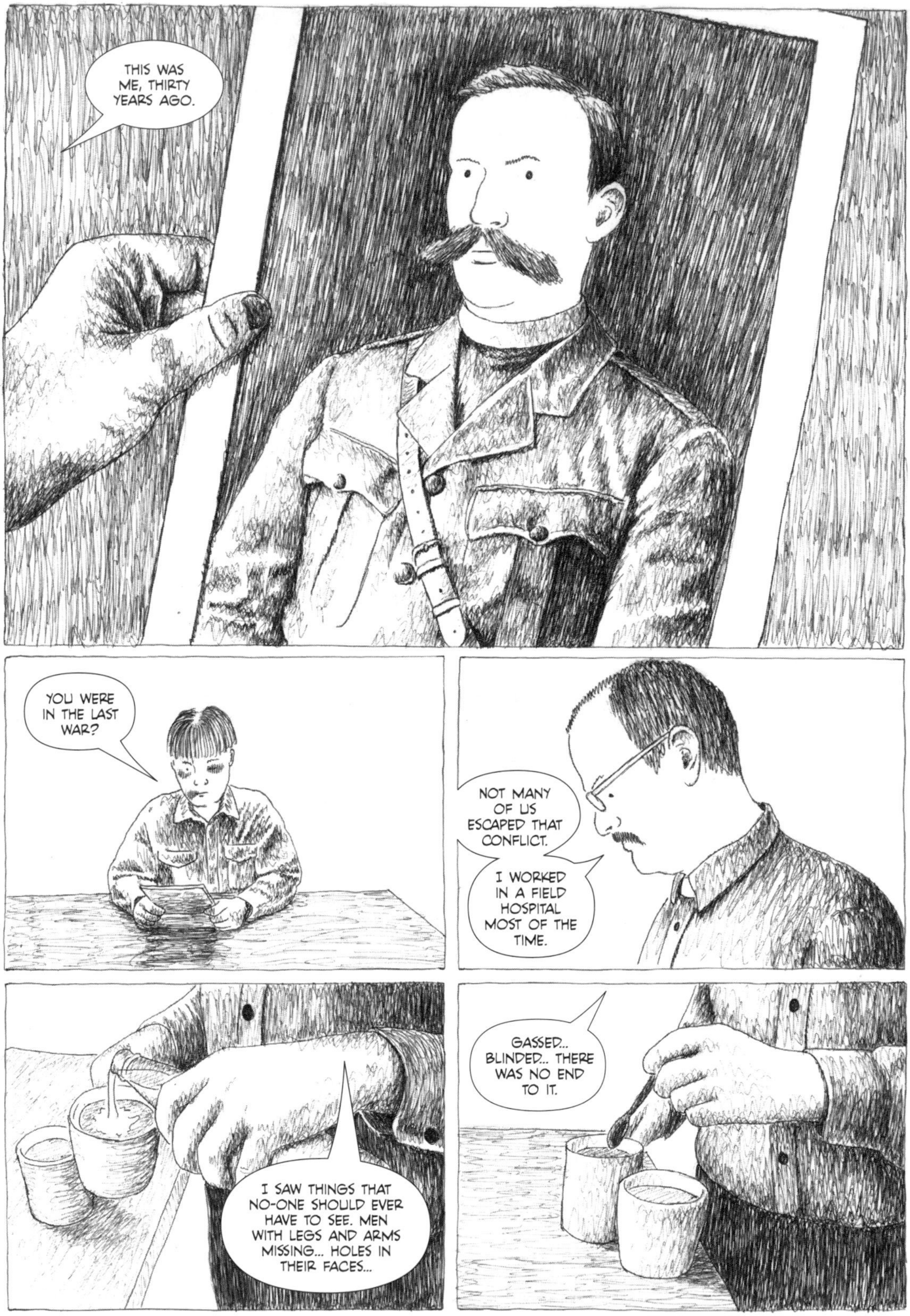
THIS WAS ME, THIRTY YEARS AGO.
YOU WERE IN THE LAST WAR?
NOT MANY OF US ESCAPED THAT CONFLICT.
I WORKED IN A FIELD HOSPITAL MOST OF THE TIME.
I SAW THINGS THAT NO-ONE SHOULD EVER HAVE TO SEE. MEN WITH LEGS AND ARMS MISSING... HOLES IN THEIR FACES...
GASSED... BLINDED... THERE WAS NO END TO IT.

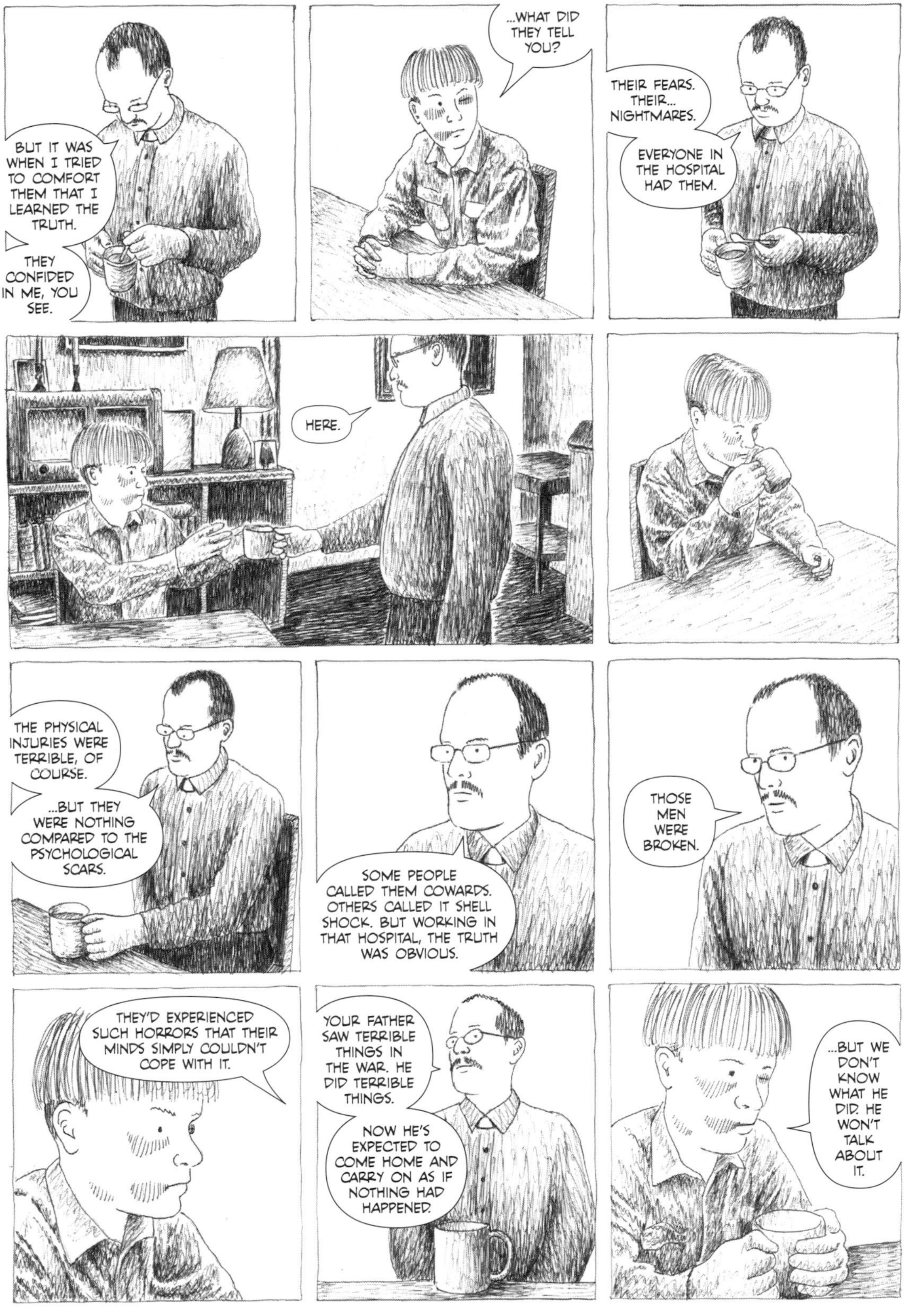
BUT IT WAS WHEN I TRIED TO COMFORT THEM THAT I LEARNED THE TRUTH.
THEY CONFIDED IN ME, YOU SEE.
...WHAT DID THEY TELL YOU?
THEIR FEARS. THEIR... NIGHTMARES.
EVERYONE IN THE HOSPITAL HAD THEM.
HERE.
THE PHYSICAL INJURIES WERE TERRIBLE, OF COURSE.
...BUT THEY WERE NOTHING COMPARED TO THE PSYCHOLOGICAL SCARS.
SOME PEOPLE CALLED THEM COWARDS. OTHERS CALLED IT SHELL SHOCK. BUT WORKING IN THAT HOSPITAL, THE TRUTH WAS OBVIOUS.
THOSE MEN WERE BROKEN.
THEY'D EXPERIENCED SUCH HORRORS THAT THEIR MINDS SIMPLY COULDN'T COPE WITH IT.
YOUR FATHER SAW TERRIBLE THINGS IN THE WAR. HE DID TERRIBLE THINGS.
NOW HE'S EXPECTED TO COME HOME AND CARRY ON AS IF NOTHING HAD HAPPENED.
...BUT WE DON'T KNOW WHAT HE DID. HE WON'T TALK ABOUT IT.

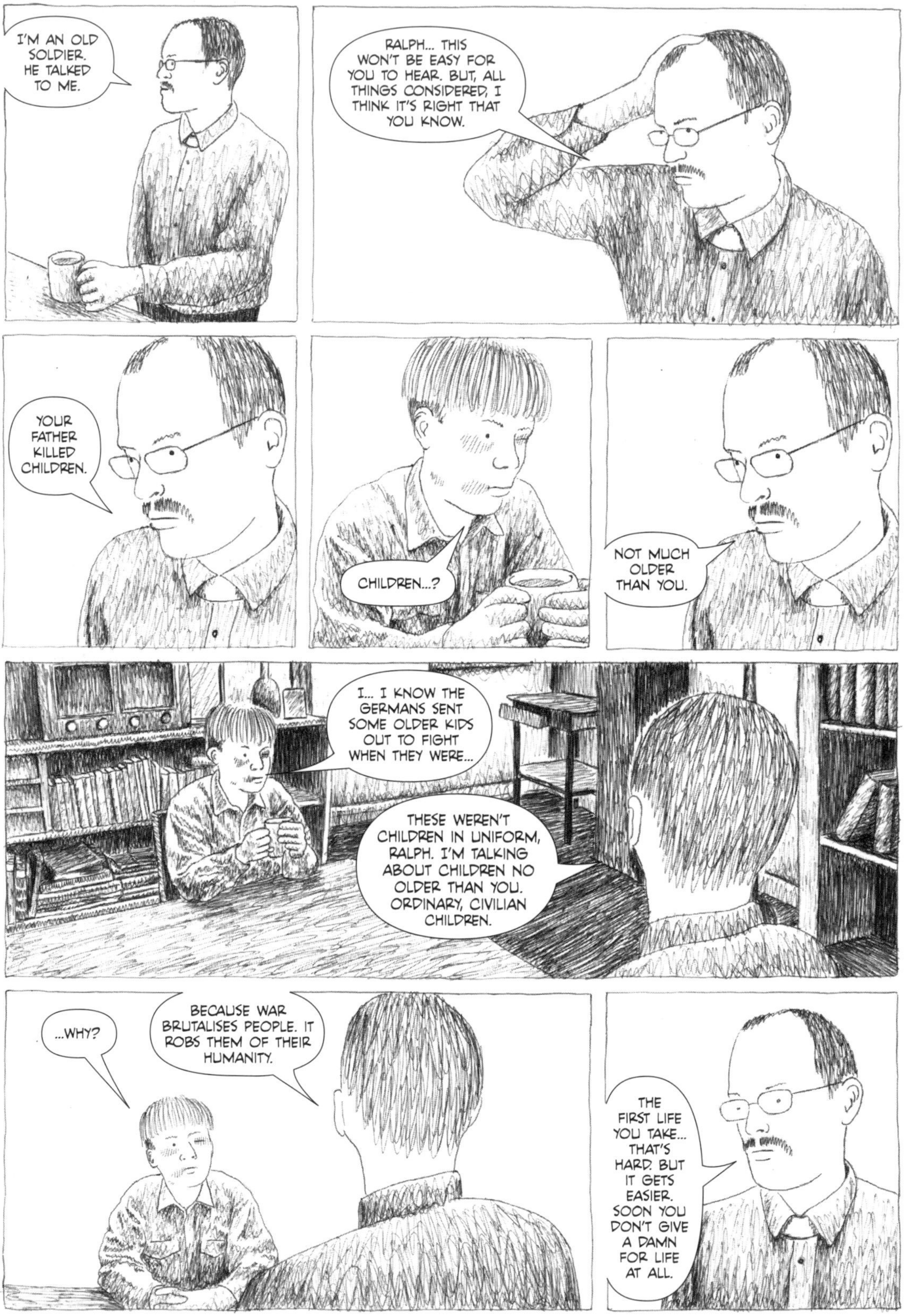
I'M AN OLD SOLDIER. HE TALKED TO ME.
RALPH... THIS WON'T BE EASY FOR YOU TO HEAR. BUT, ALL THINGS CONSIDERED, I THINK IT'S RIGHT THAT YOU KNOW.
YOUR FATHER KILLED CHILDREN.
CHILDREN...?
NOT MUCH OLDER THAN YOU.
I... I KNOW THE GERMANS SENT SOME OLDER KIDS OUT TO FIGHT WHEN THEY WERE...
THESE WEREN'T CHILDREN IN UNIFORM, RALPH. I'M TALKING ABOUT CHILDREN NO OLDER THAN YOU. ORDINARY, CIVILIAN CHILDREN.
...WHY?
BECAUSE WAR BRUTALISES PEOPLE. IT ROBS THEM OF THEIR HUMANITY.
THE FIRST LIFE YOU TAKE... THAT'S HARD. BUT IT GETS EASIER. SOON YOU DON'T GIVE A DAMN FOR LIFE AT ALL.

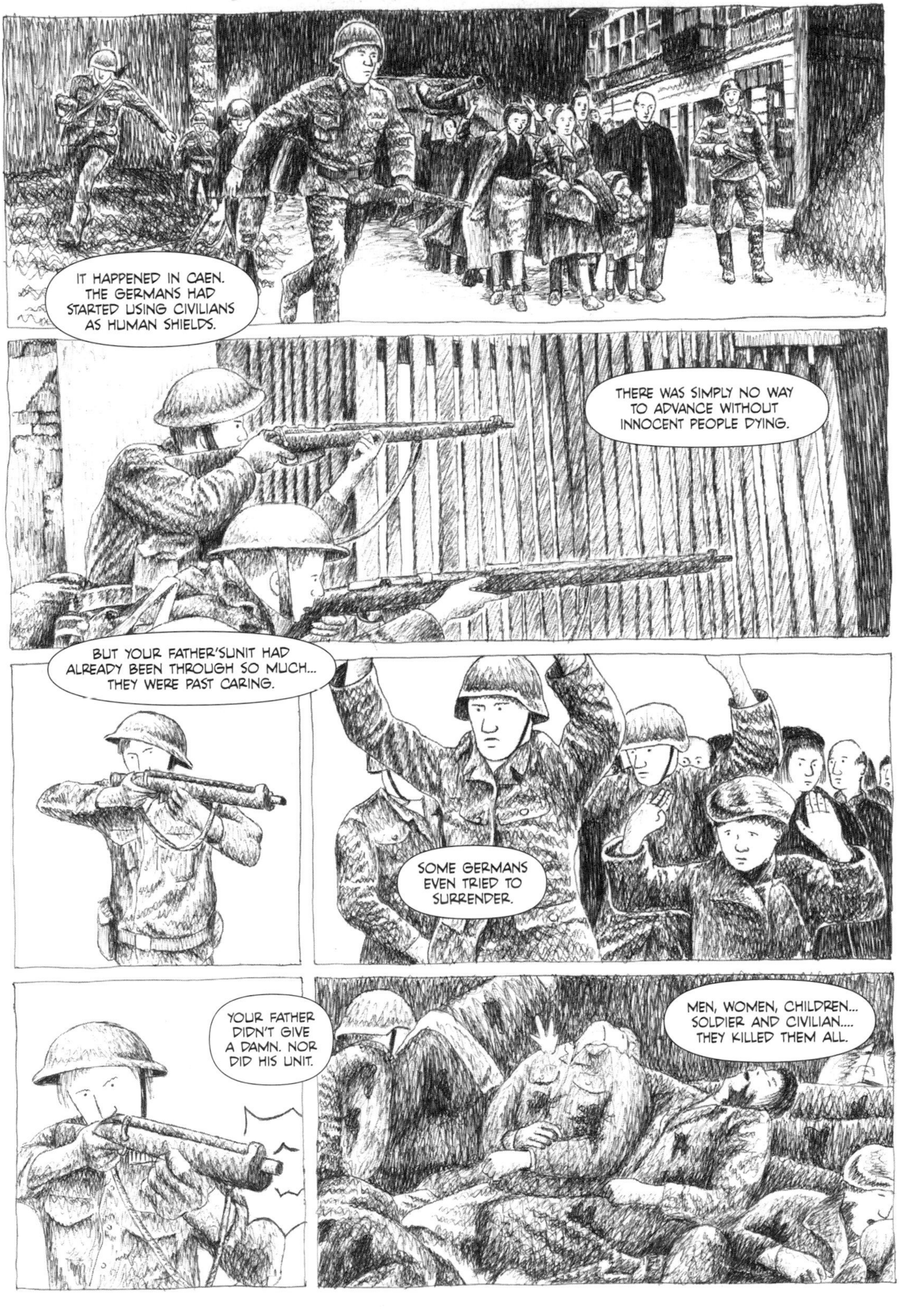
IT HAPPENED IN CAEN. THE GERMANS HAD STARTED USING CIVILIANS AS HUMAN SHIELDS.
THERE WAS SIMPLY NO WAY TO ADVANCE WITHOUT INNOCENT PEOPLE DYING.
BUT YOUR FATHER'SUNIT HAD ALREADY BEEN THROUGH SO MUCH... THEY WERE PAST CARING.
SOME GERMANS EVEN TRIED TO SURRENDER.
YOUR FATHER DIDN'T GIVE A DAMN. NOR DID HIS UNIT.
MEN, WOMEN, CHILDREN... SOLDIER AND CIVILIAN.... THEY KILLED THEM ALL.

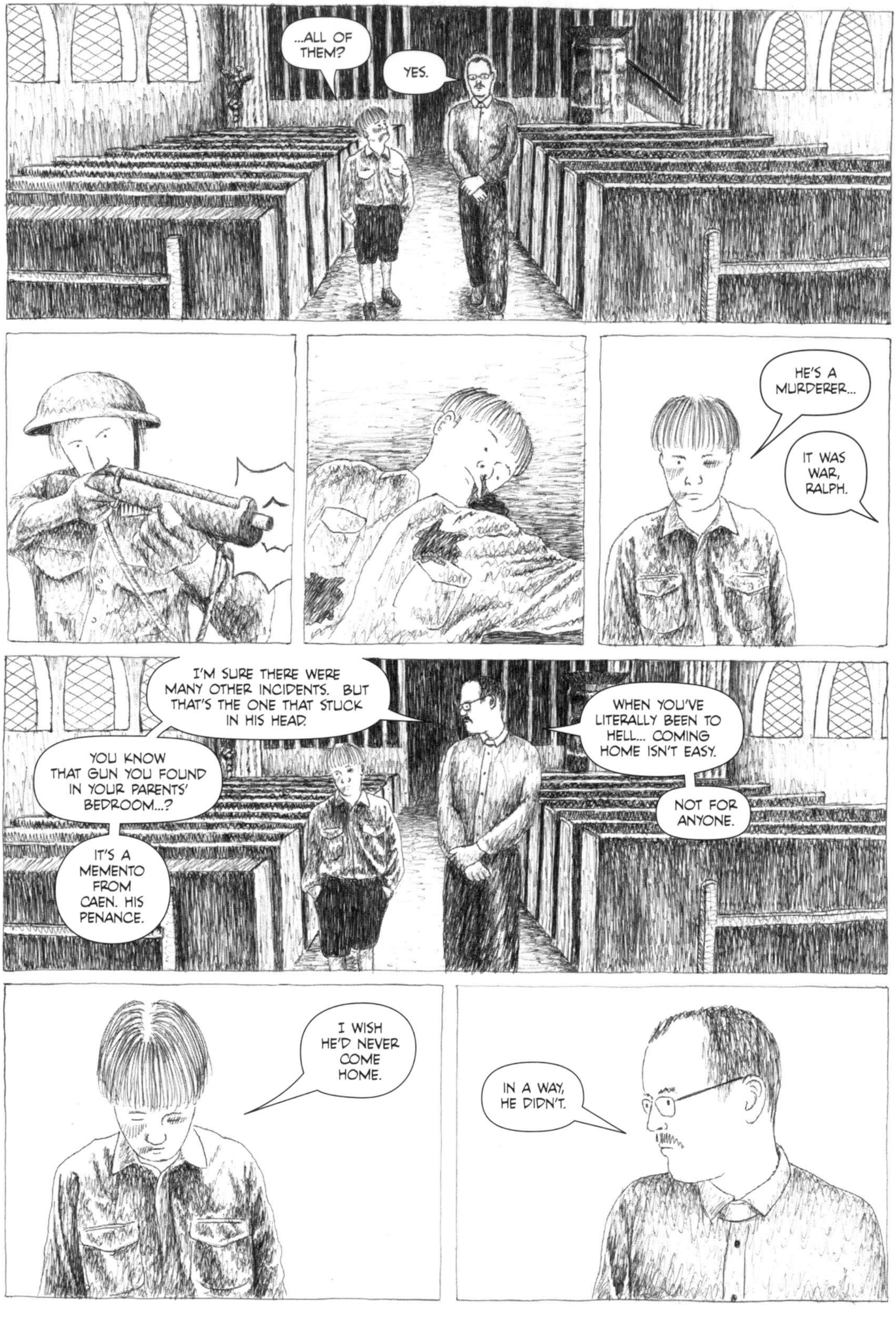
...ALL OF THEM?
YES.
HE'S A MURDERER...
IT WAS WAR, RALPH.
I'M SURE THERE WERE MANY OTHER INCIDENTS. BUT THAT'S THE ONE THAT STUCK IN HIS HEAD.
YOU KNOW THAT GUN YOU FOUND IN YOUR PARENTS' BEDROOM...?
IT'S A MEMENTO FROM CAEN. HIS PENANCE.
WHEN YOU'VE LITERALLY BEEN TO HELL... COMING HOME ISN'T EASY.
NOT FOR ANYONE.
I WISH HE'D NEVER COME HOME.
IN A WAY, HE DIDN'T.

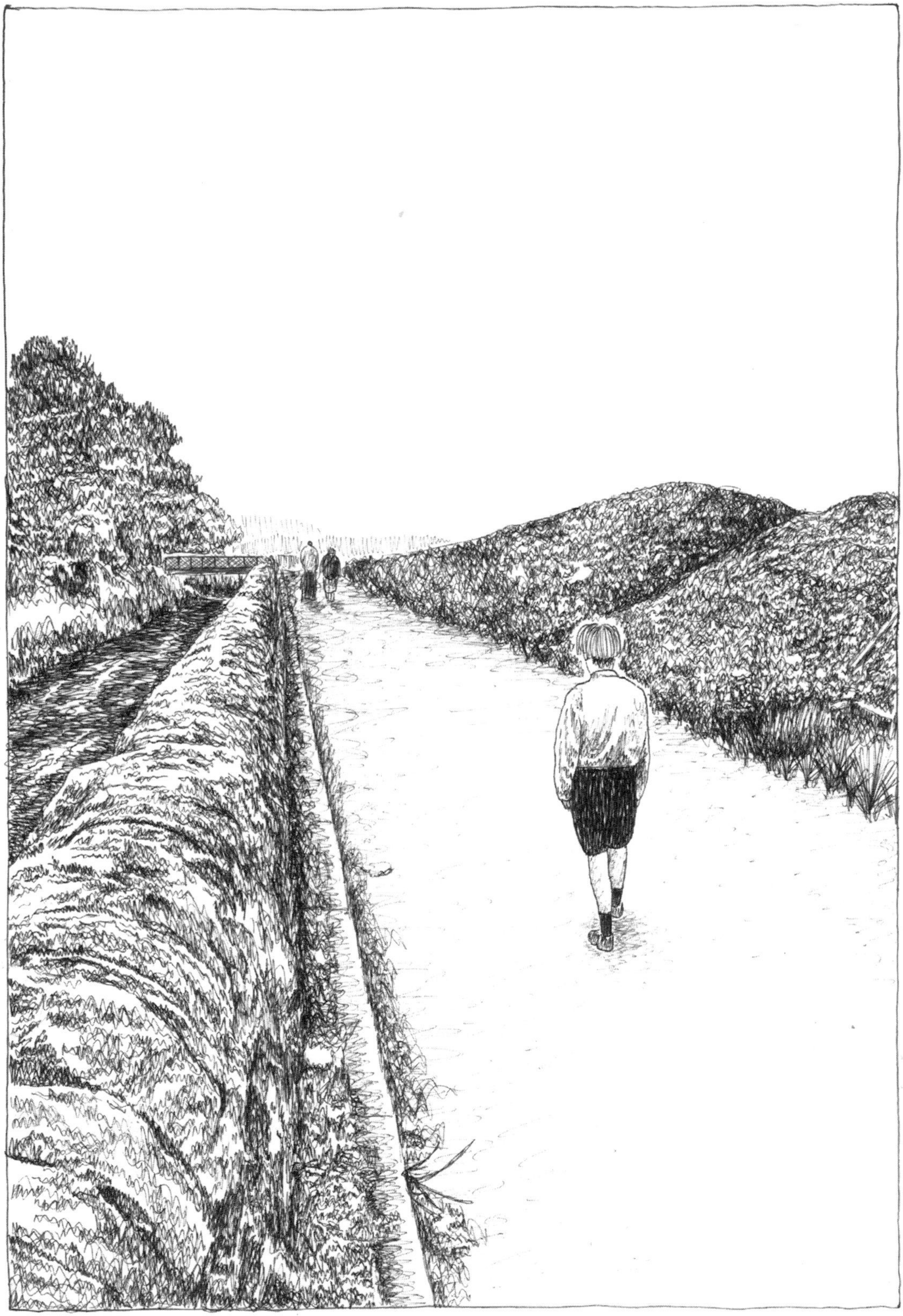

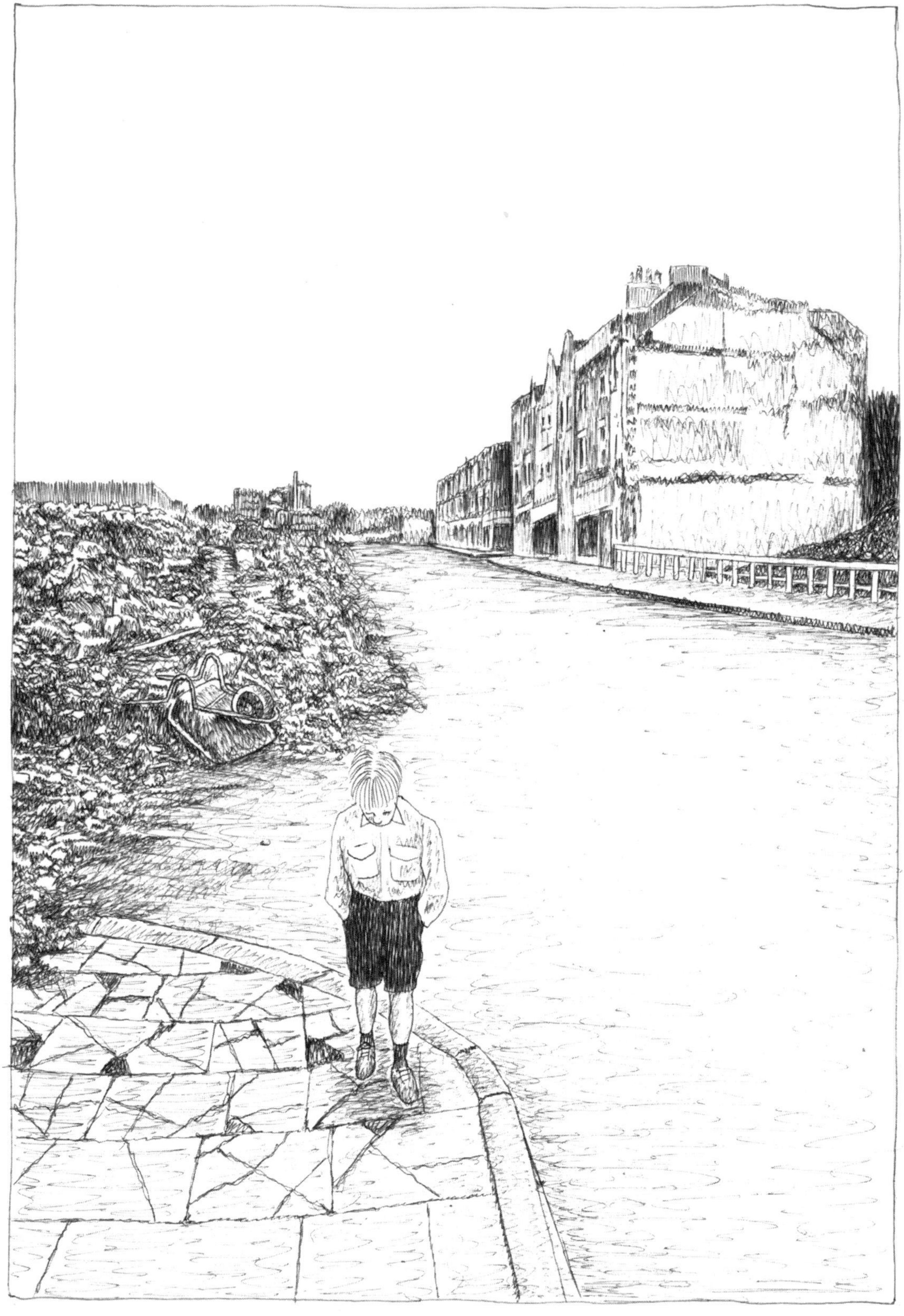

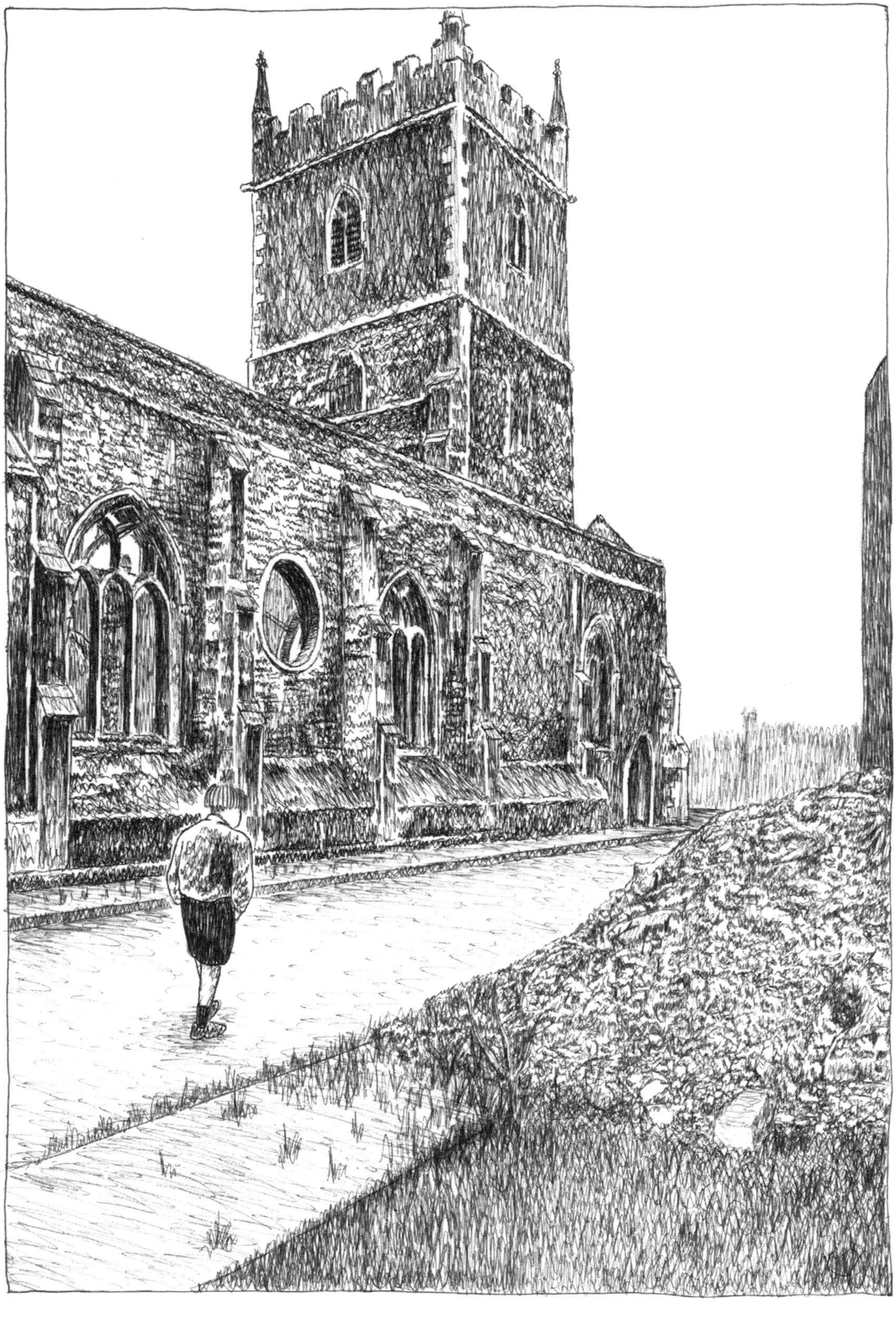

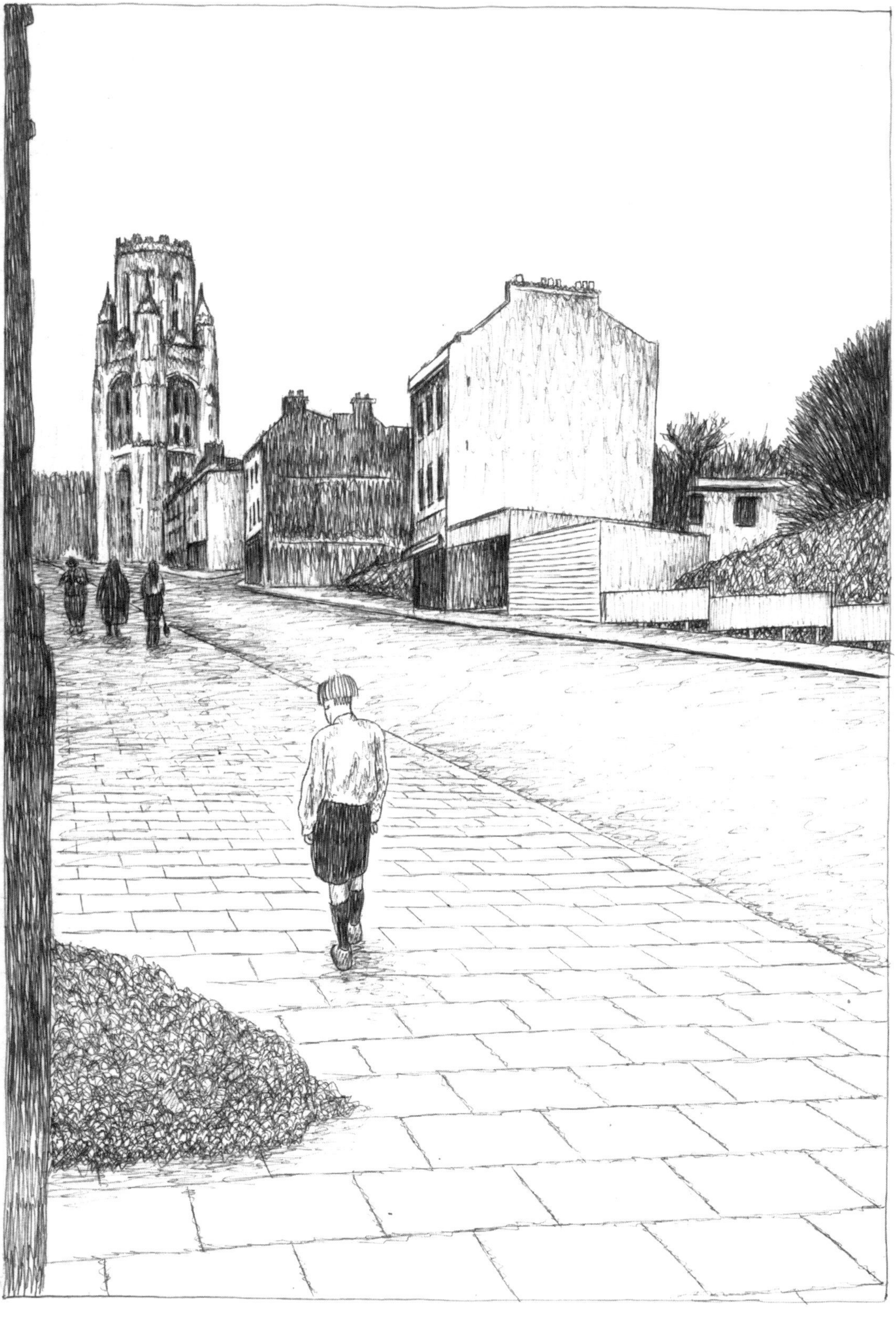

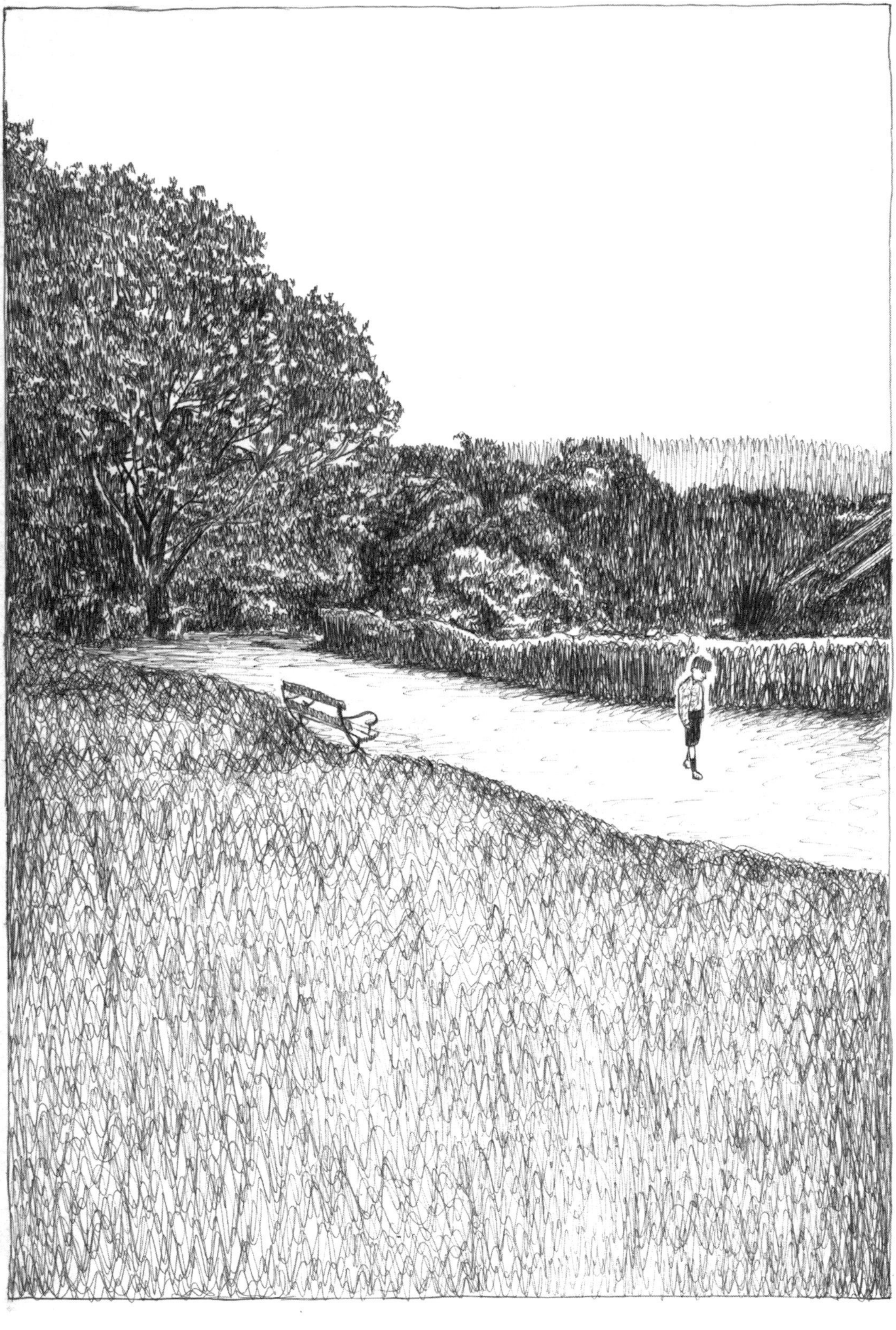

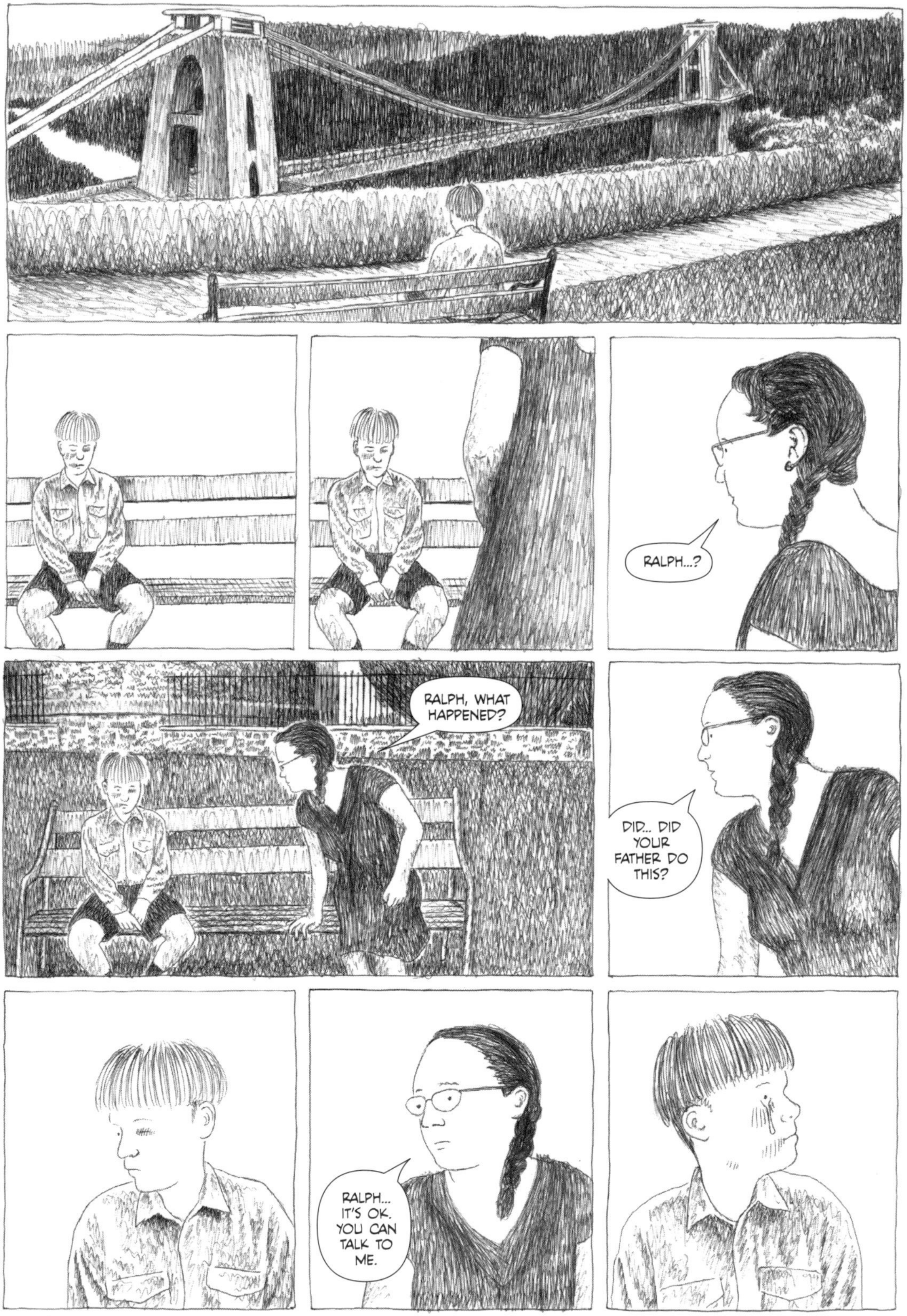
RALPH...?
RALPH, WHAT HAPPENED?
DID... DID YOUR FATHER DO THIS?
RALPH... IT'S OK. YOU CAN TALK TO ME.

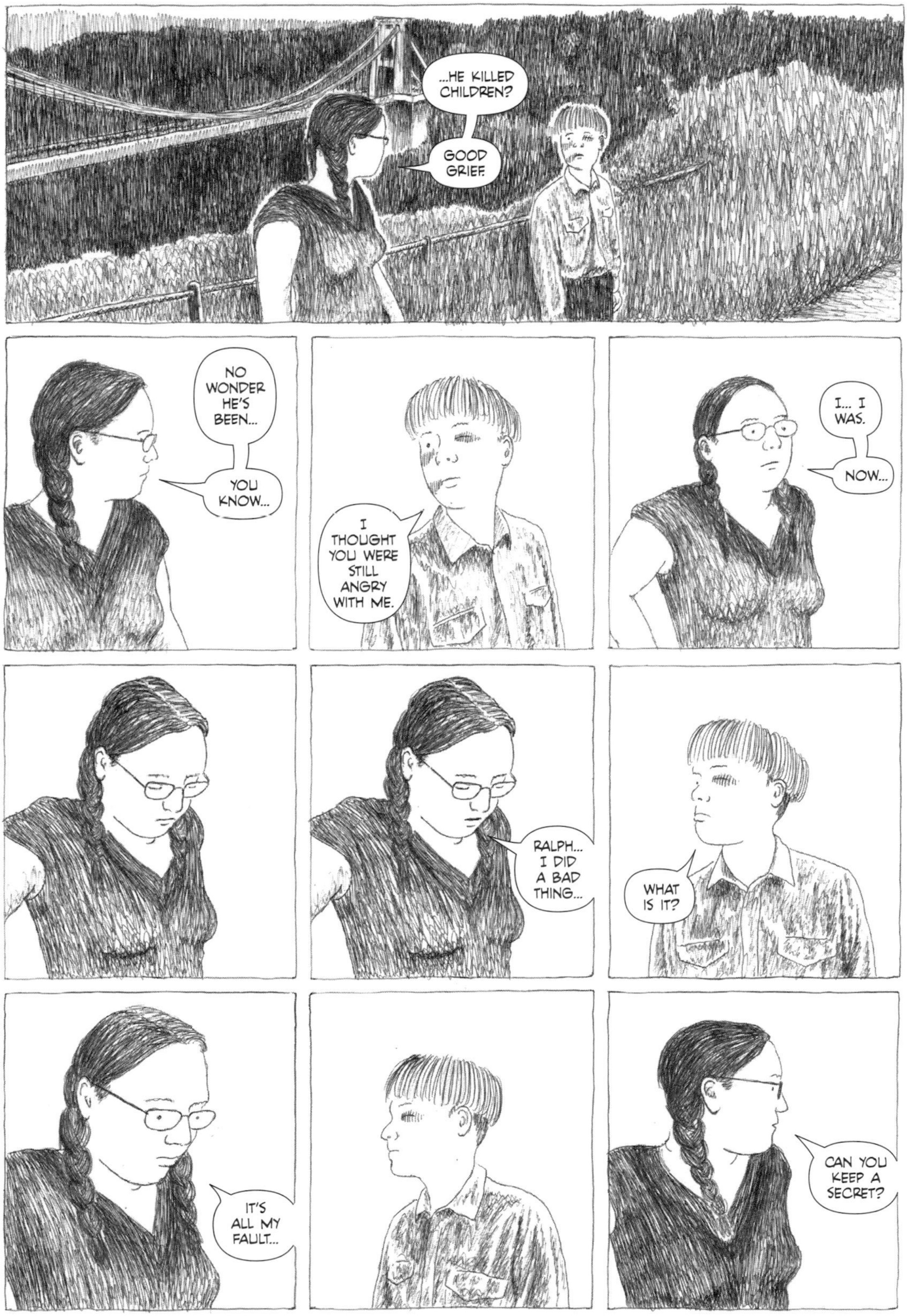
...HE KILLED CHILDREN?
GOOD GRIEF.
NO WONDER HE'S BEEN...
YOU KNOW...
I THOUGHT YOU WERE STILL ANGRY WITH ME.
I... I WAS.
NOW...
RALPH... I DID A BAD THING...
WHAT IS IT?
IT'S ALL MY FAULT...
CAN YOU KEEP A SECRET?

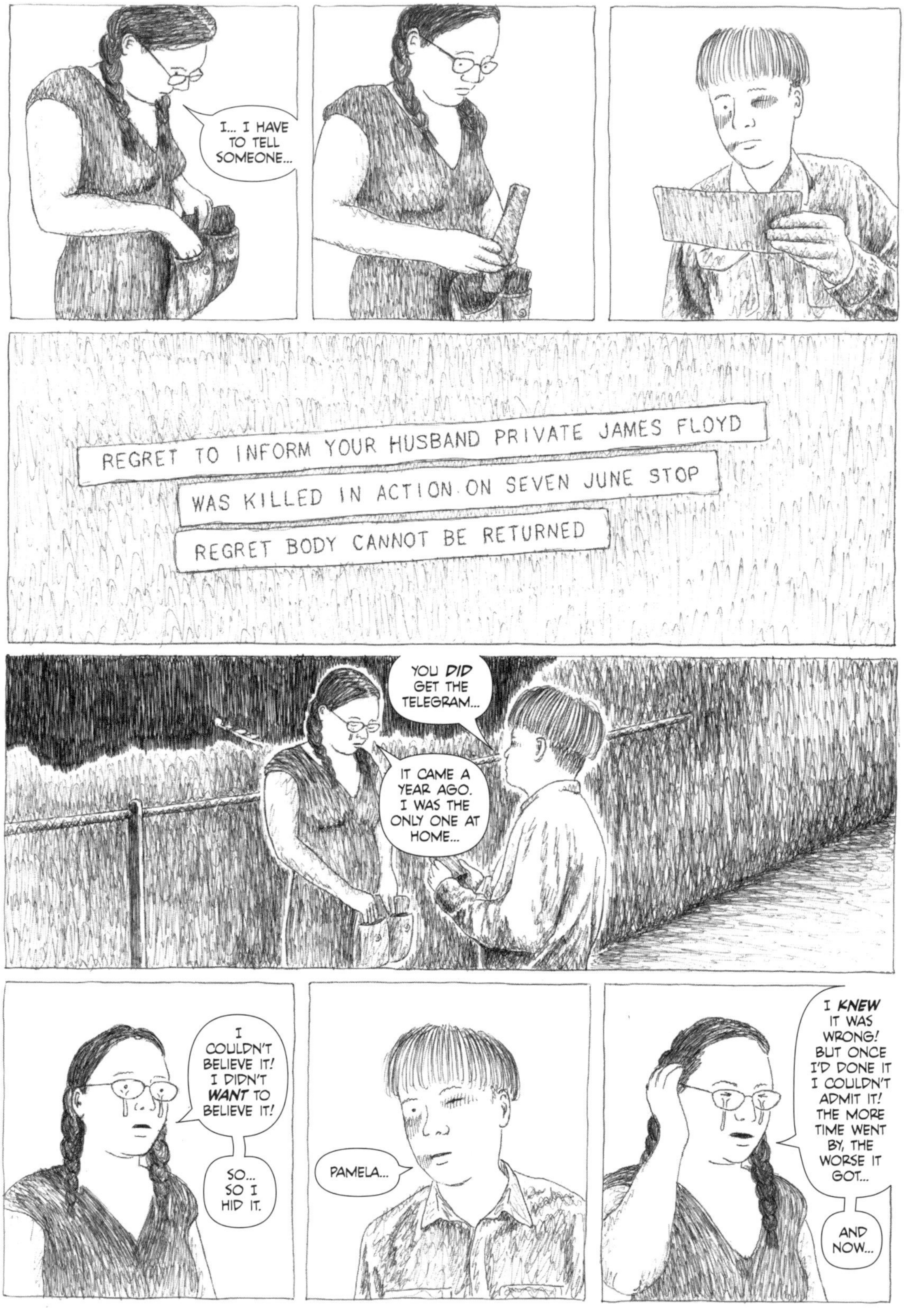
I... I HAVE TO TELL SOMEONE...
REGRET TO INFORM YOUR HUSBAND PRIVATE JAMES FLOYD
WAS KILLED IN ACTION ON SEVEN JUNE STOP
REGRET BODY CANNOT BE RETURNED
YOU DID GET THE TELEGRAM...
IT CAME A YEAR AGO. I WAS THE ONLY ONE AT HOME...
I COULDN'T BELIEVE IT! I DIDN'T WANT TO BELIEVE IT!
SO... SO I HID IT.
PAMELA...
I KNEW IT WAS WRONG! BUT ONCE I'D DONE IT I COULDN'T ADMIT IT! THE MORE TIME WENT BY, THE WORSE IT GOT...
AND NOW...

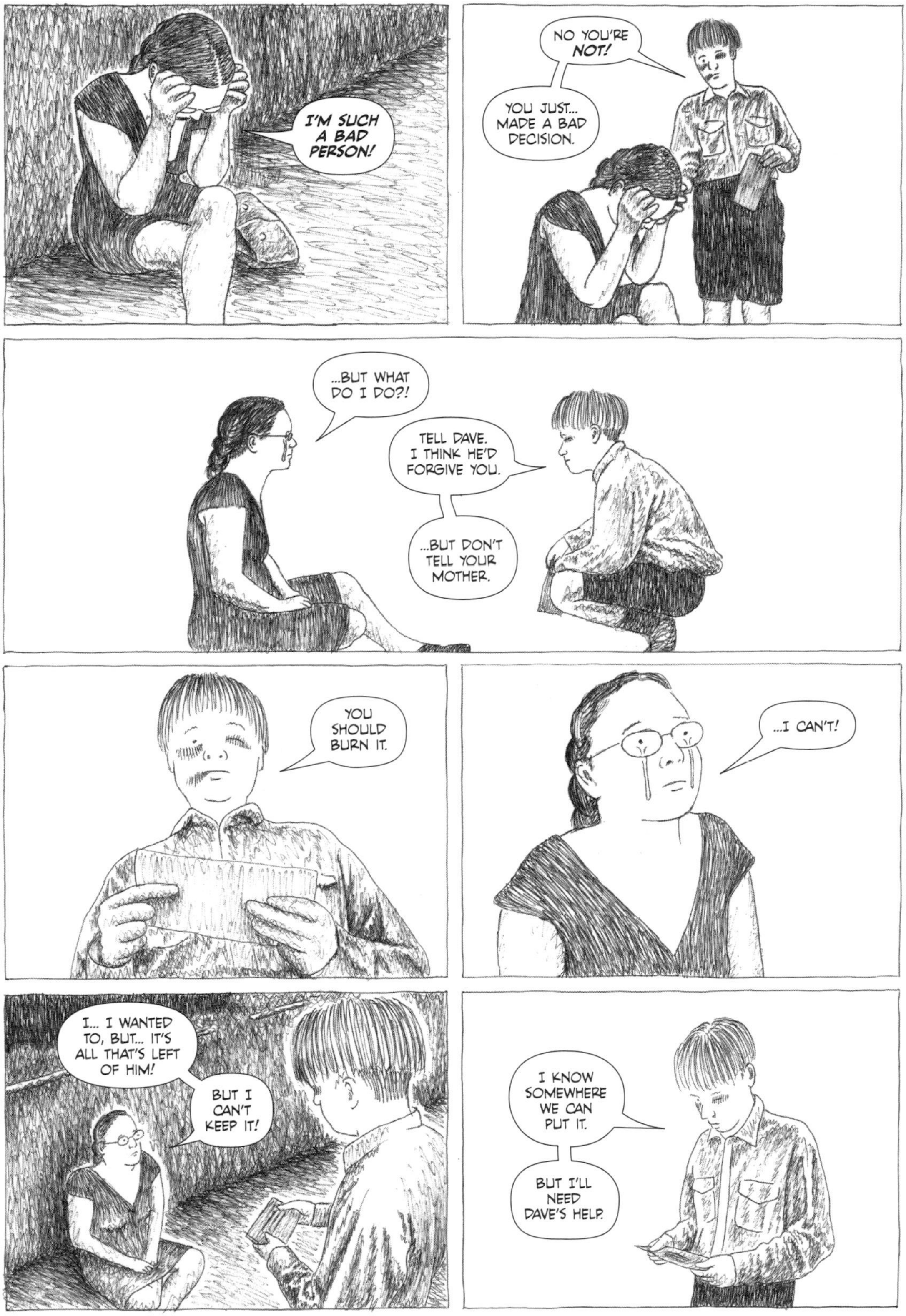
I'M SUCH A BAD PERSON!
NO YOU'RE NOT!
YOU JUST... MADE A BAD DECISION.
...BUT WHAT DO I DO?!
TELL DAVE. I THINK HE'D FORGIVE YOU.
...BUT DON'T TELL YOUR MOTHER.
YOU SHOULD BURN IT.
...I CAN'T!
I... I WANTED TO, BUT... IT'S ALL THAT'S LEFT OF HIM!
BUT I CAN'T KEEP IT!
I KNOW SOMEWHERE WE CAN PUT IT.
BUT I'LL NEED DAVE'S HELP.

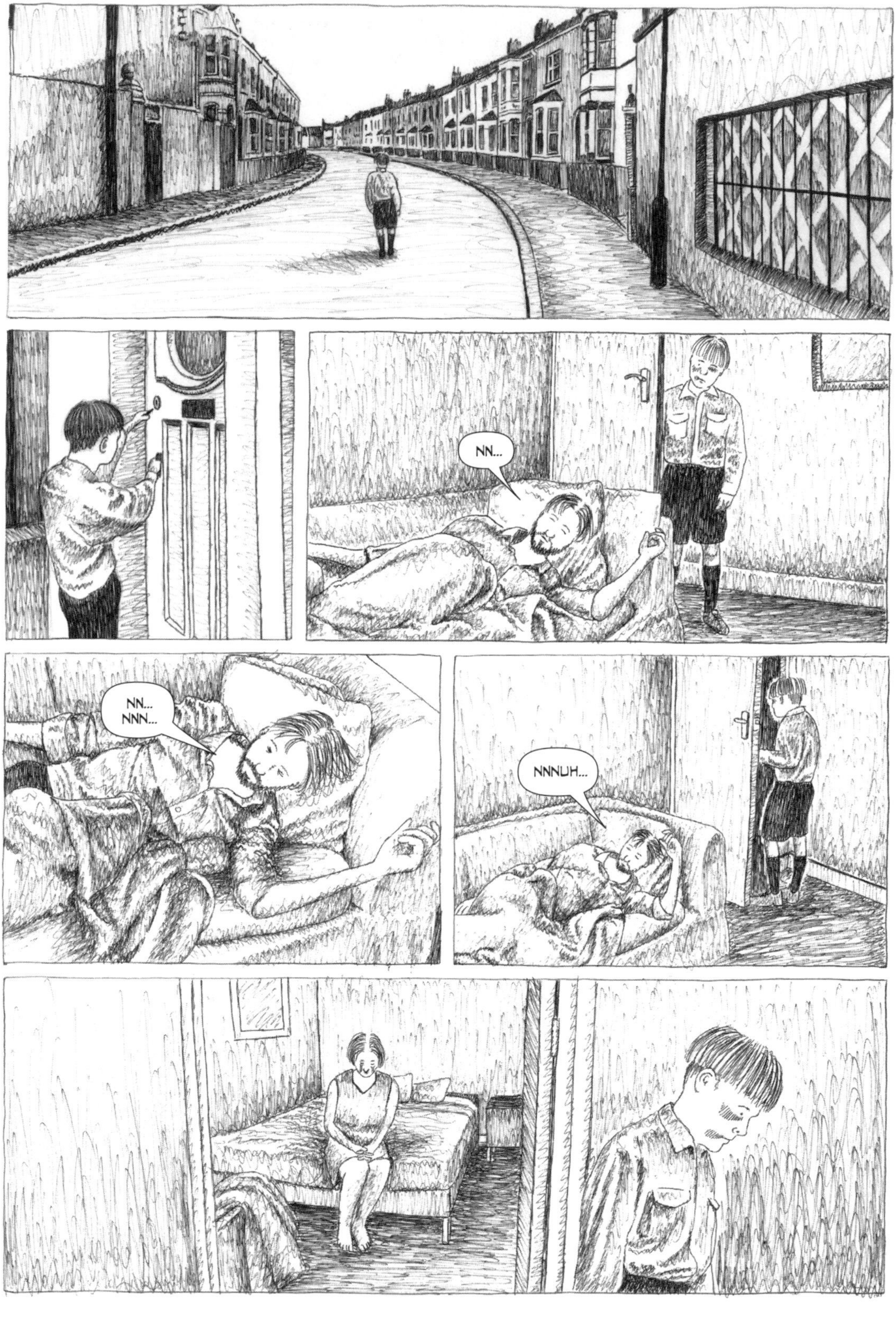
NN...
NN...
NNN...
NNNUH...

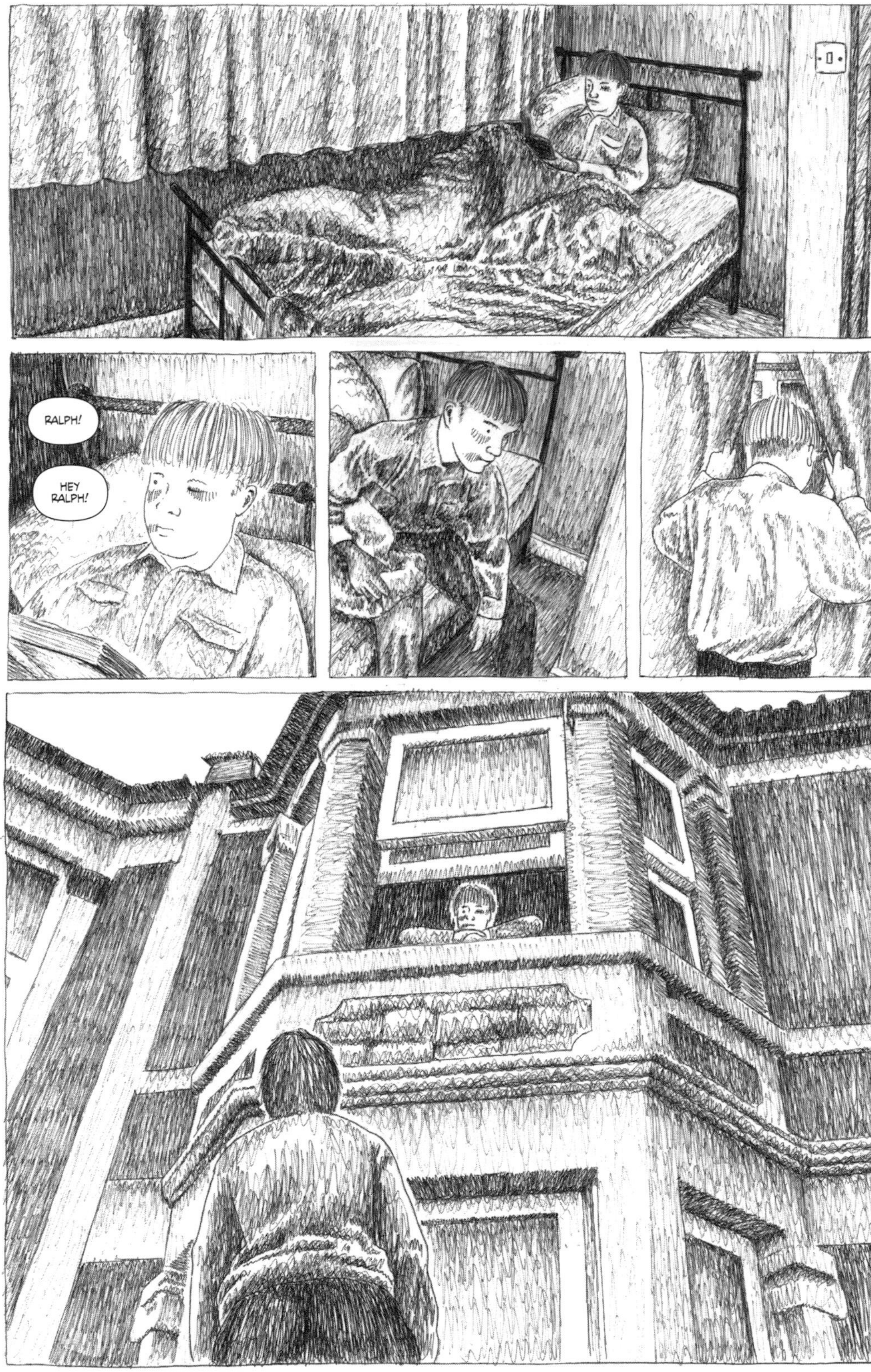
RALPH!
HEY RALPH!

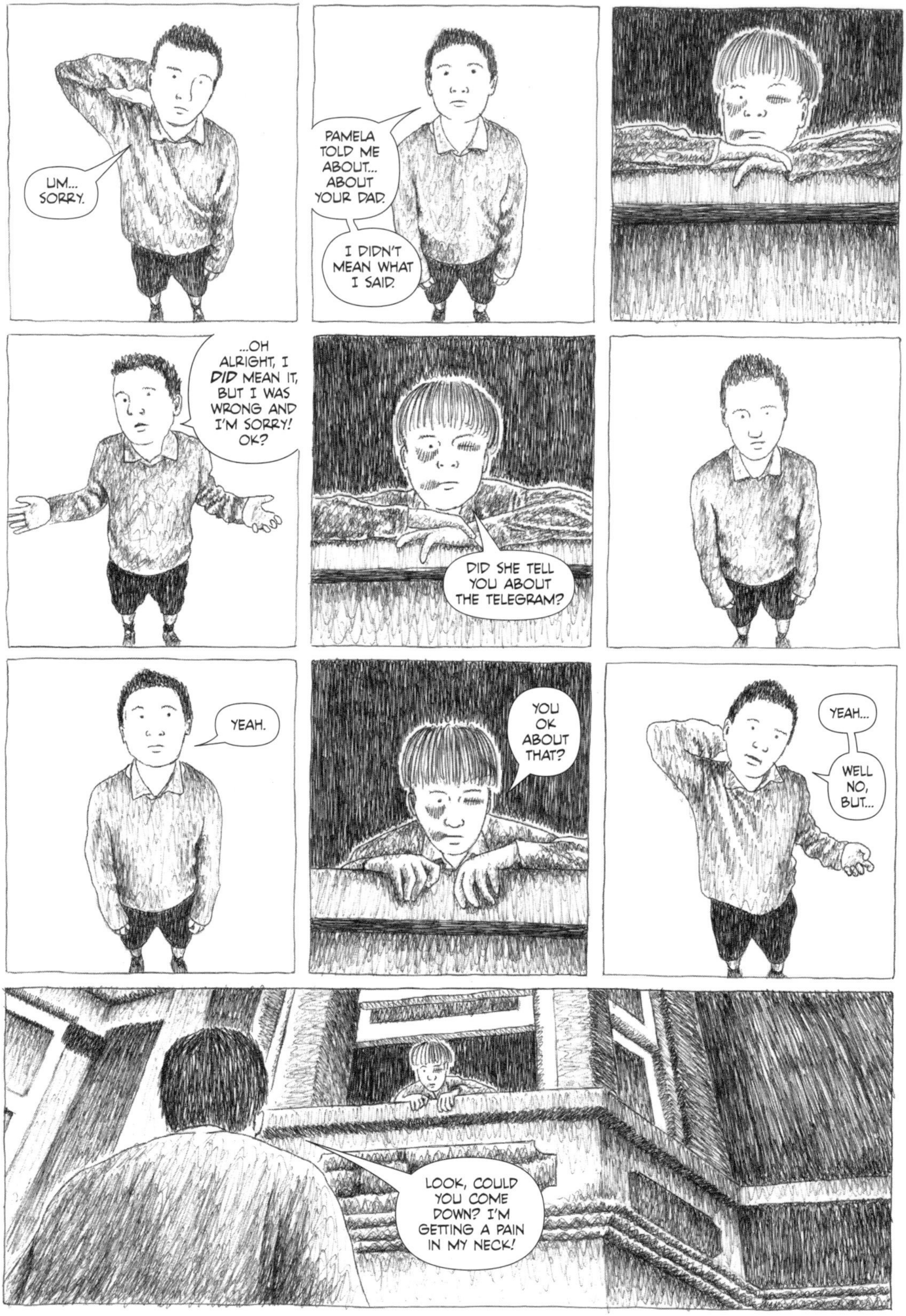
UM... SORRY.
PAMELA TOLD ME ABOUT... ABOUT YOUR DAD.
I DIDN'T MEAN WHAT I SAID.
...OH ALRIGHT, I DID MEAN IT, BUT I WAS WRONG AND I'M SORRY! OK?
DID SHE TELL YOU ABOUT THE TELEGRAM?
YEAH.
YOU OK ABOUT THAT?
YEAH...
WELL NO, BUT...
LOOK, COULD YOU COME DOWN? I'M GETTING A PAIN IN MY NECK!

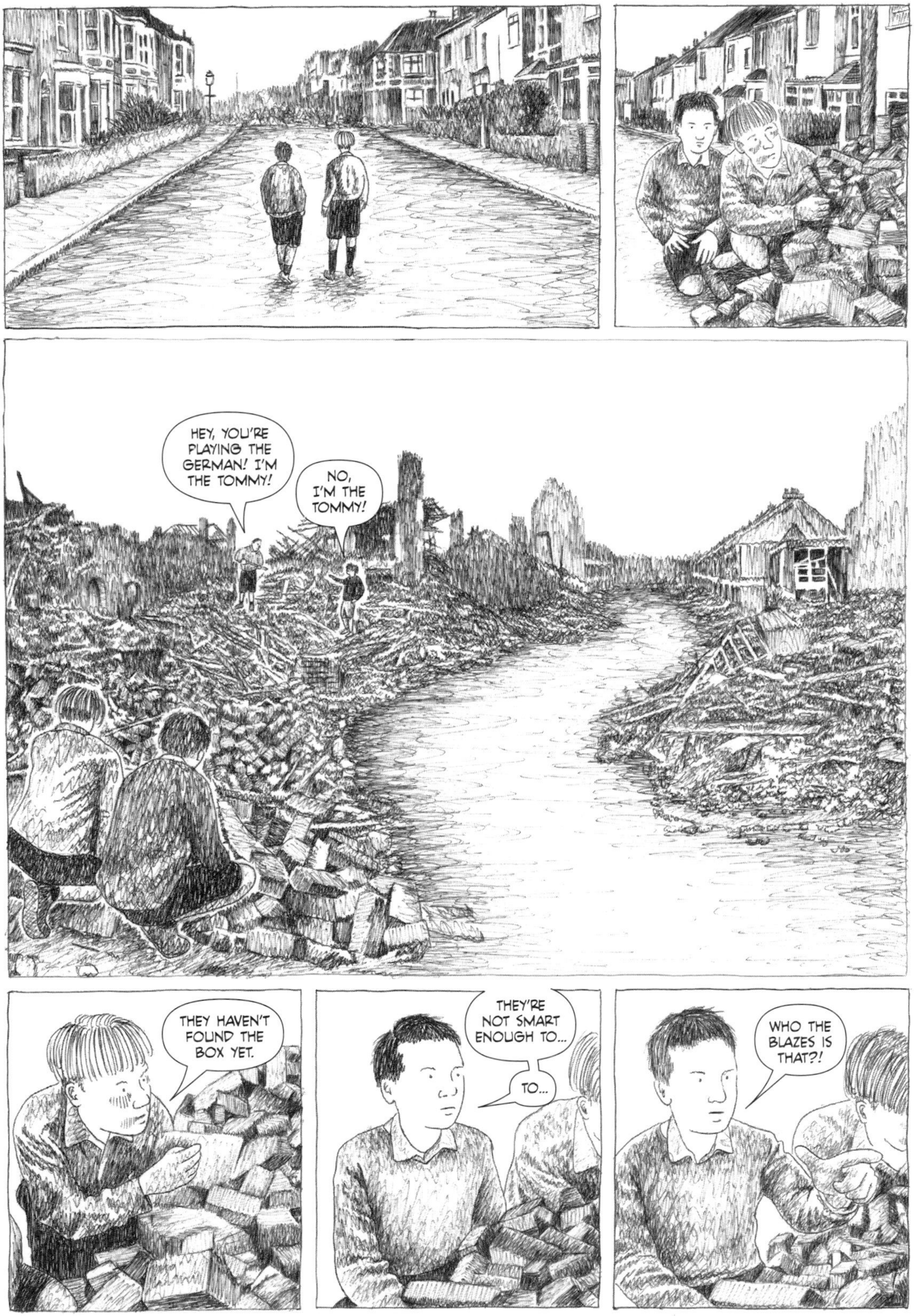
HEY, YOU'RE PLAYING THE GERMAN! I'M THE TOMMY!
NO, I'M THE TOMMY!
THEY HAVEN'T FOUND THE BOX YET.
THEY'RE NOT SMART ENOUGH TO...
TO...
WHO THE BLAZES IS THAT?!

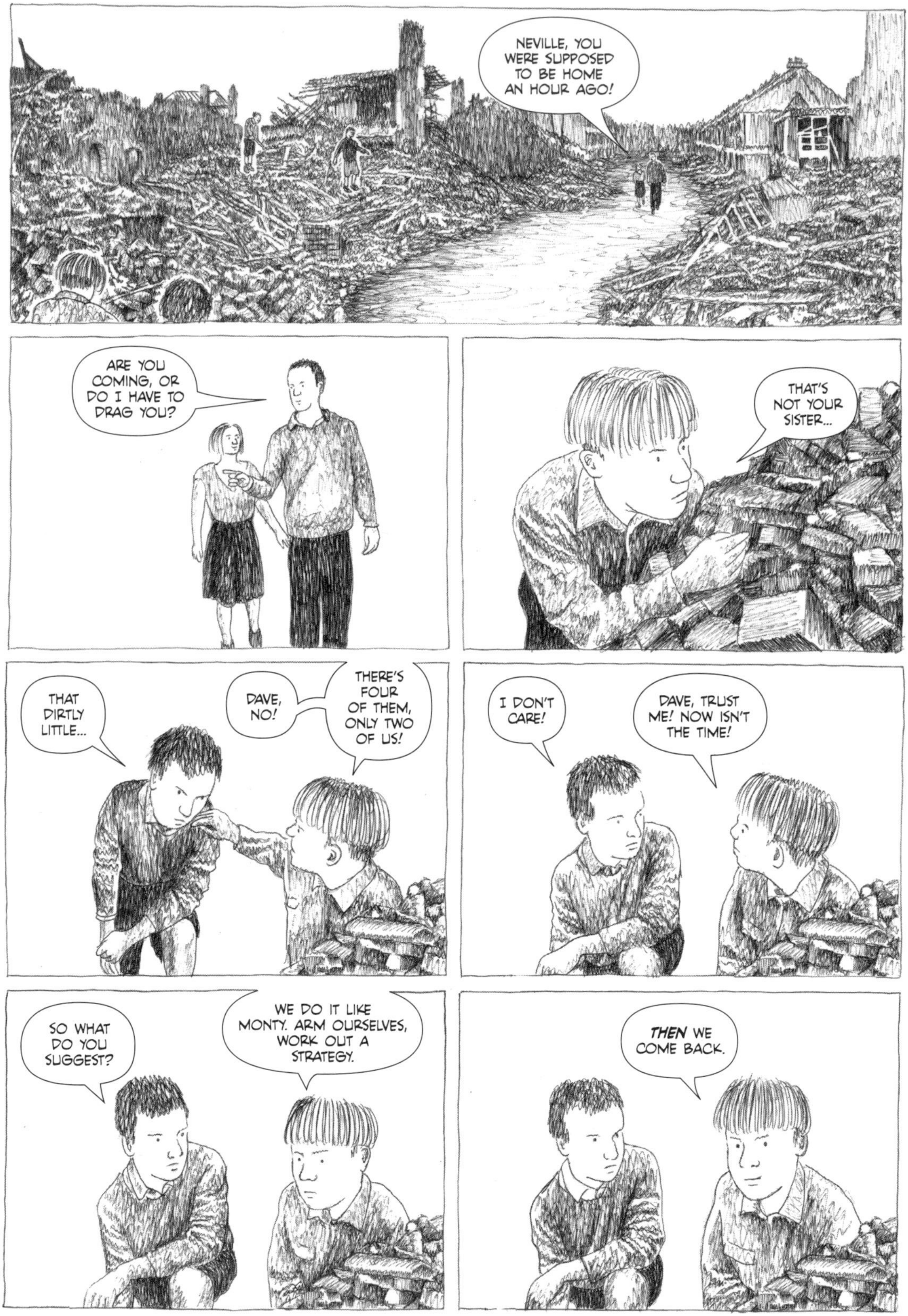
NEVILLE, YOU WERE SUPPOSED TO BE HOME AN HOUR AGO!
ARE YOU COMING, OR DO I HAVE TO DRAG YOU?
THAT'S NOT YOUR SISTER...
THAT DIRTLY LITTLE...
DAVE, NO!
THERE'S FOUR OF THEM, ONLY TWO OF US!
I DON'T CARE!
DAVE, TRUST ME! NOW ISN'T THE TIME!
SO WHAT DO YOU SUGGEST?
WE DO IT LIKE MONTY. ARM OURSELVES, WORK OUT A STRATEGY.
THEN WE COME BACK.

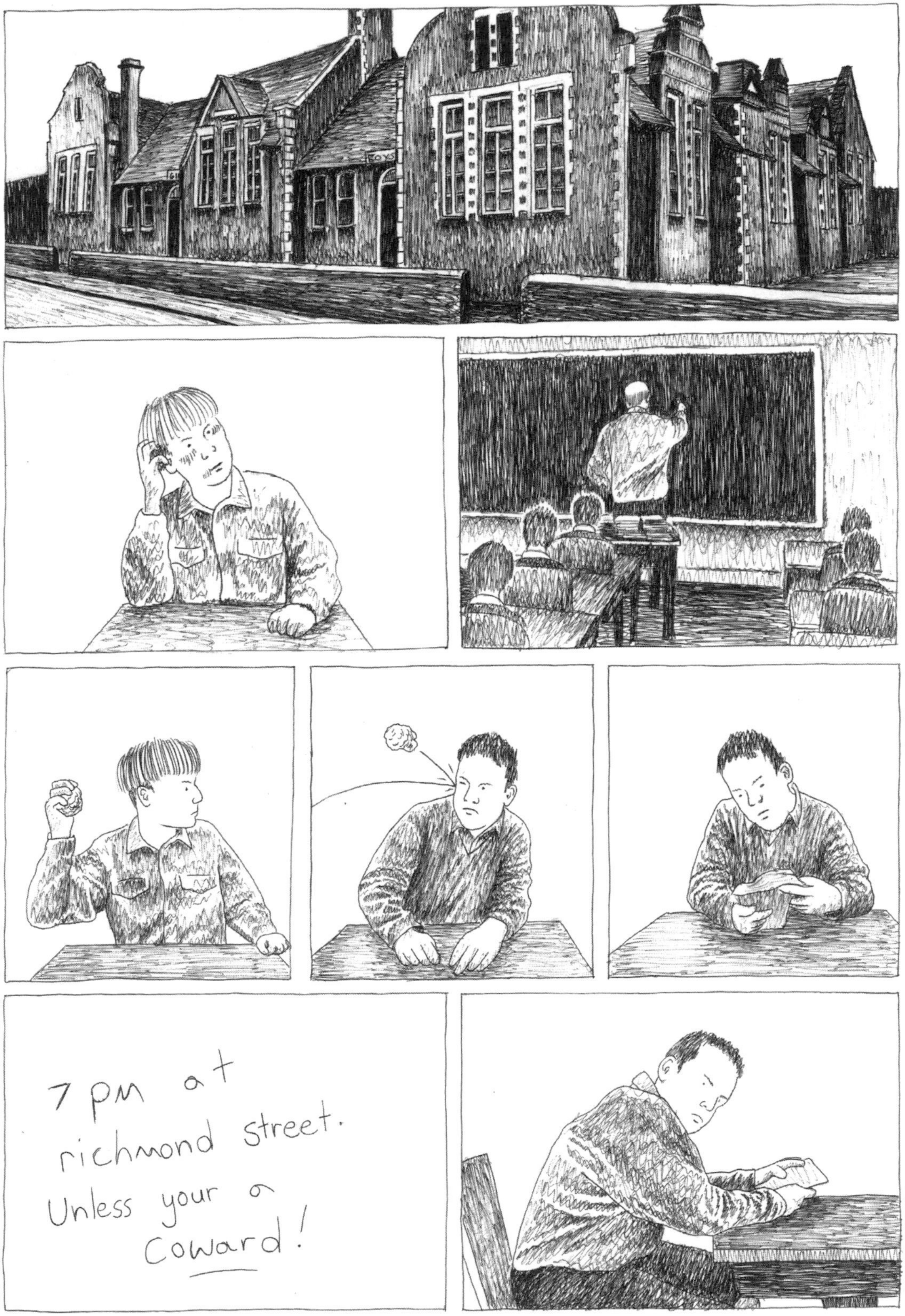
7 pm at
richmond street.
Unless your a
coward!

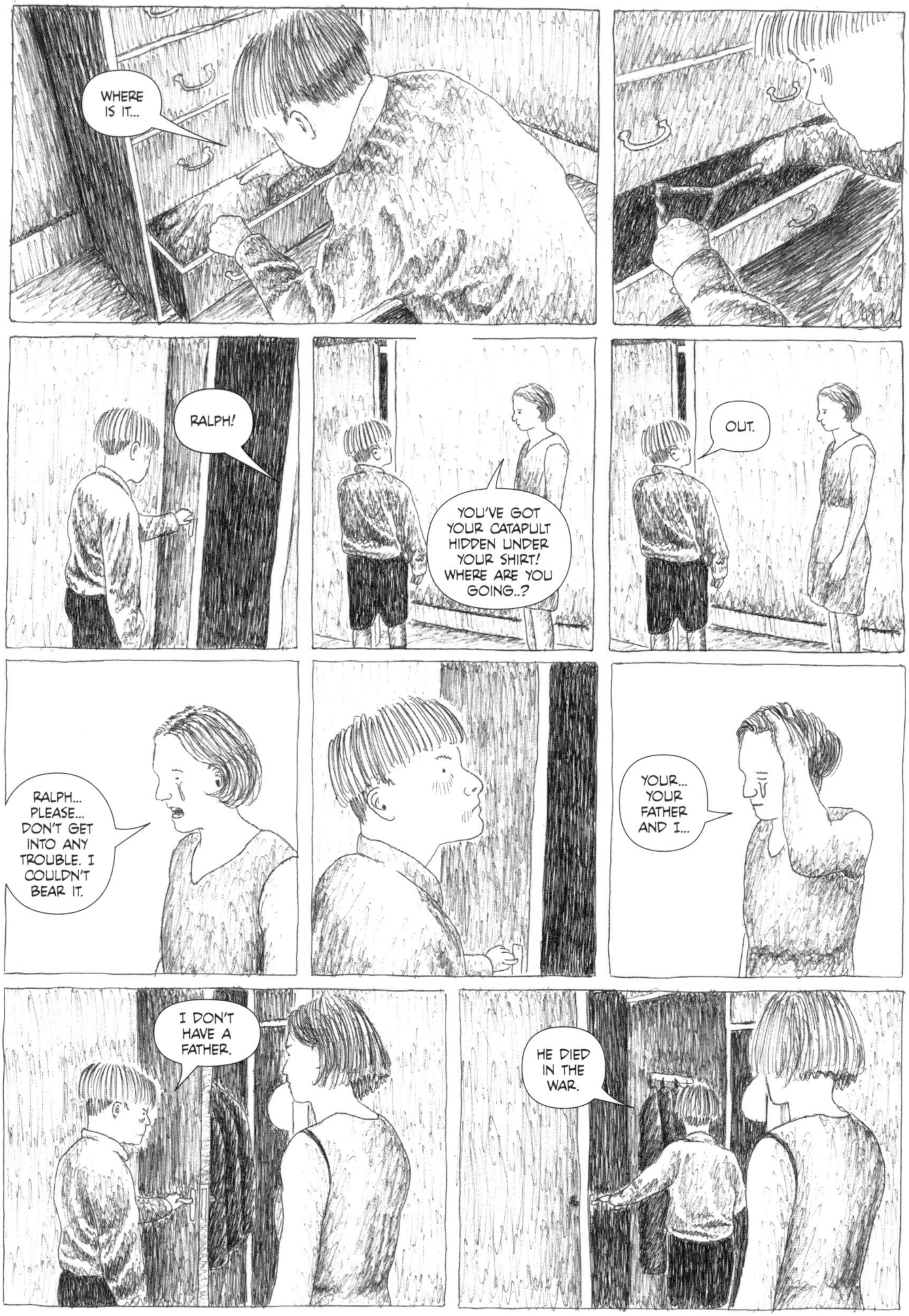
WHERE IS IT...
RALPH!
YOU'VE GOT YOUR CATAPULT HIDDEN UNDER YOUR SHIRT! WHERE ARE YOU GOING..?
OUT.
RALPH... PLEASE... DON'T GET INTO ANY TROUBLE. I COULDN'T BEAR IT.
YOUR... YOUR FATHER AND I...
I DON'T HAVE A FATHER.
HE DIED IN THE WAR.

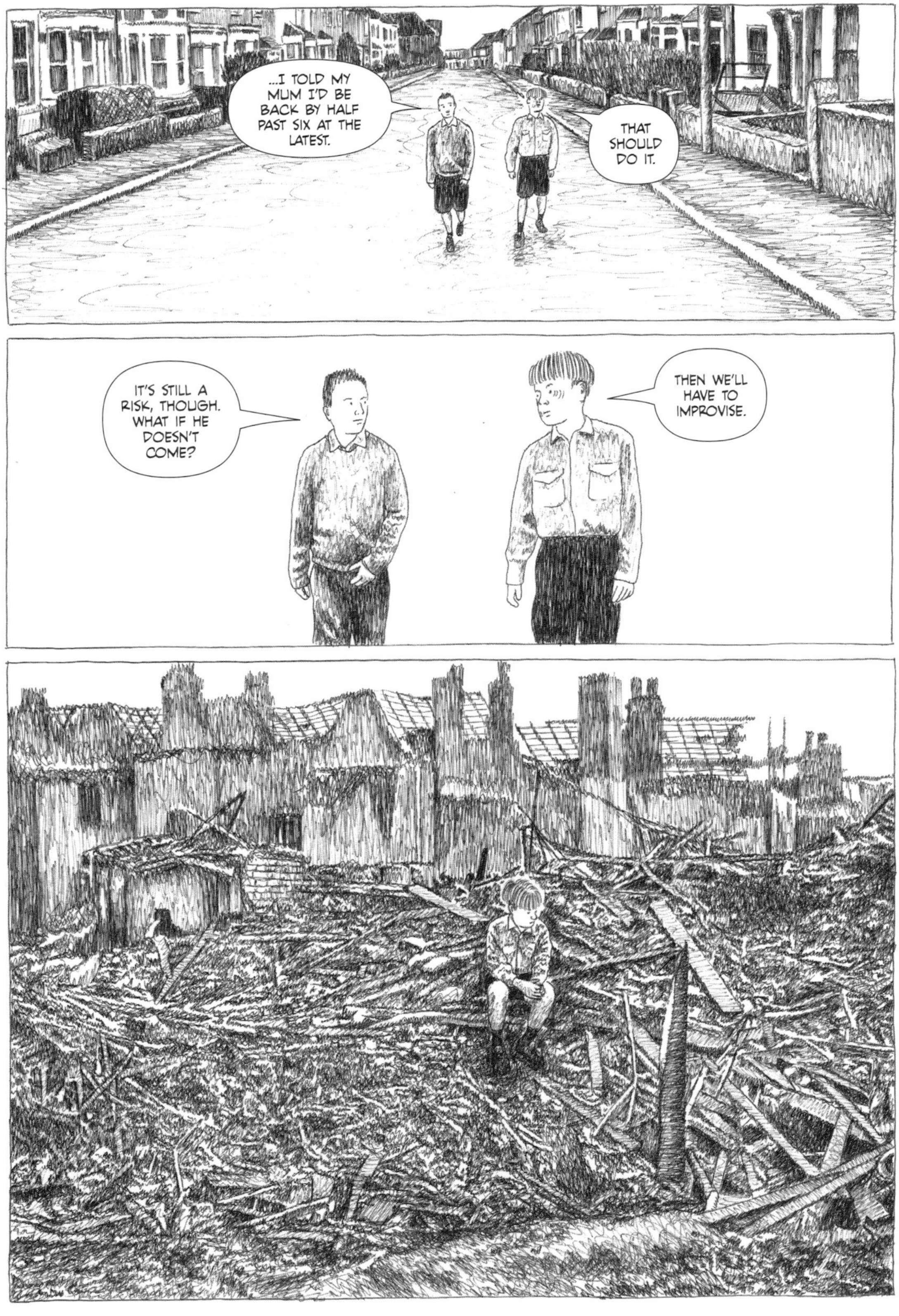
...I TOLD MY MUM I'D BE BACK BY HALF PAST SIX AT THE LATEST.
THAT SHOULD DO IT.
IT'S STILL A RISK, THOUGH. WHAT IF HE DOESN'T COME?
THEN WE'LL HAVE TO IMPROVISE.

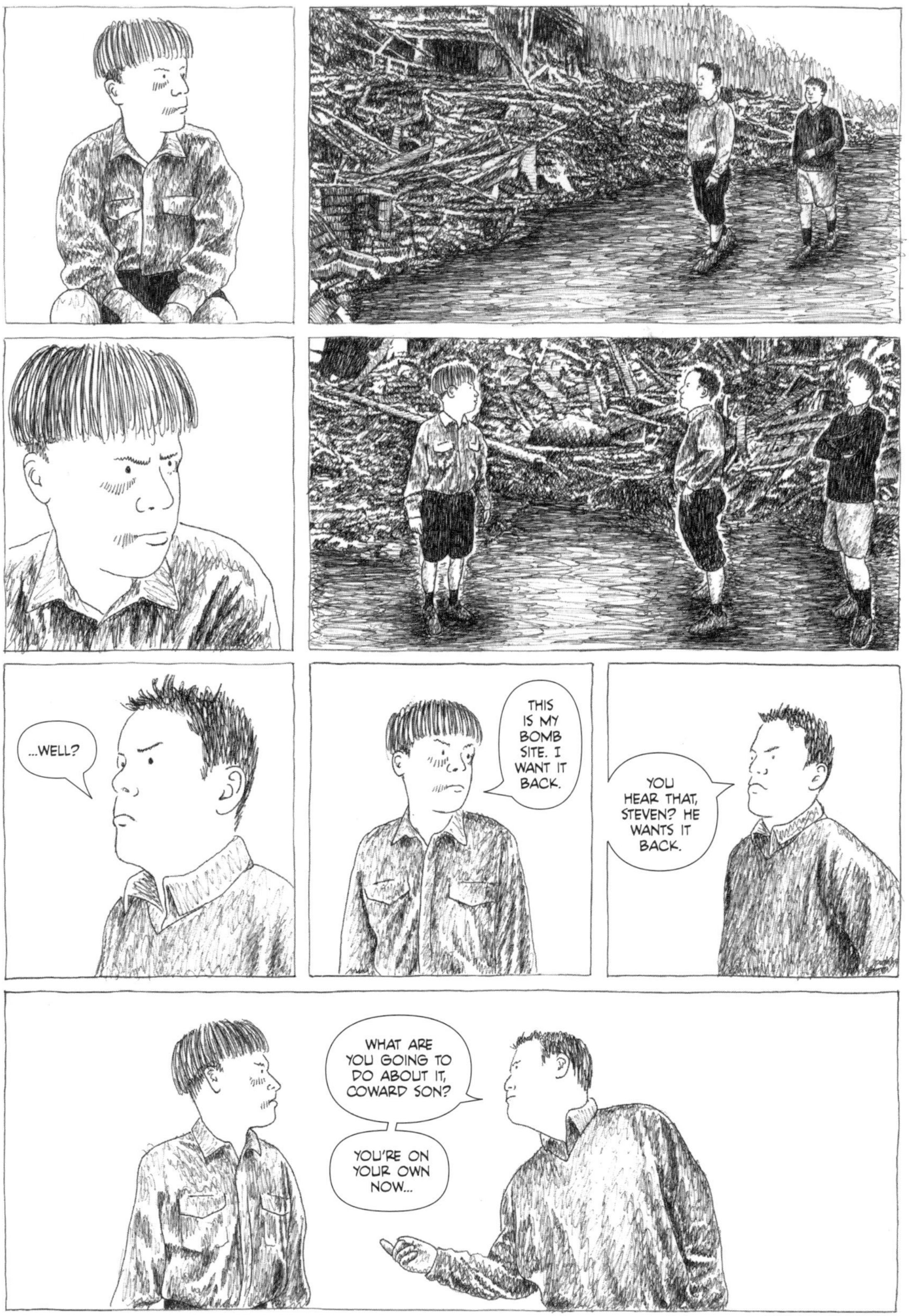
...WELL?
THIS IS MY BOMB SITE. I WANT IT BACK.
YOU HEAR THAT, STEVEN? HE WANTS IT BACK.
WHAT ARE YOU GOING TO DO ABOUT IT, COWARD SON?
YOU'RE ON YOUR OWN NOW...

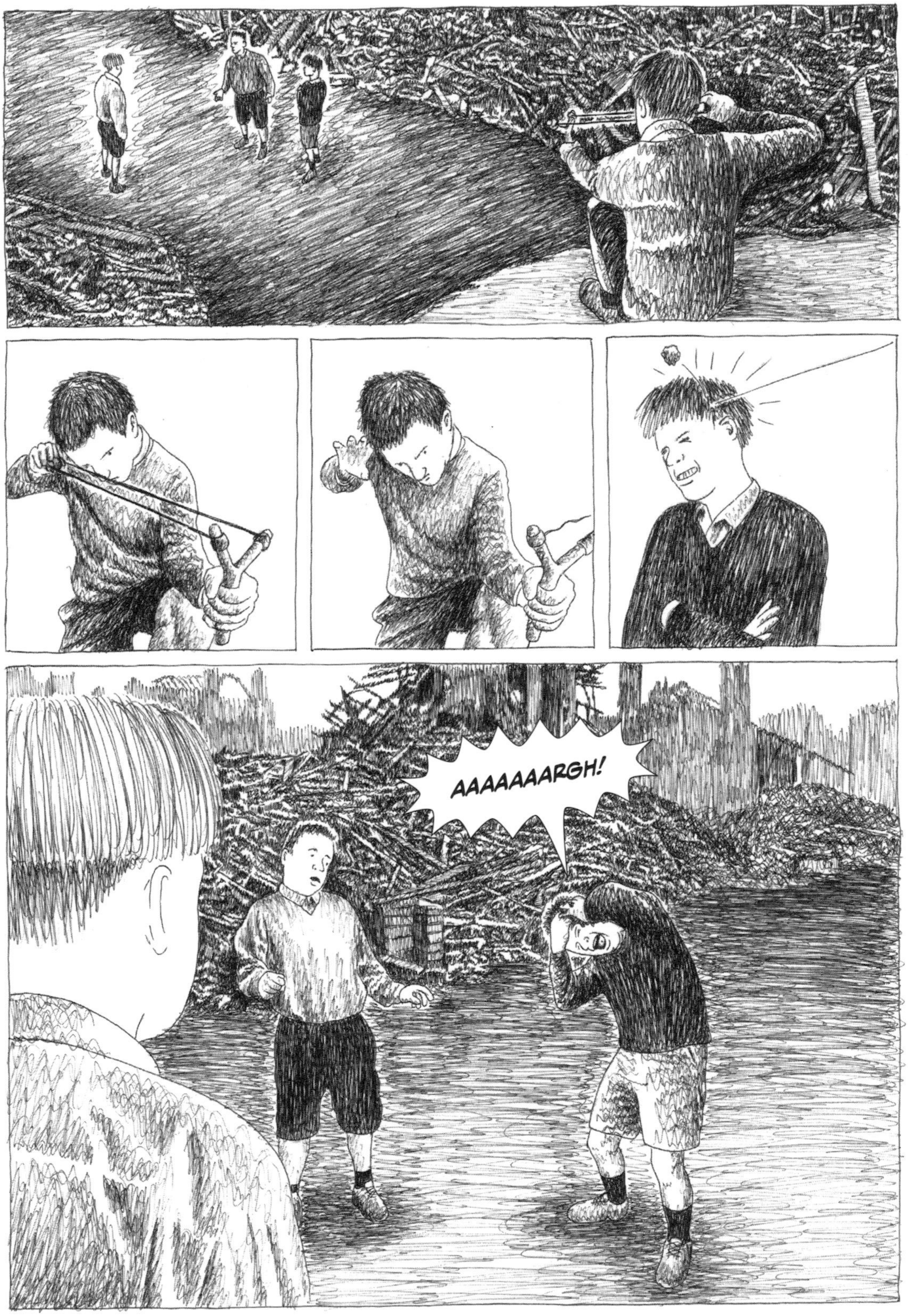
AAAAAAARGH!

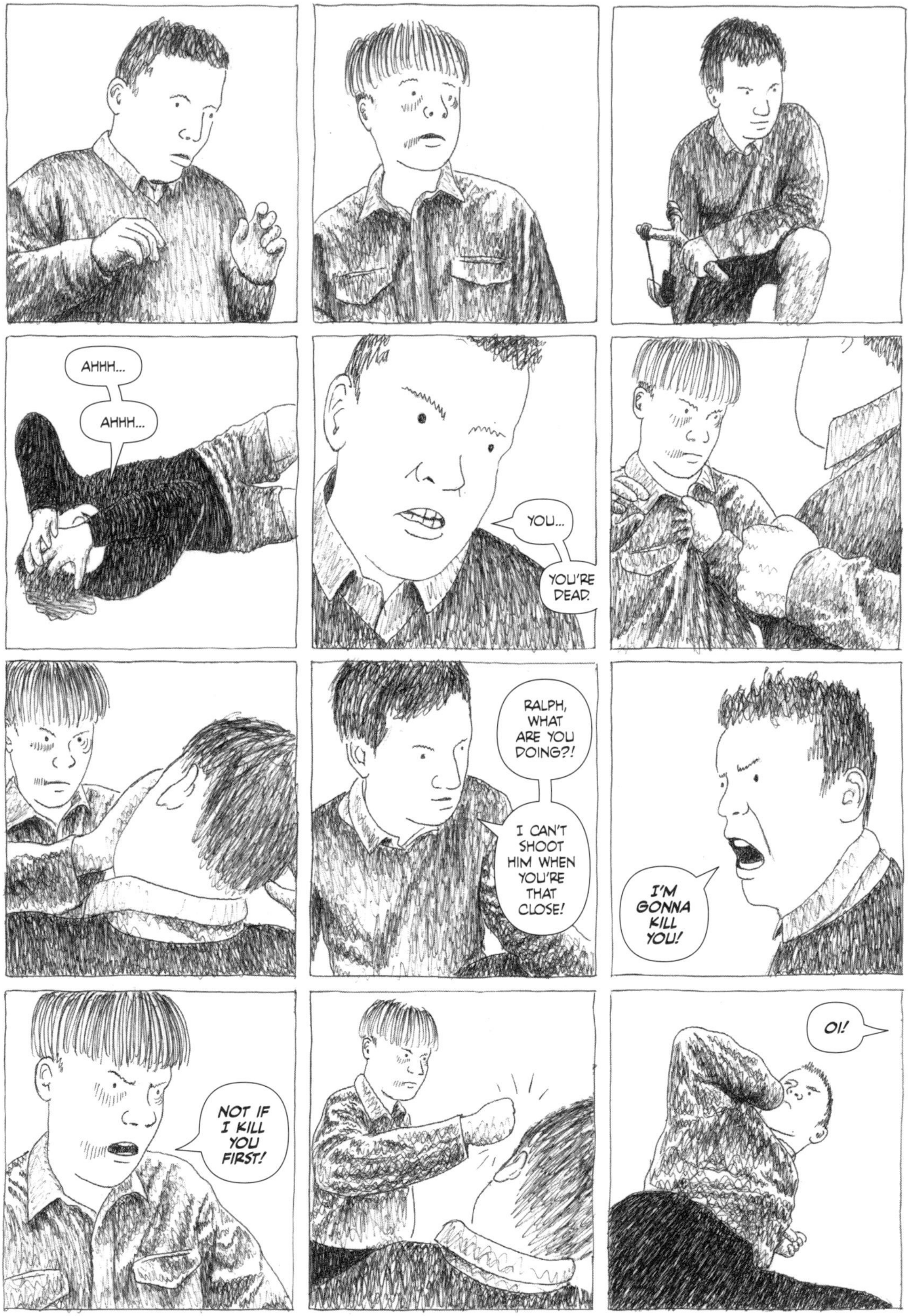
AHHH...
AHHH...
YOU...
YOU'RE DEAD.
RALPH, WHAT ARE YOU DOING?!
I CAN'T SHOOT HIM WHEN YOU'RE THAT CLOSE!
I'M GONNA KILL YOU!
NOT IF I KILL YOU FIRST!
OI!

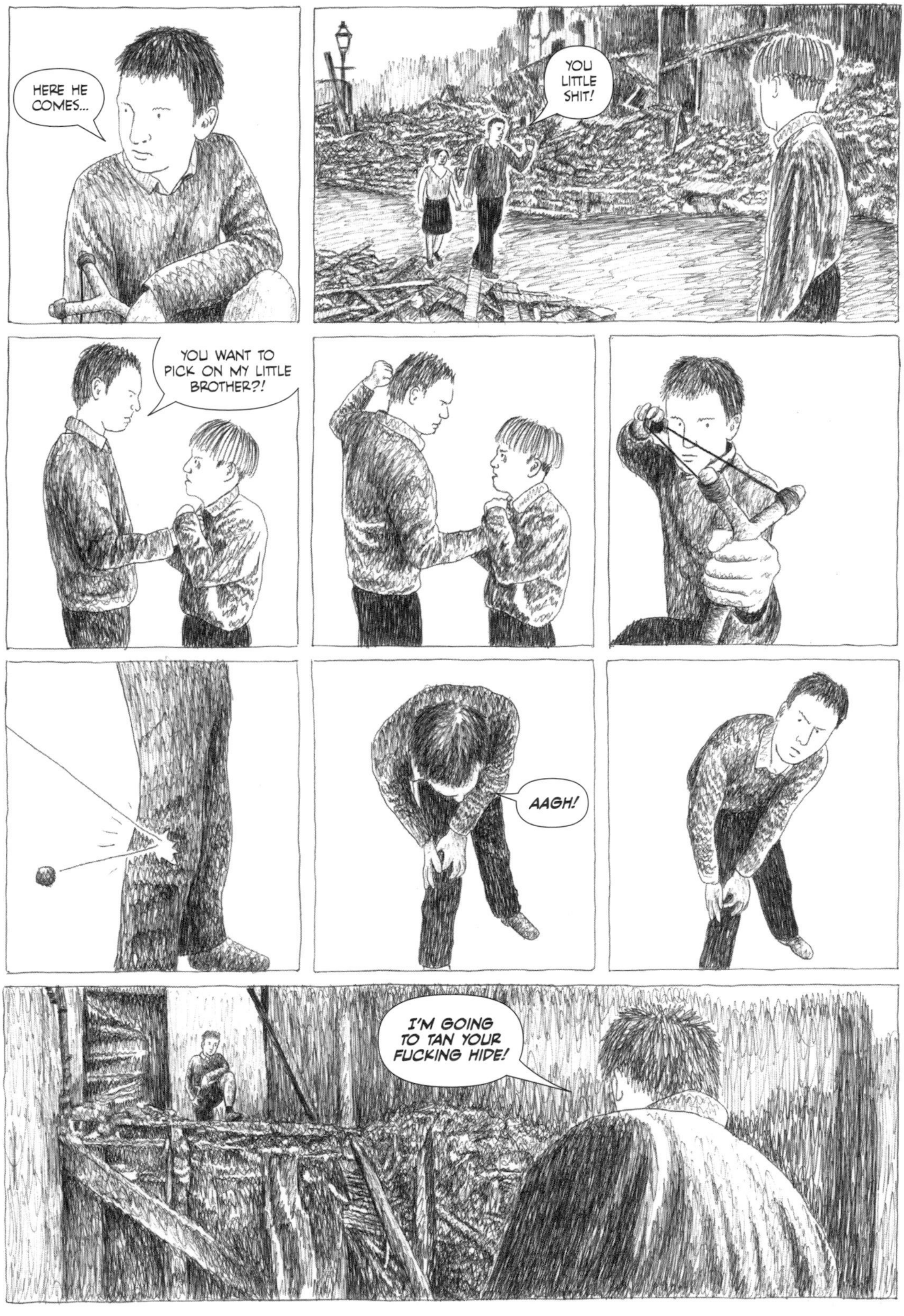
HERE HE COMES...
YOU LITTLE SHIT!
YOU WANT TO PICK ON MY LITTLE BROTHER?!
AAGH!
I'M GOING TO TAN YOUR FUCKING HIDE!

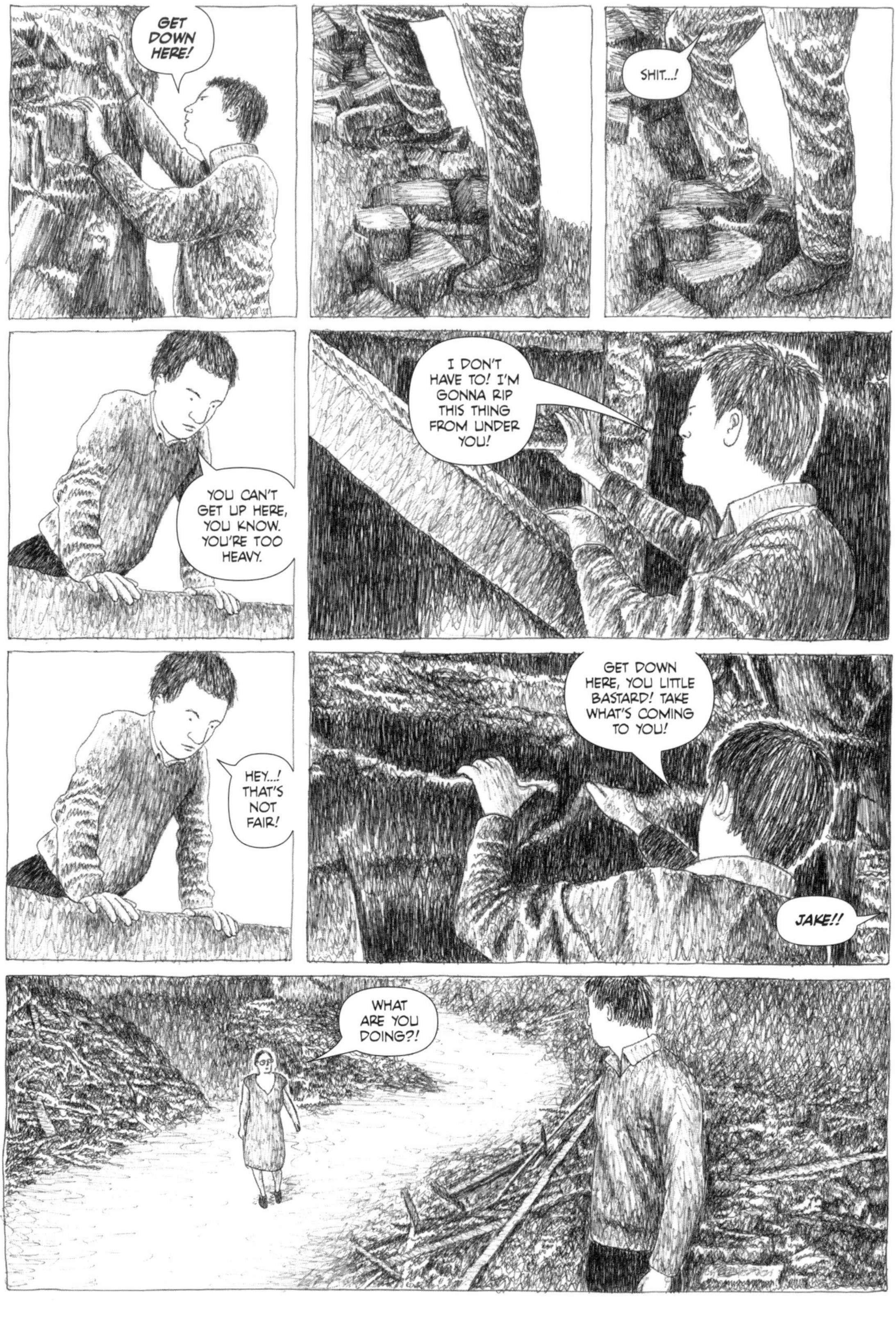
GET DOWN HERE!
SHIT...!
YOU CAN'T GET UP HERE, YOU KNOW. YOU'RE TOO HEAVY.
I DON'T HAVE TO! I'M GONNA RIP THIS THING FROM UNDER YOU!
HEY...! THAT'S NOT FAIR!
GET DOWN HERE, YOU LITTLE BASTARD! TAKE WHAT'S COMING TO YOU!
JAKE!!
WHAT ARE YOU DOING?!

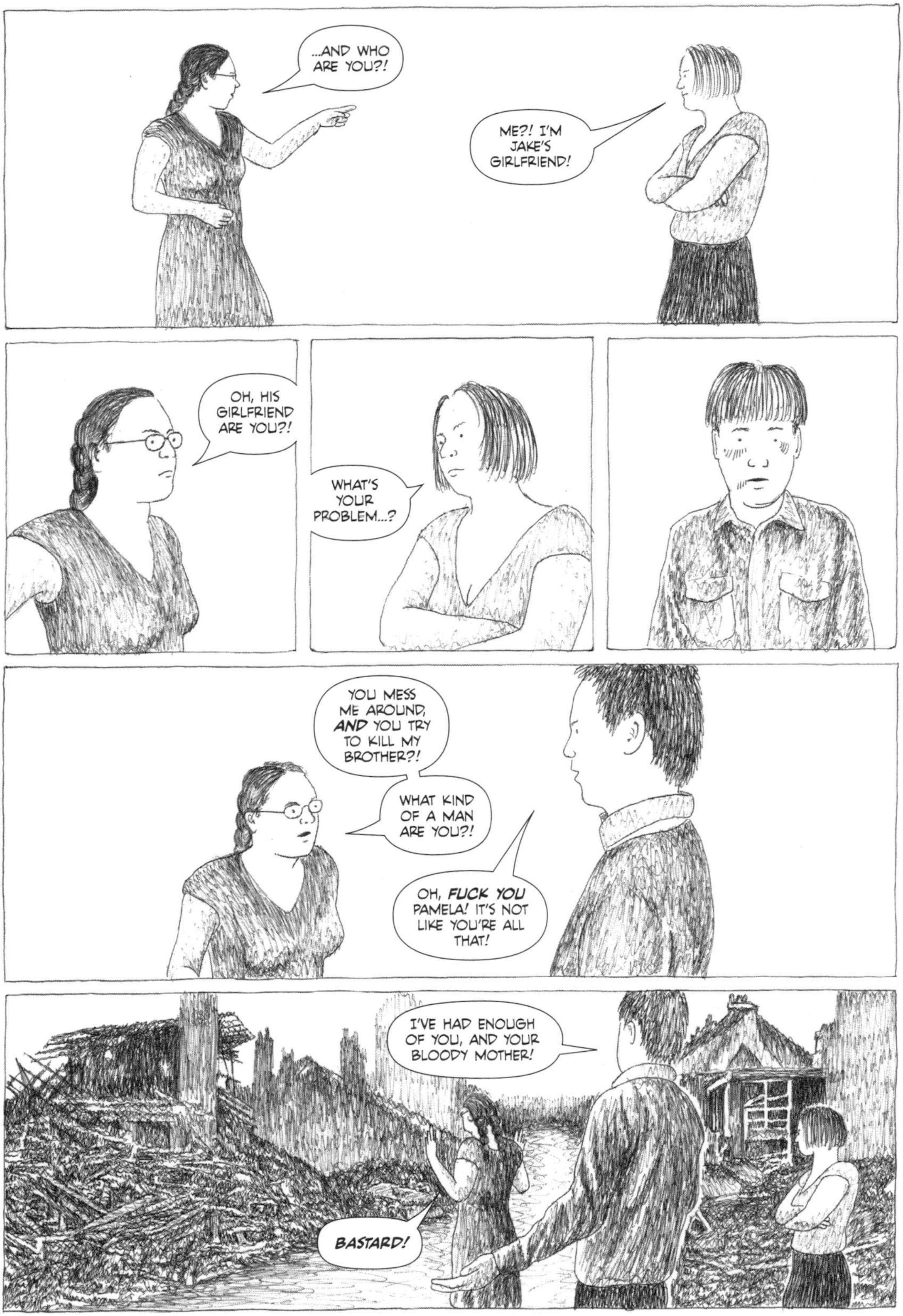

...AND WHO ARE YOU?!
ME?! I'M JAKE'S GIRLFRIEND!
OH, HIS GIRLFRIEND ARE YOU?!
WHAT'S YOUR PROBLEM...?
YOU MESS ME AROUND, AND YOU TRY TO KILL MY BROTHER?!
WHAT KIND OF A MAN ARE YOU?!
OH, FUCK YOU PAMELA! IT'S NOT LIKE YOU'RE ALL THAT!
I'VE HAD ENOUGH OF YOU, AND YOUR BLOODY MOTHER!
BASTARD!

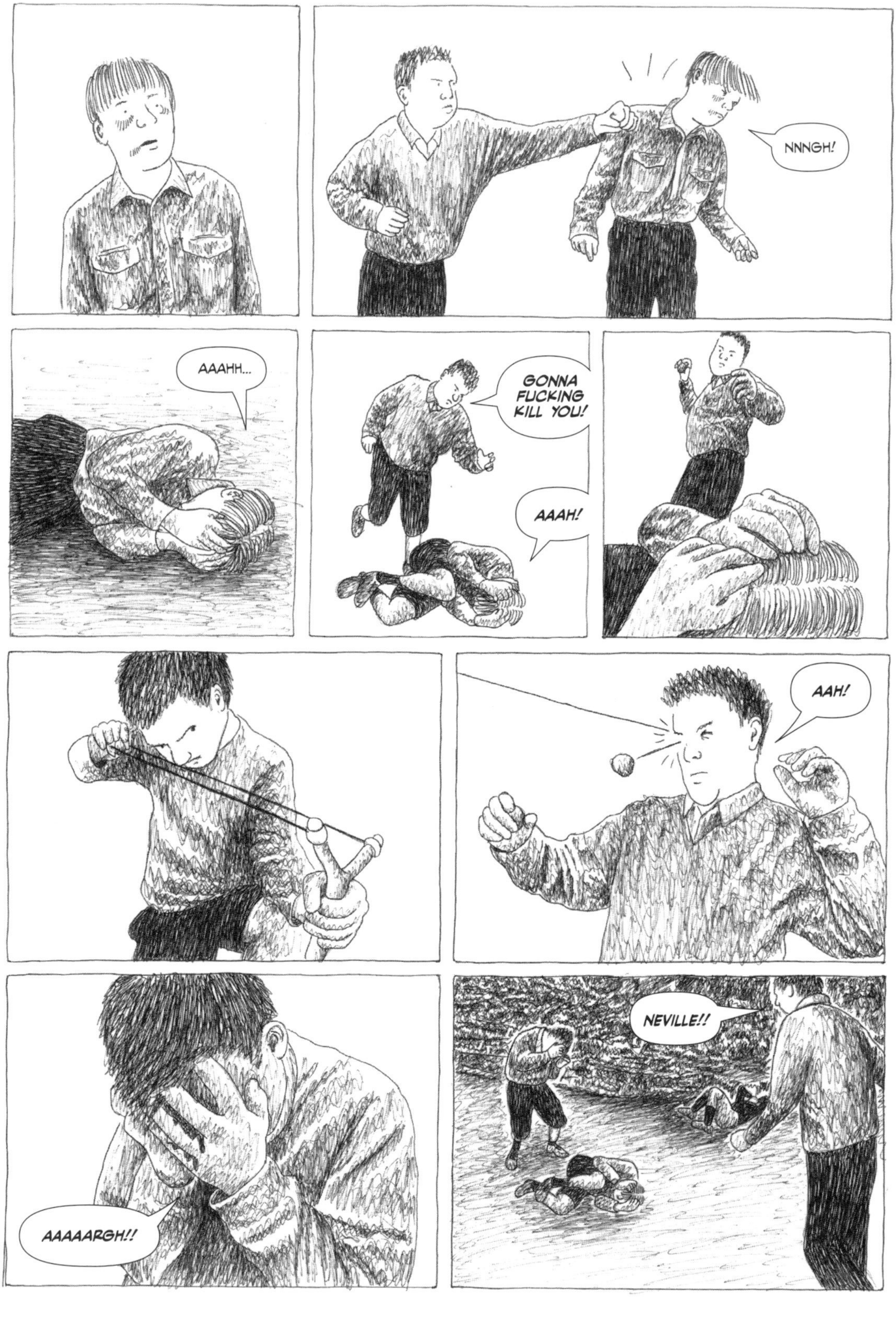
NNNGH!
AAAHH...
GONNA FUCKING KILL YOU!
AAAH!
AAH!
AAAAARGH!!
NEVILLE!!

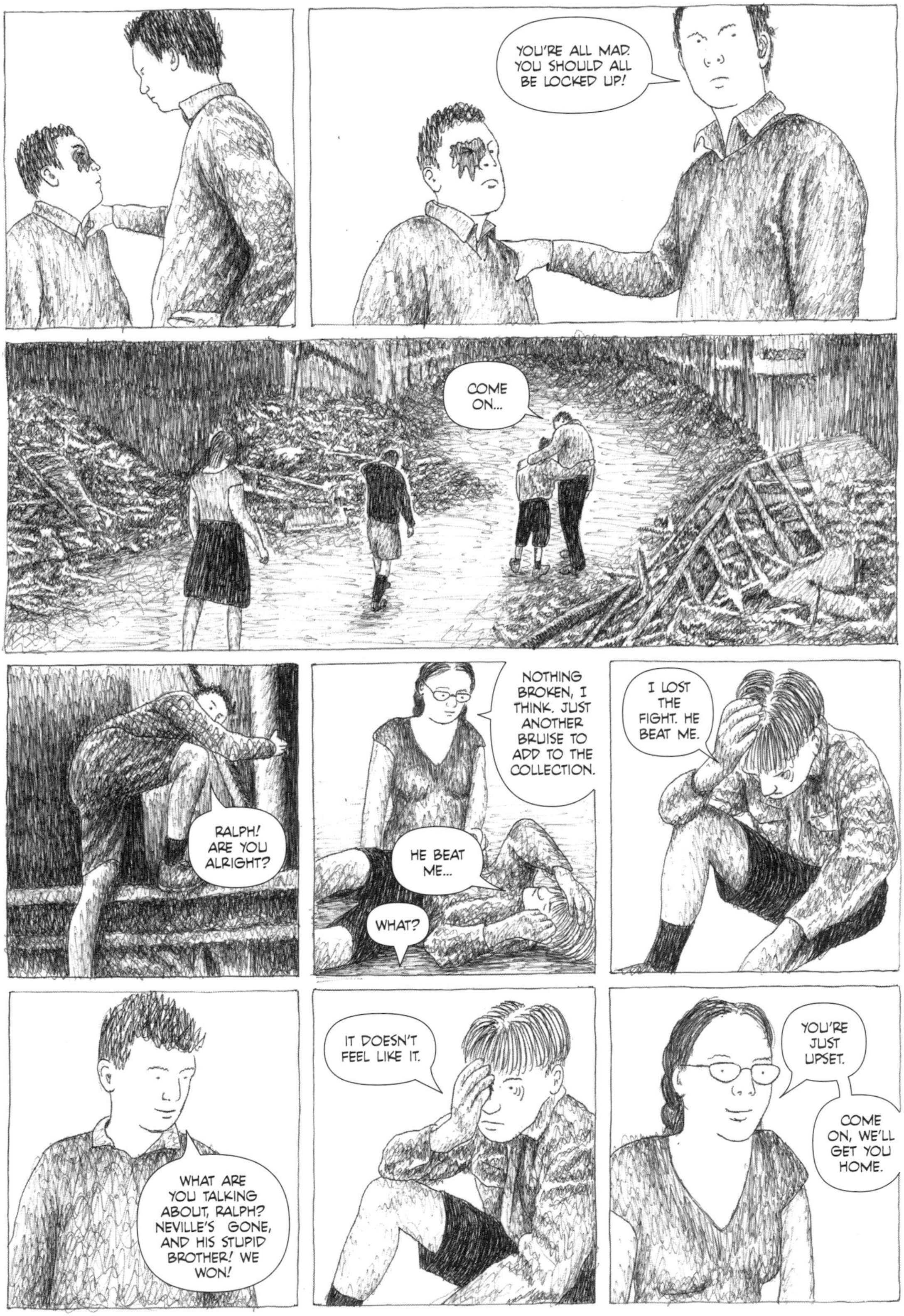
YOU'RE ALL MAD. YOU SHOULD ALL BE LOCKED UP!
COME ON...
RALPH! ARE YOU ALRIGHT?
NOTHING BROKEN, I THINK. JUST ANOTHER BRUISE TO ADD TO THE COLLECTION.
HE BEAT ME...
WHAT?
I LOST THE FIGHT. HE BEAT ME.
WHAT ARE YOU TALKING ABOUT, RALPH? NEVILLE'S GONE, AND HIS STUPID BROTHER! WE WON!
IT DOESN'T FEEL LIKE IT.
YOU'RE JUST UPSET.
COME ON, WE'LL GET YOU HOME.

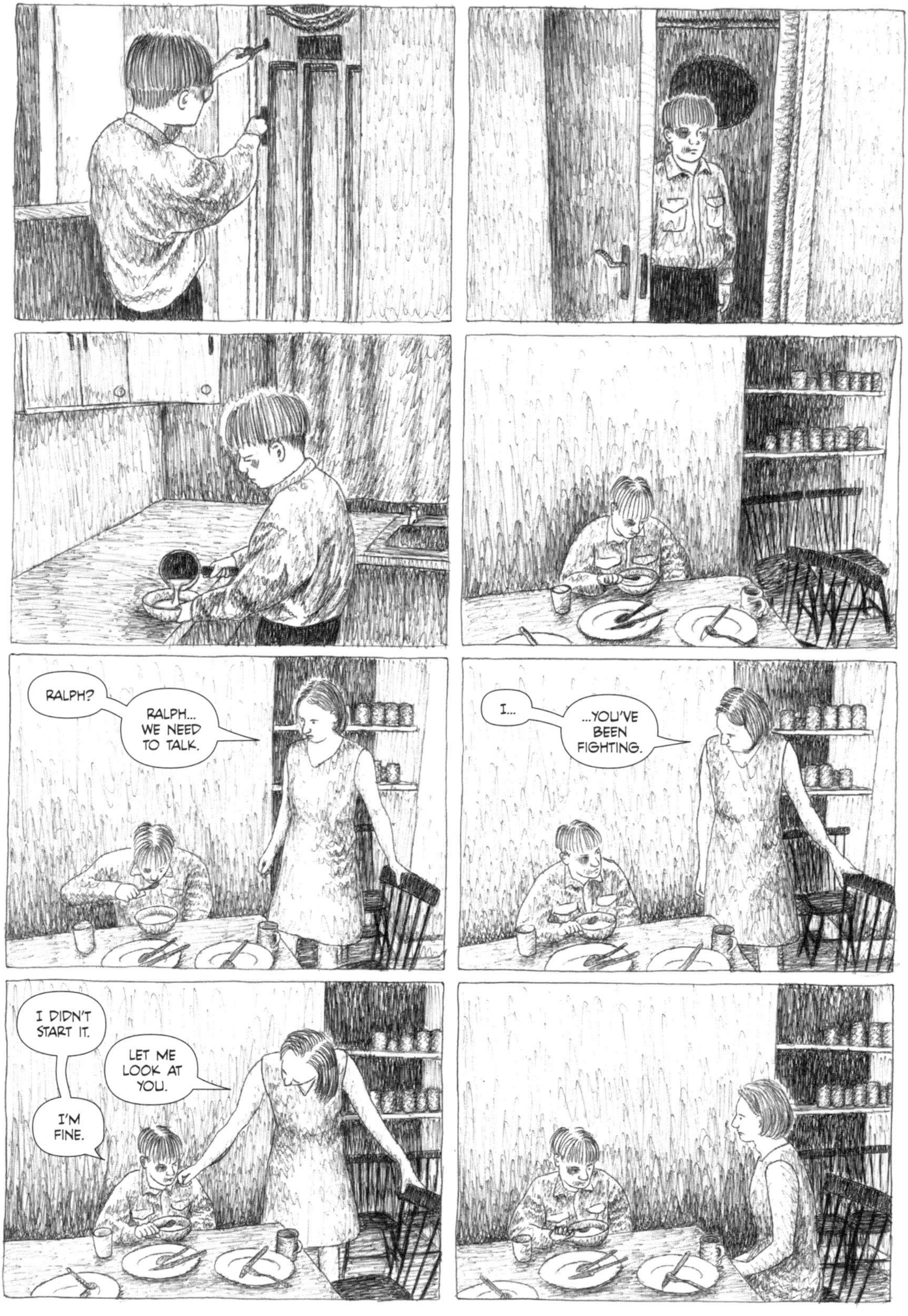
RALPH?
RALPH... WE NEED TO TALK.
I...
...YOU'VE BEEN FIGHTING.
I DIDN'T START IT.
LET ME LOOK AT YOU.
I'M FINE.

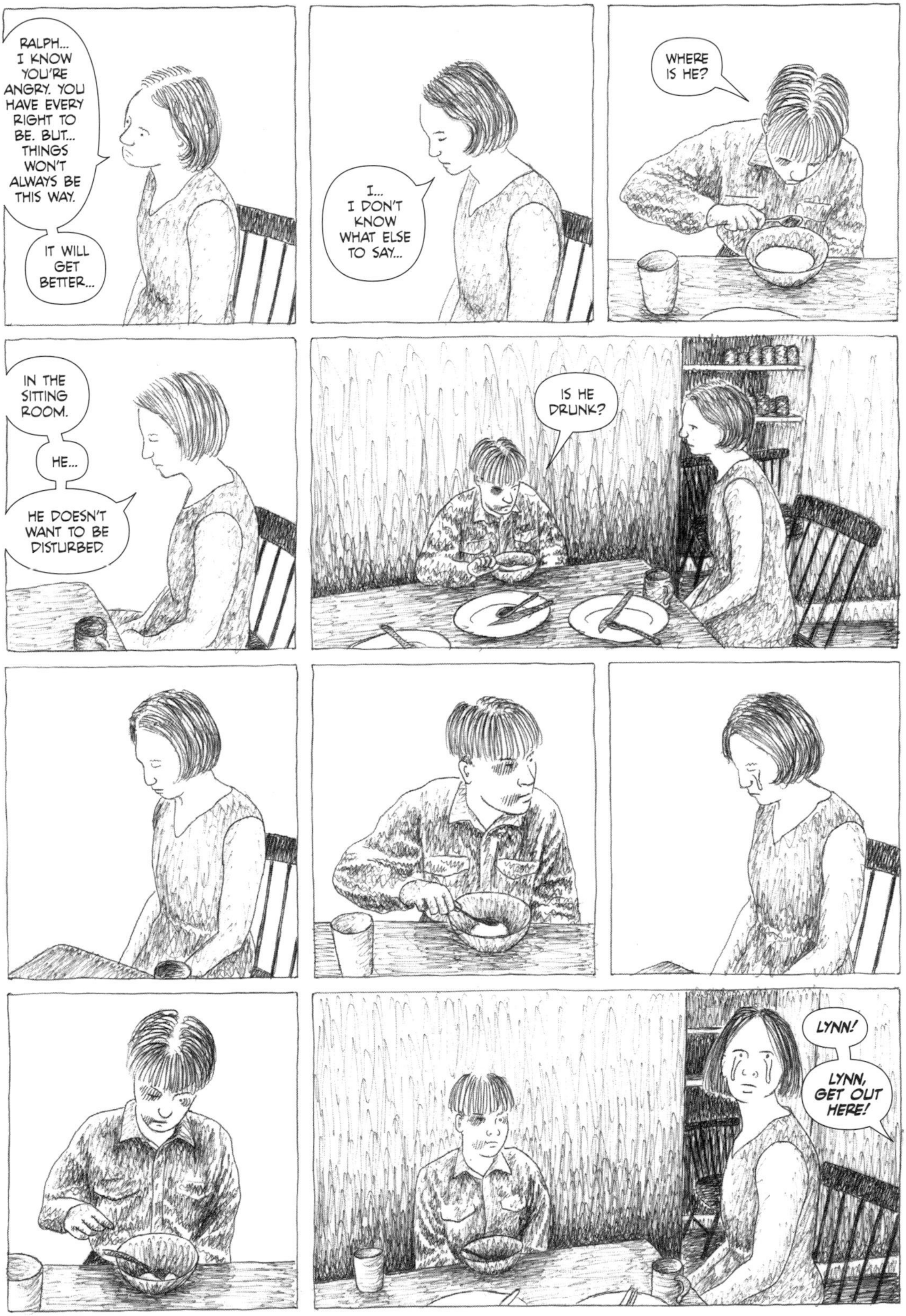
RALPH... I KNOW YOU'RE ANGRY. YOU HAVE EVERY RIGHT TO BE. BUT... THINGS WON'T ALWAYS BE THIS WAY.
IT WILL GET BETTER...
I... I DON'T KNOW WHAT ELSE TO SAY...
WHERE IS HE?
IN THE SITTING ROOM.
HE...
HE DOESN'T WANT TO BE DISTURBED.
IS HE DRUNK?
LYNN!
LYNN, GET OUT HERE!

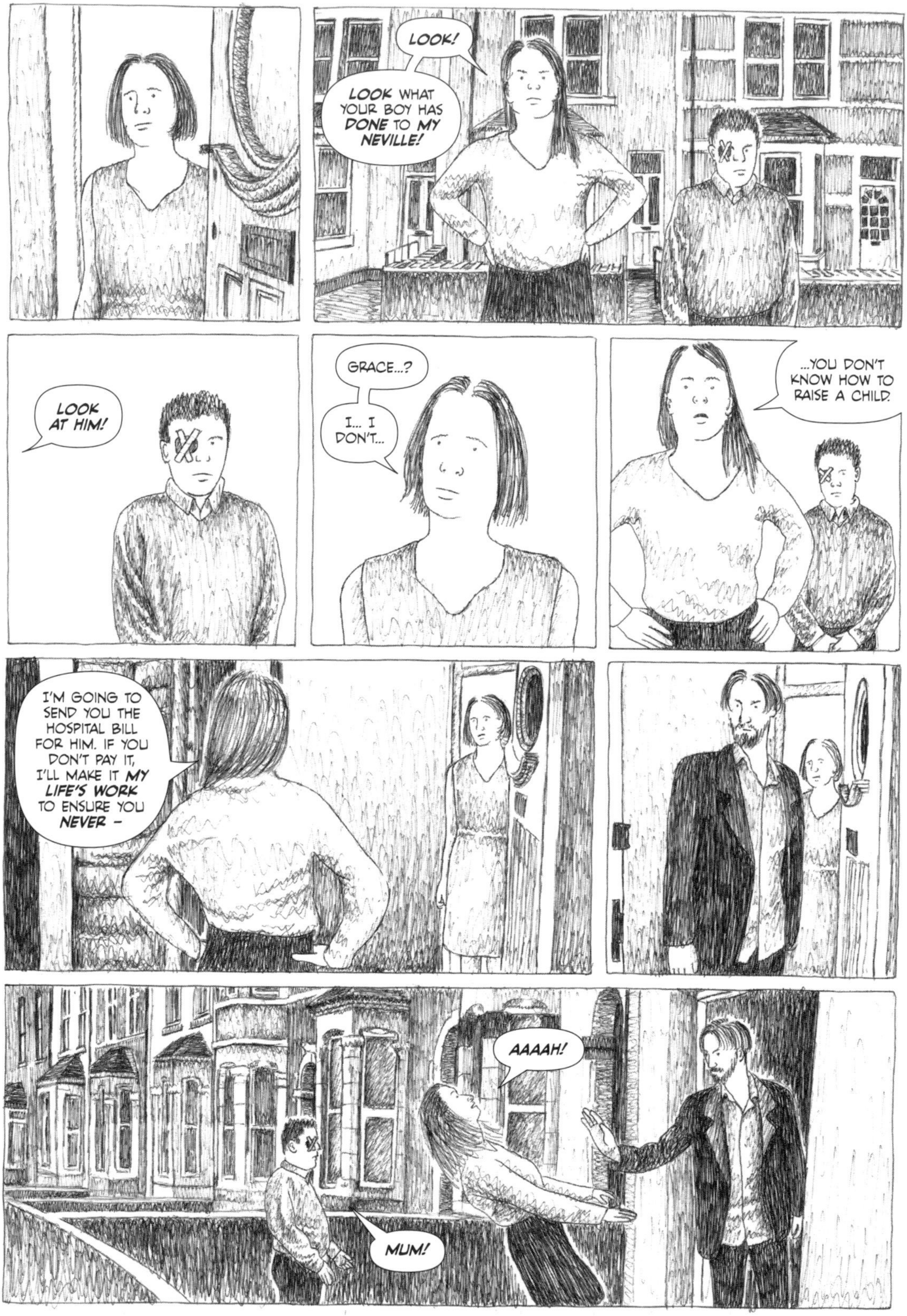
LOOK!
LOOK WHAT YOUR BOY HAS DONE TO MY NEVILLE!
LOOK AT HIM!
GRACE...?
I... I DON'T...
...YOU DON'T KNOW HOW TO RAISE A CHILD.
I'M GOING TO SEND YOU THE HOSPITAL BILL FOR HIM. IF YOU DON'T PAY IT, I'LL MAKE IT MY LIFE'S WORK TO ENSURE YOU NEVER –
AAAAH!
MUM!

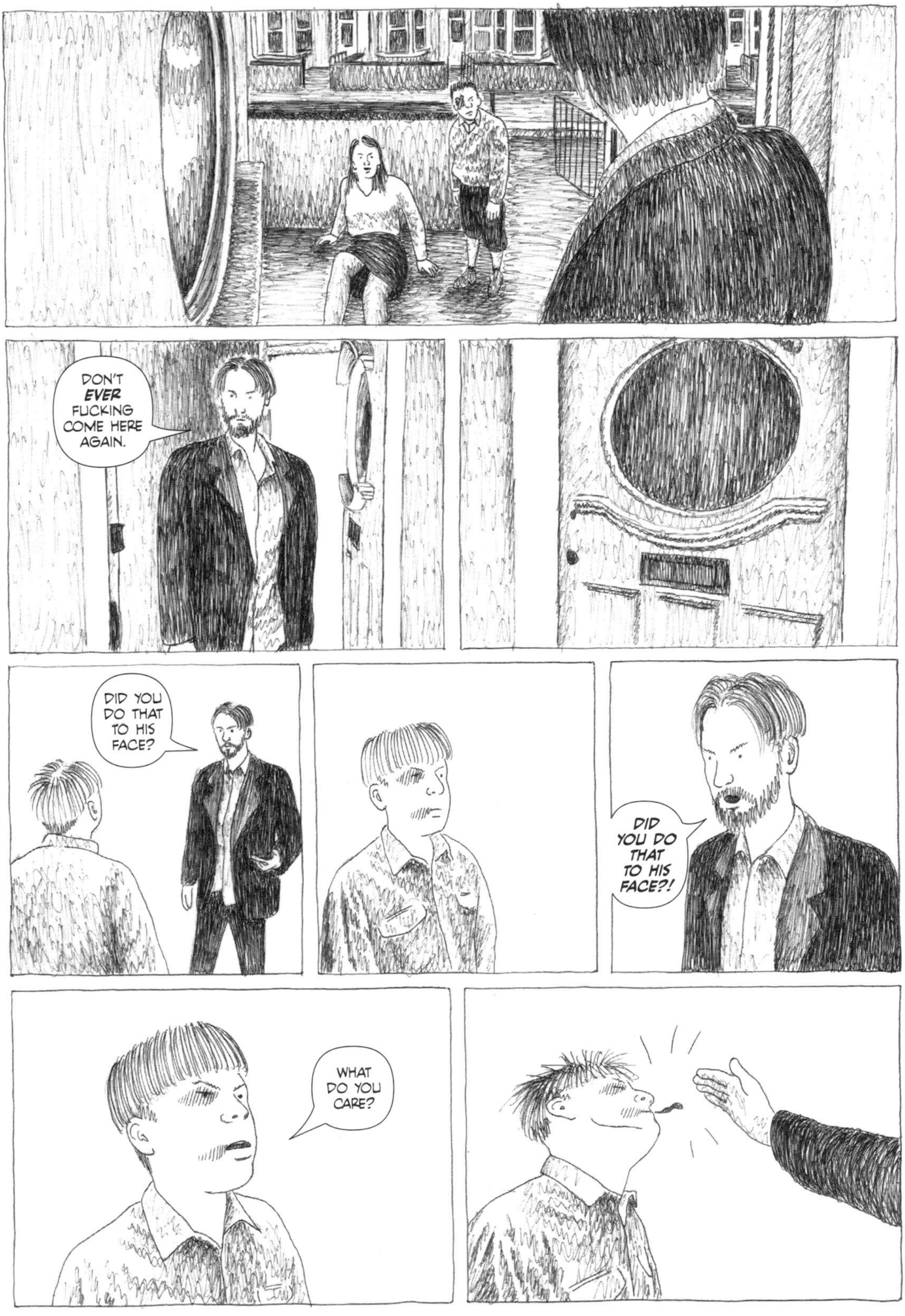
DON'T **EVER** FUCKING COME HERE AGAIN.
DID YOU DO THAT TO HIS FACE?
DID YOU DO THAT TO HIS FACE?!
WHAT DO YOU CARE?

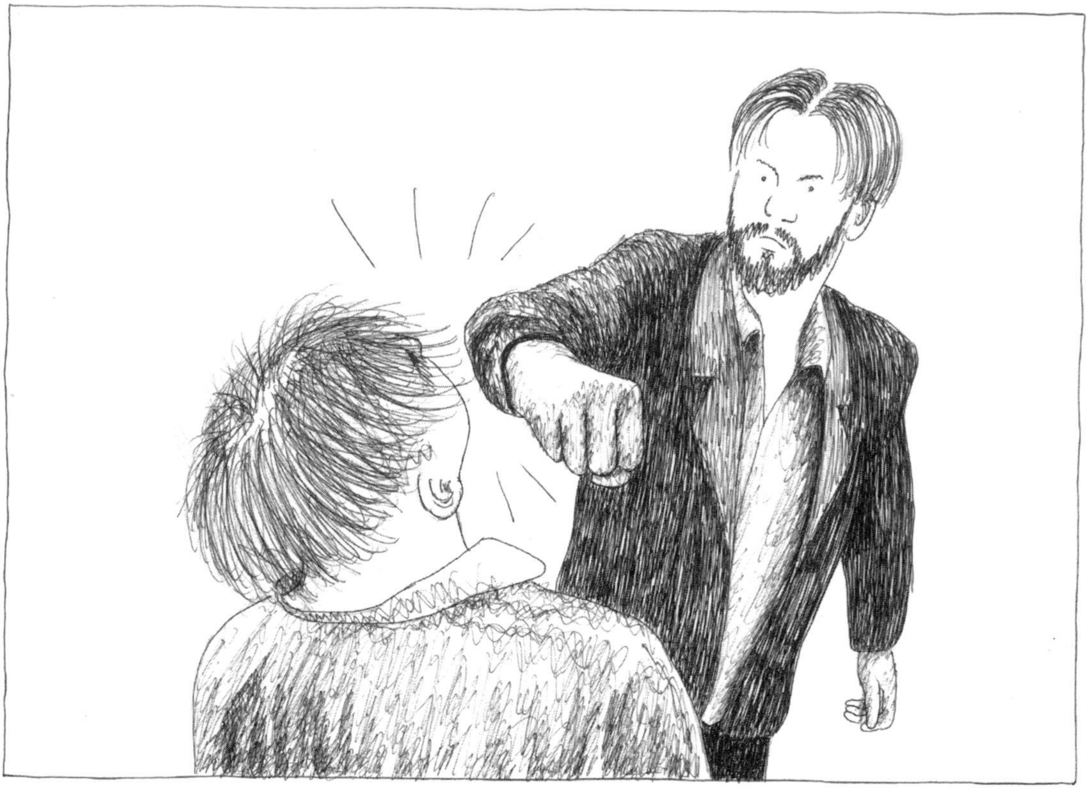

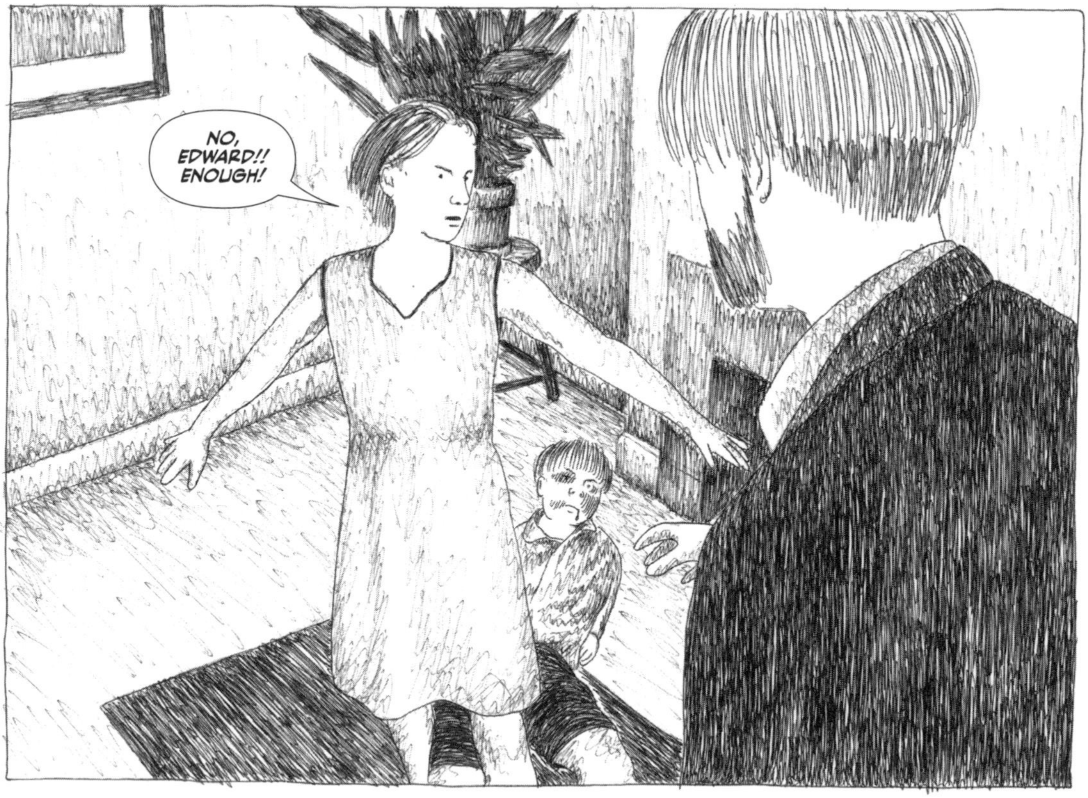
NO, EDWARD!! ENOUGH!

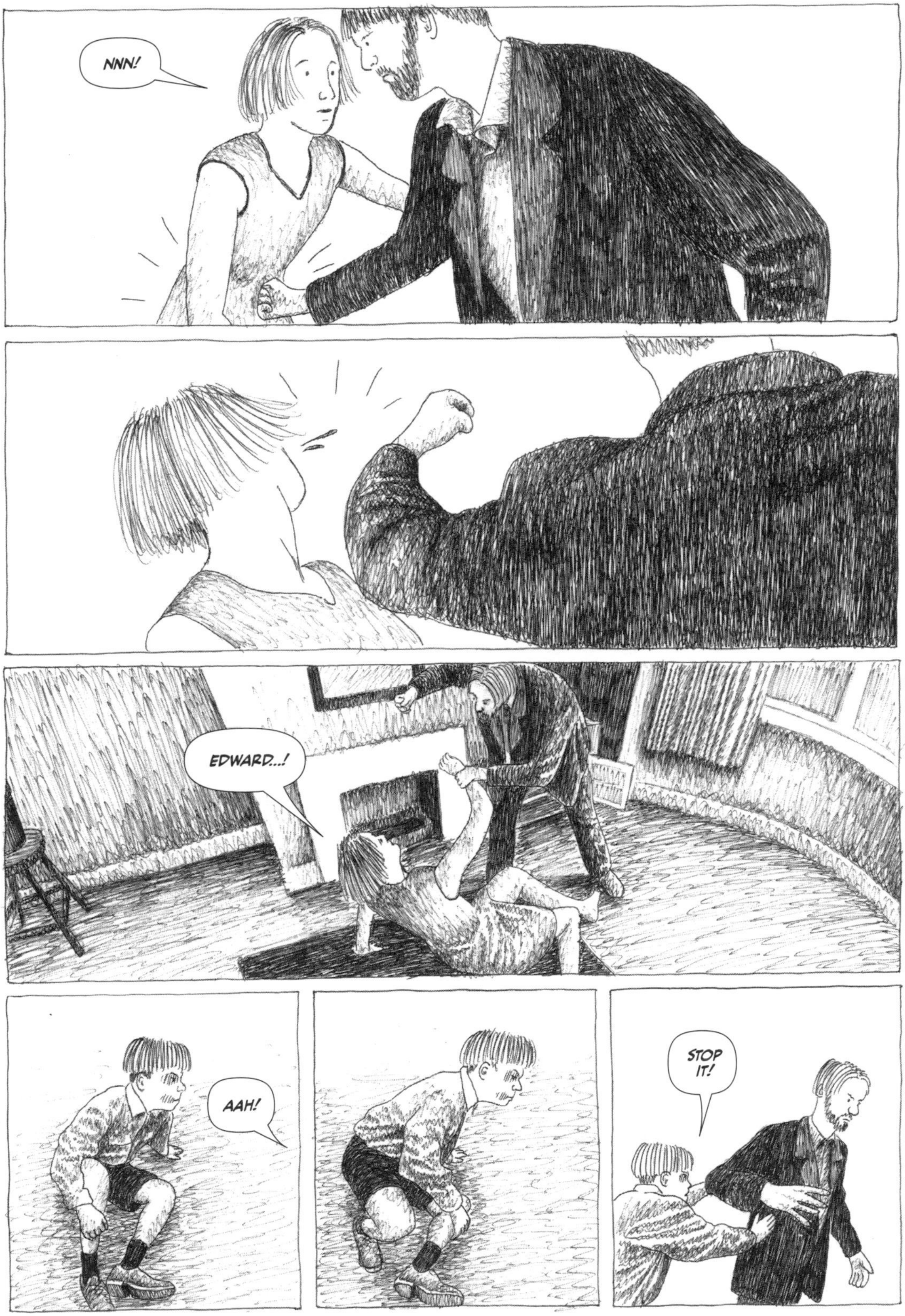
NNN!
EDWARD...!
AAH!
STOP IT!

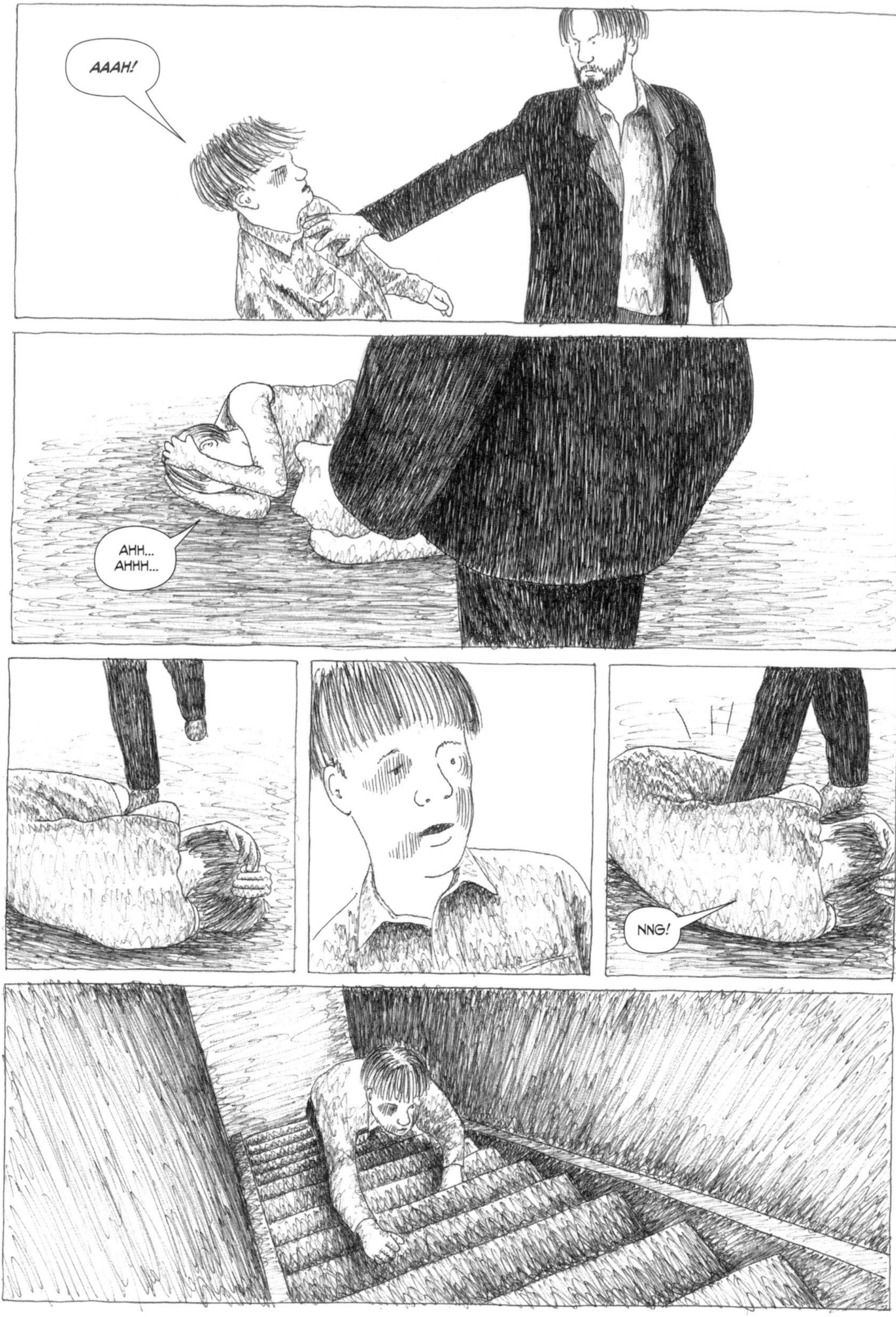
AAAH!
AHH... AHHH...
NNG!

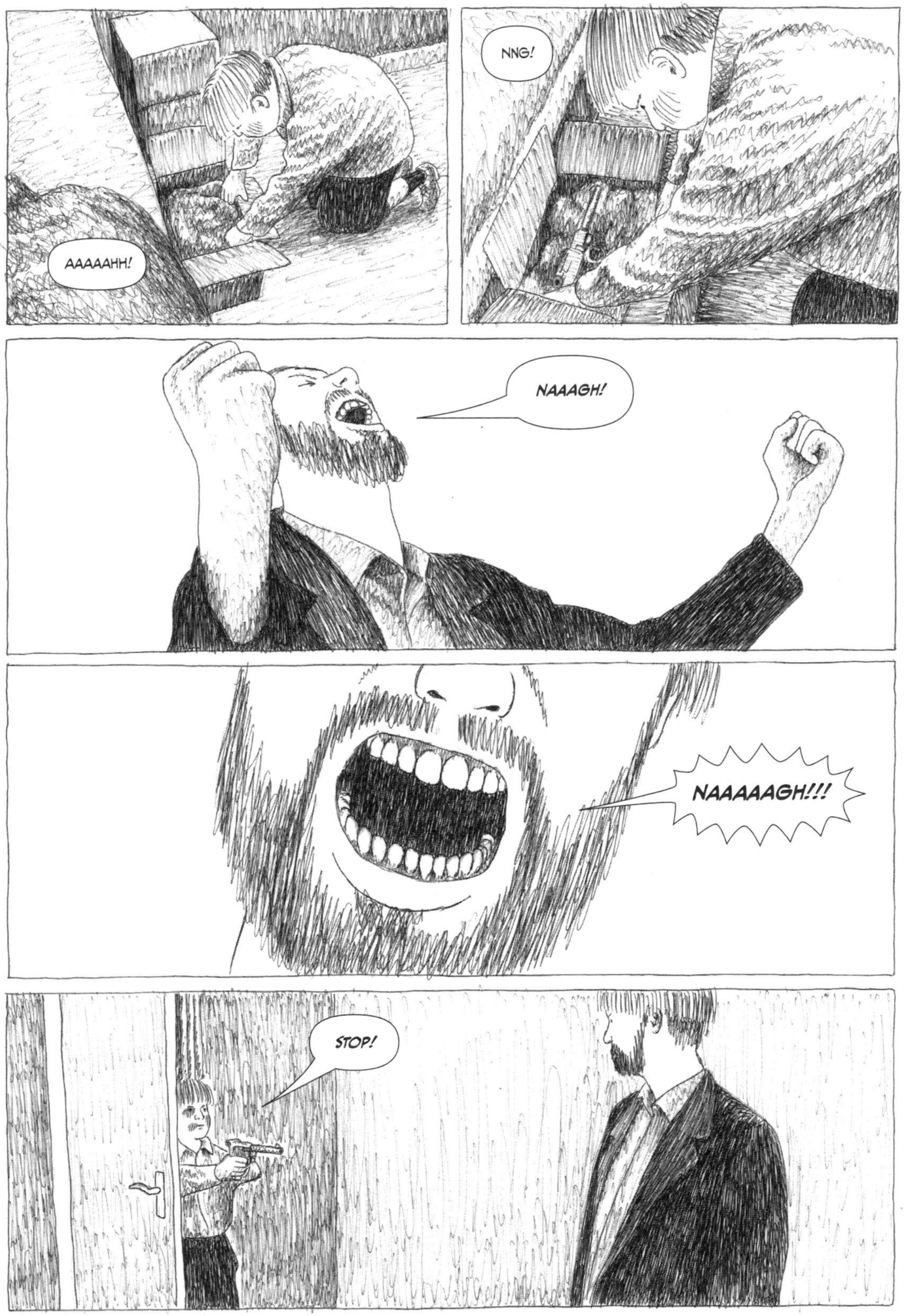
AAAAAHH!
NNG!
NAAAGH!
NAAAAAGH!!!
STOP!

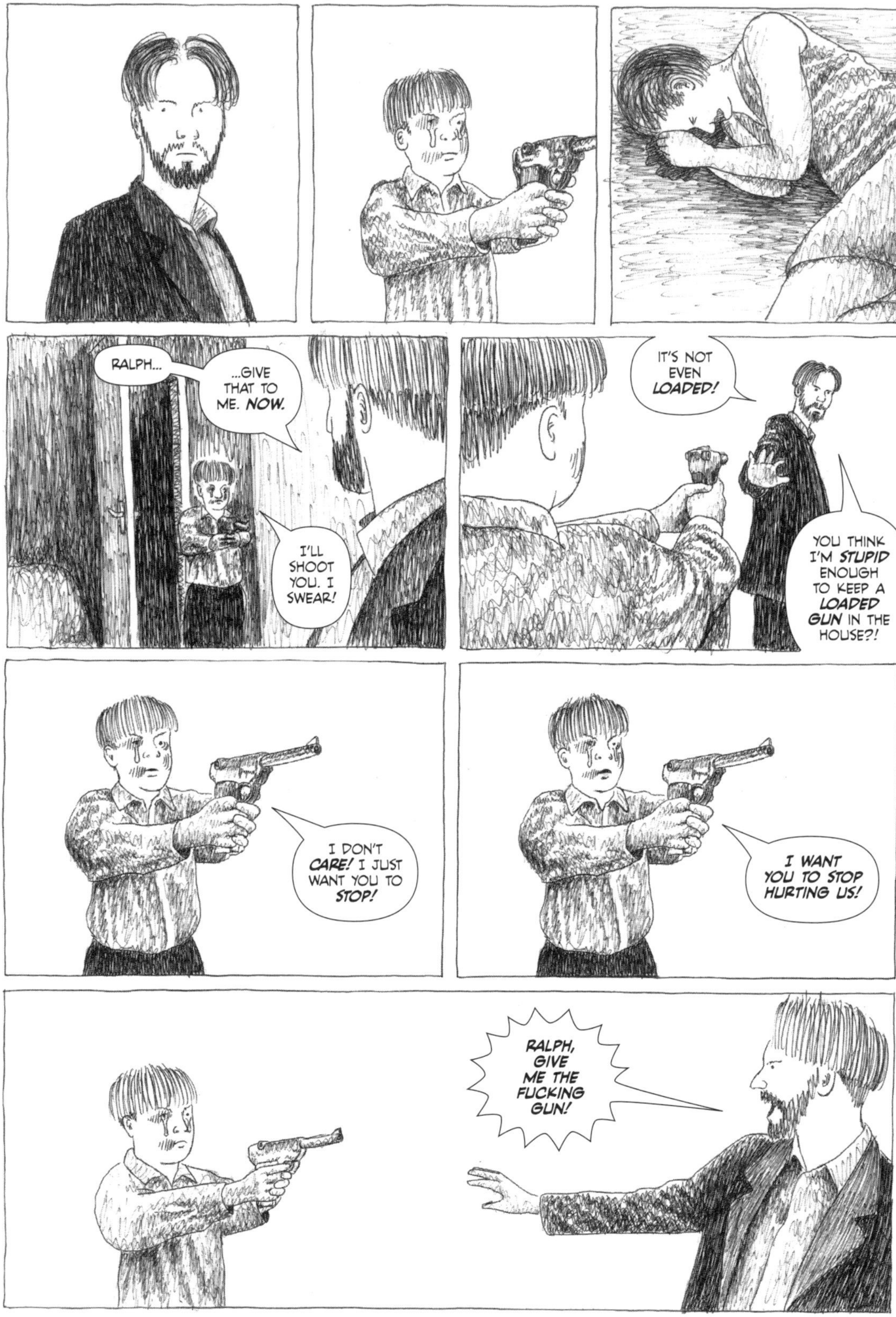
RALPH...
...GIVE THAT TO ME. NOW.
I'LL SHOOT YOU. I SWEAR!
IT'S NOT EVEN LOADED!
YOU THINK I'M STUPID ENOUGH TO KEEP A LOADED GUN IN THE HOUSE?!
I DON'T CARE! I JUST WANT YOU TO STOP!
I WANT YOU TO STOP HURTING US!
RALPH, GIVE ME THE FUCKING GUN!

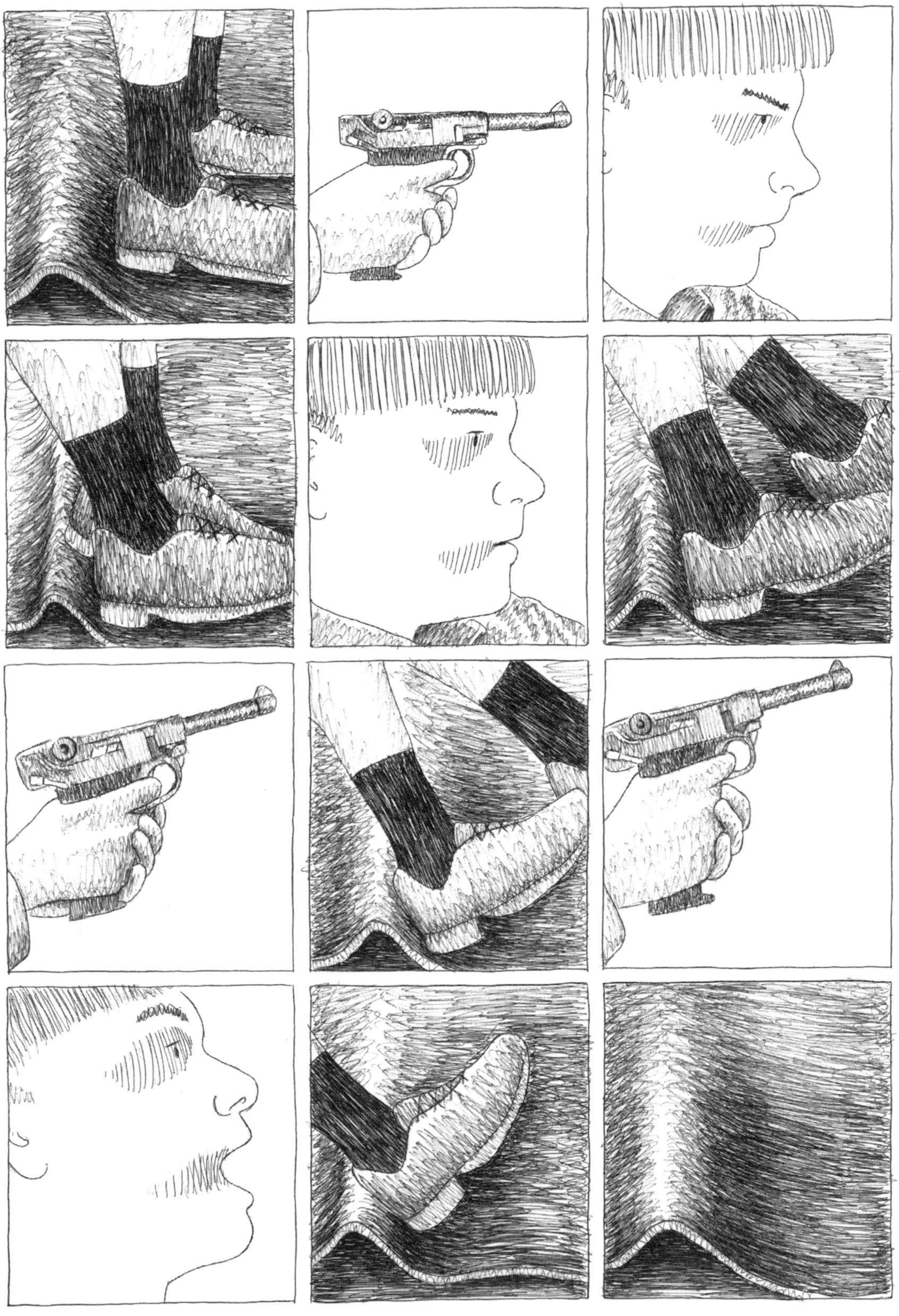

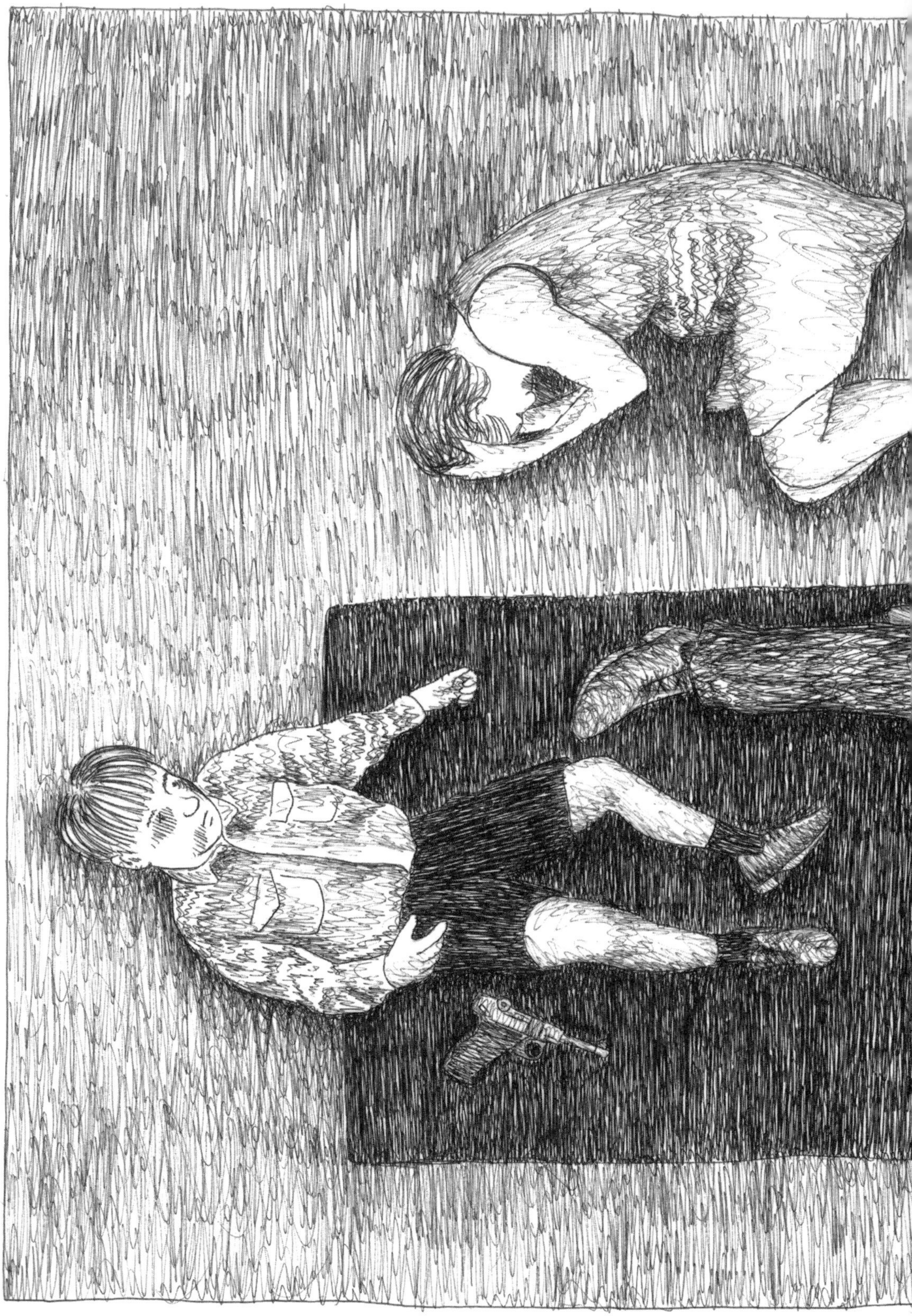

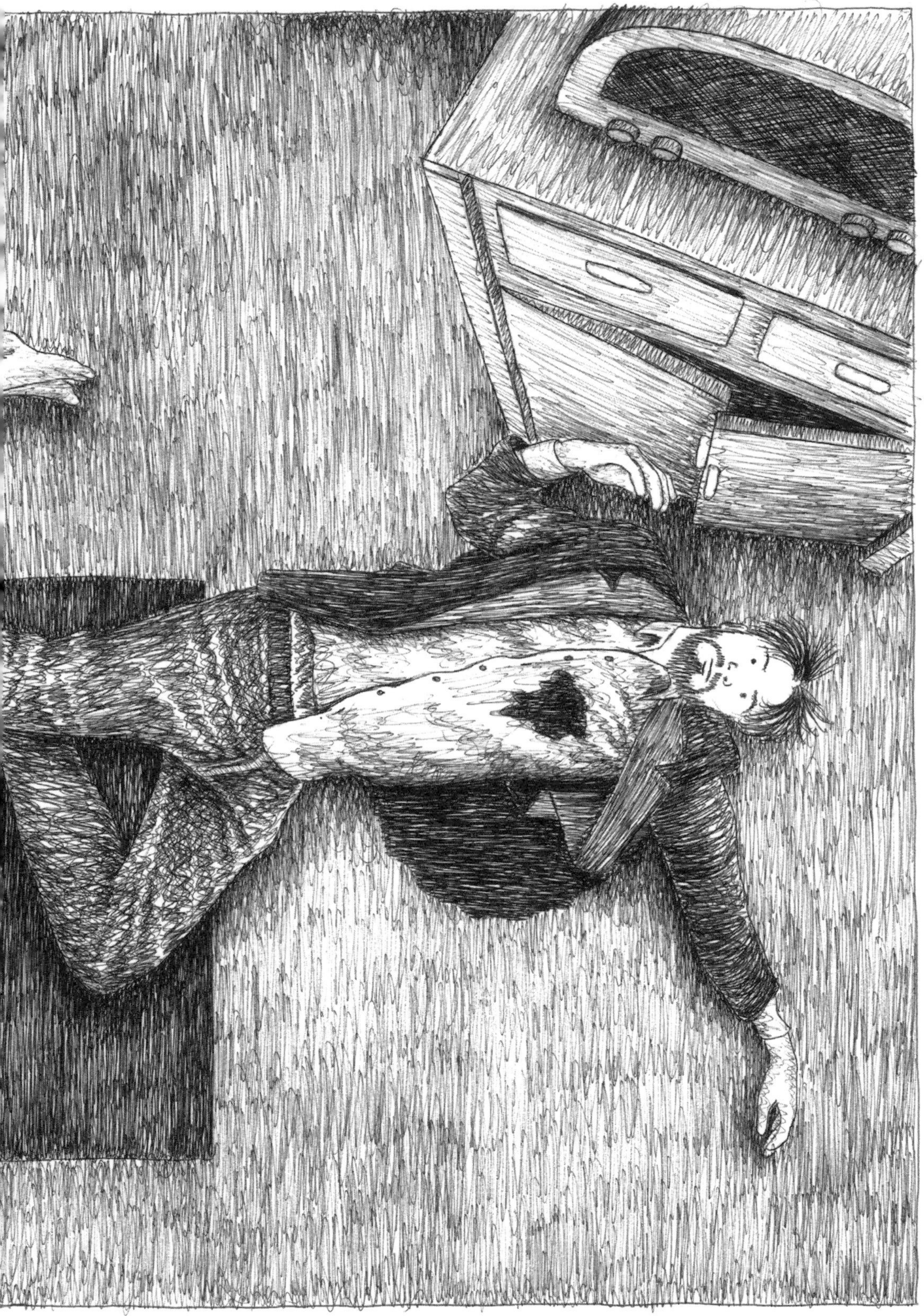

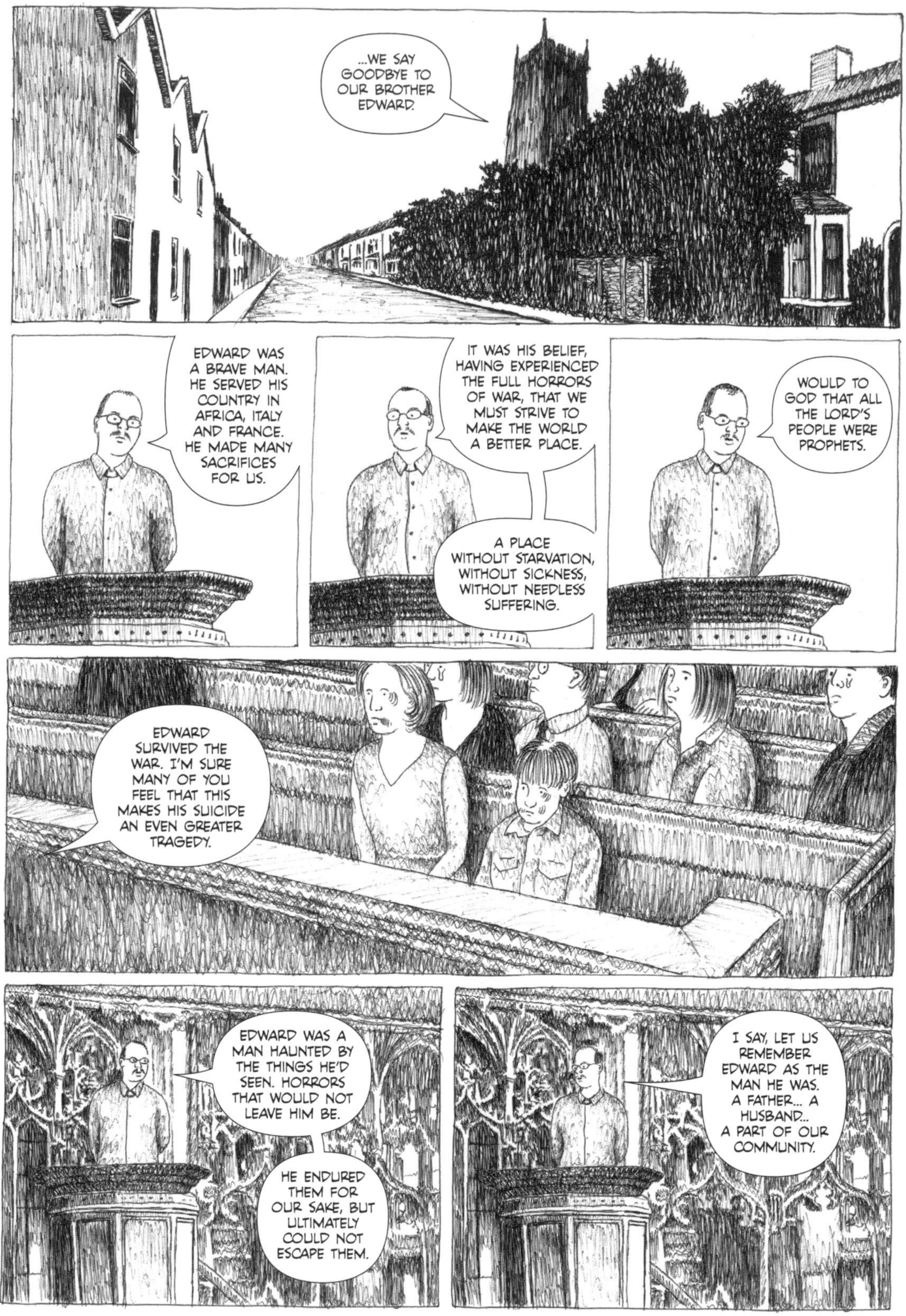
...WE SAY GOODBYE TO OUR BROTHER EDWARD.
EDWARD WAS A BRAVE MAN. HE SERVED HIS COUNTRY IN AFRICA, ITALY AND FRANCE. HE MADE MANY SACRIFICES FOR US.
IT WAS HIS BELIEF, HAVING EXPERIENCED THE FULL HORRORS OF WAR, THAT WE MUST STRIVE TO MAKE THE WORLD A BETTER PLACE.
A PLACE WITHOUT STARVATION, WITHOUT SICKNESS, WITHOUT NEEDLESS SUFFERING.
WOULD TO GOD THAT ALL THE LORD'S PEOPLE WERE PROPHETS.
EDWARD SURVIVED THE WAR. I'M SURE MANY OF YOU FEEL THAT THIS MAKES HIS SUICIDE AN EVEN GREATER TRAGEDY.
EDWARD WAS A MAN HAUNTED BY THE THINGS HE'D SEEN. HORRORS THAT WOULD NOT LEAVE HIM BE.
HE ENDURED THEM FOR OUR SAKE, BUT ULTIMATELY COULD NOT ESCAPE THEM.
I SAY, LET US REMEMBER EDWARD AS THE MAN HE WAS. A FATHER... A HUSBAND... A PART OF OUR COMMUNITY.

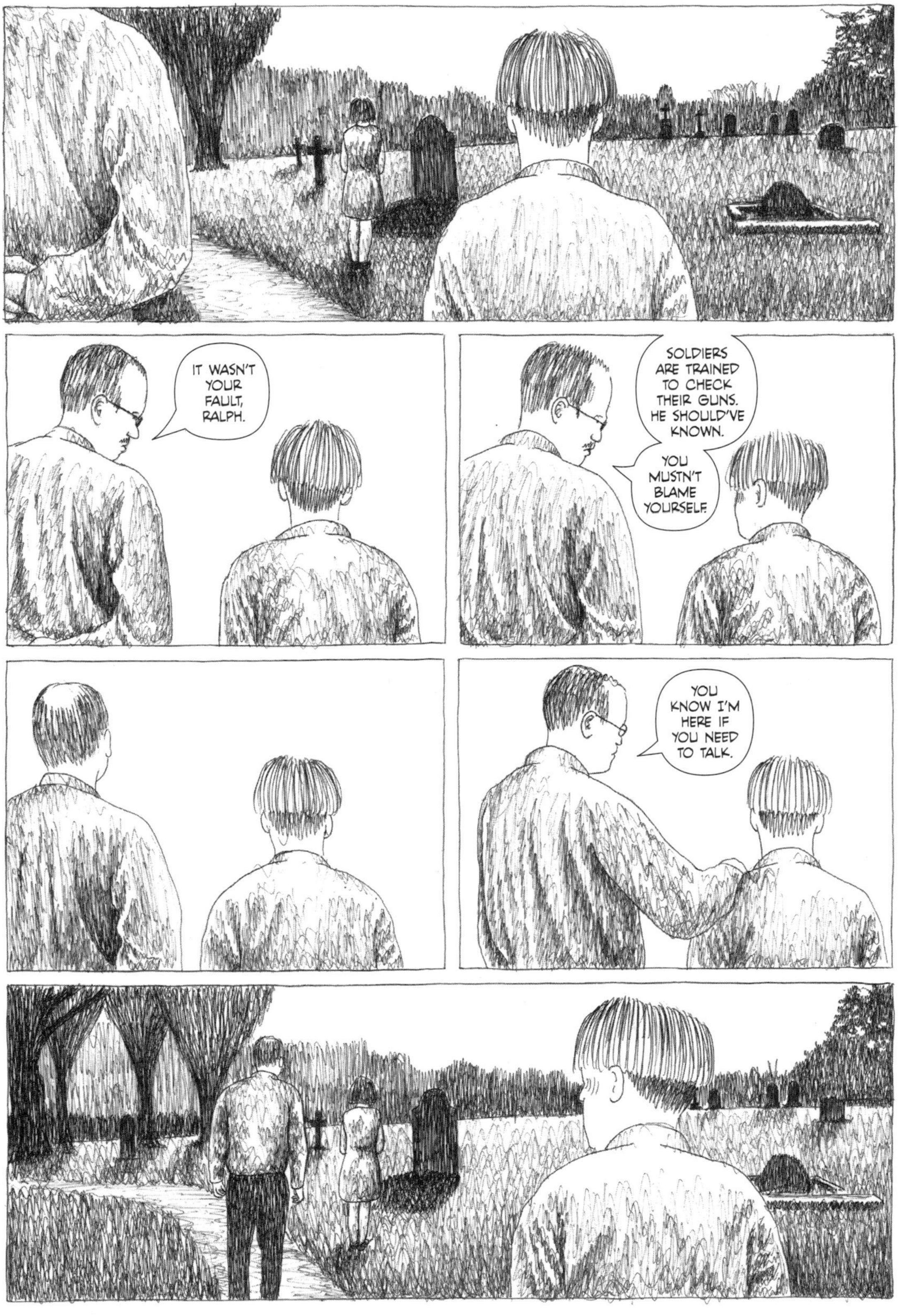
IT WASN'T YOUR FAULT, RALPH.
SOLDIERS ARE TRAINED TO CHECK THEIR GUNS. HE SHOULD'VE KNOWN.
YOU MUSTN'T BLAME YOURSELF.
YOU KNOW I'M HERE IF YOU NEED TO TALK.

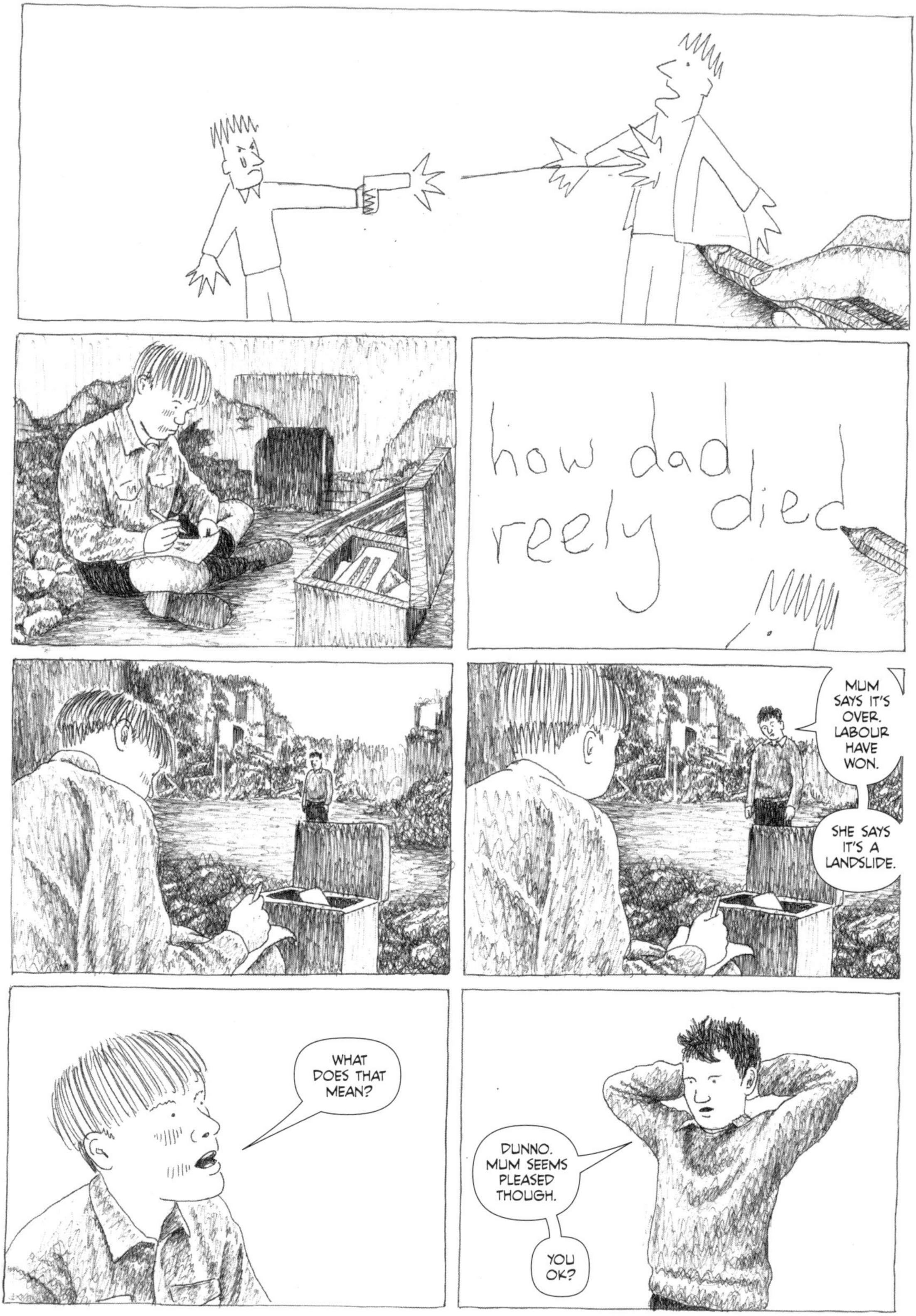
how dad
reely died
MUM SAYS IT'S OVER. LABOUR HAVE WON.
SHE SAYS IT'S A LANDSLIDE.
WHAT DOES THAT MEAN?
DUNNO. MUM SEEMS PLEASED THOUGH.
YOU OK?

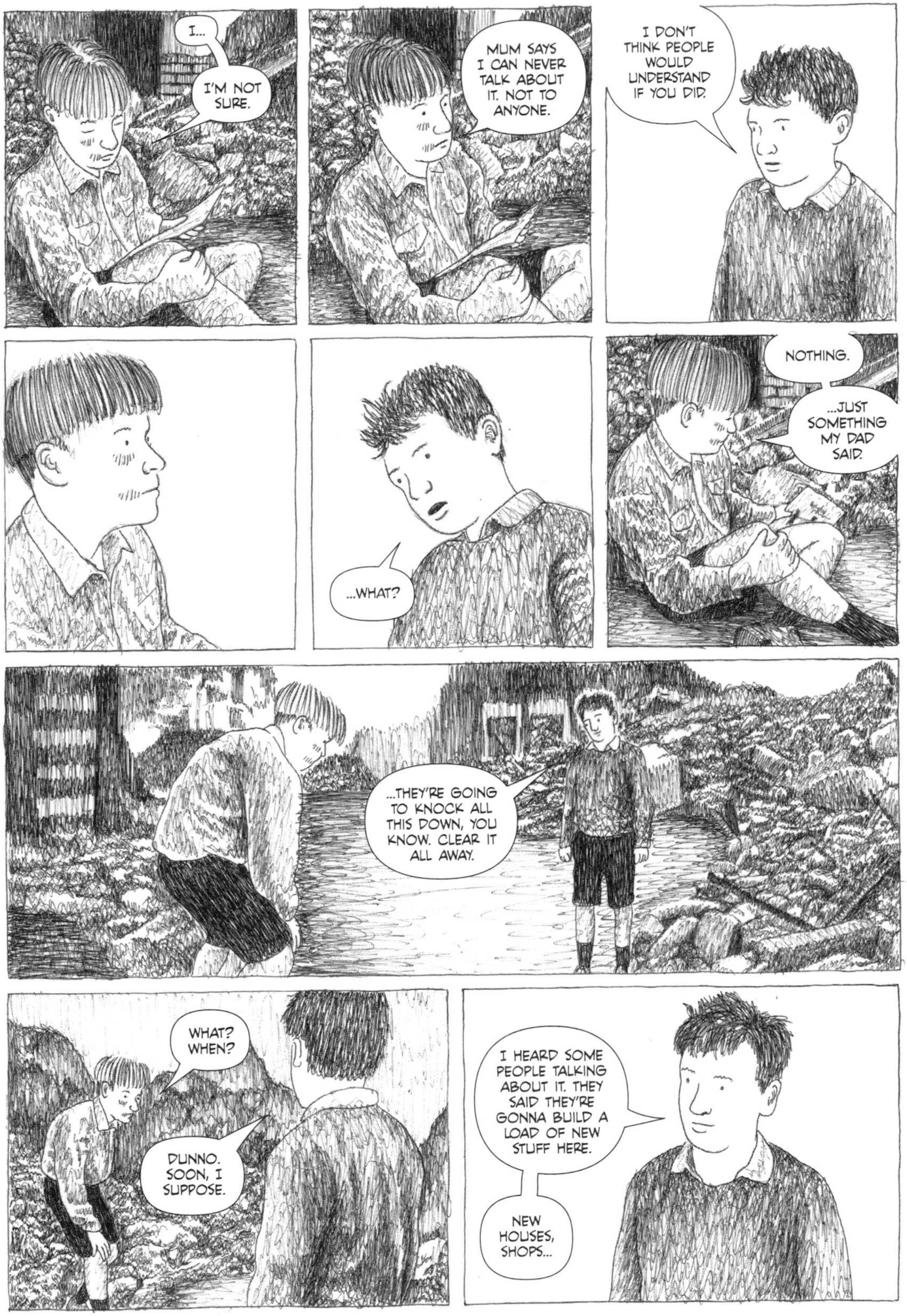
I...
I'M NOT SURE.
MUM SAYS I CAN NEVER TALK ABOUT IT. NOT TO ANYONE.
I DON'T THINK PEOPLE WOULD UNDERSTAND IF YOU DID.
...WHAT?
NOTHING.
...JUST SOMETHING MY DAD SAID.
...THEY'RE GOING TO KNOCK ALL THIS DOWN, YOU KNOW. CLEAR IT ALL AWAY.
WHAT? WHEN?
DUNNO. SOON, I SUPPOSE.
I HEARD SOME PEOPLE TALKING ABOUT IT. THEY SAID THEY'RE GONNA BUILD A LOAD OF NEW STUFF HERE.
NEW HOUSES, SHOPS...

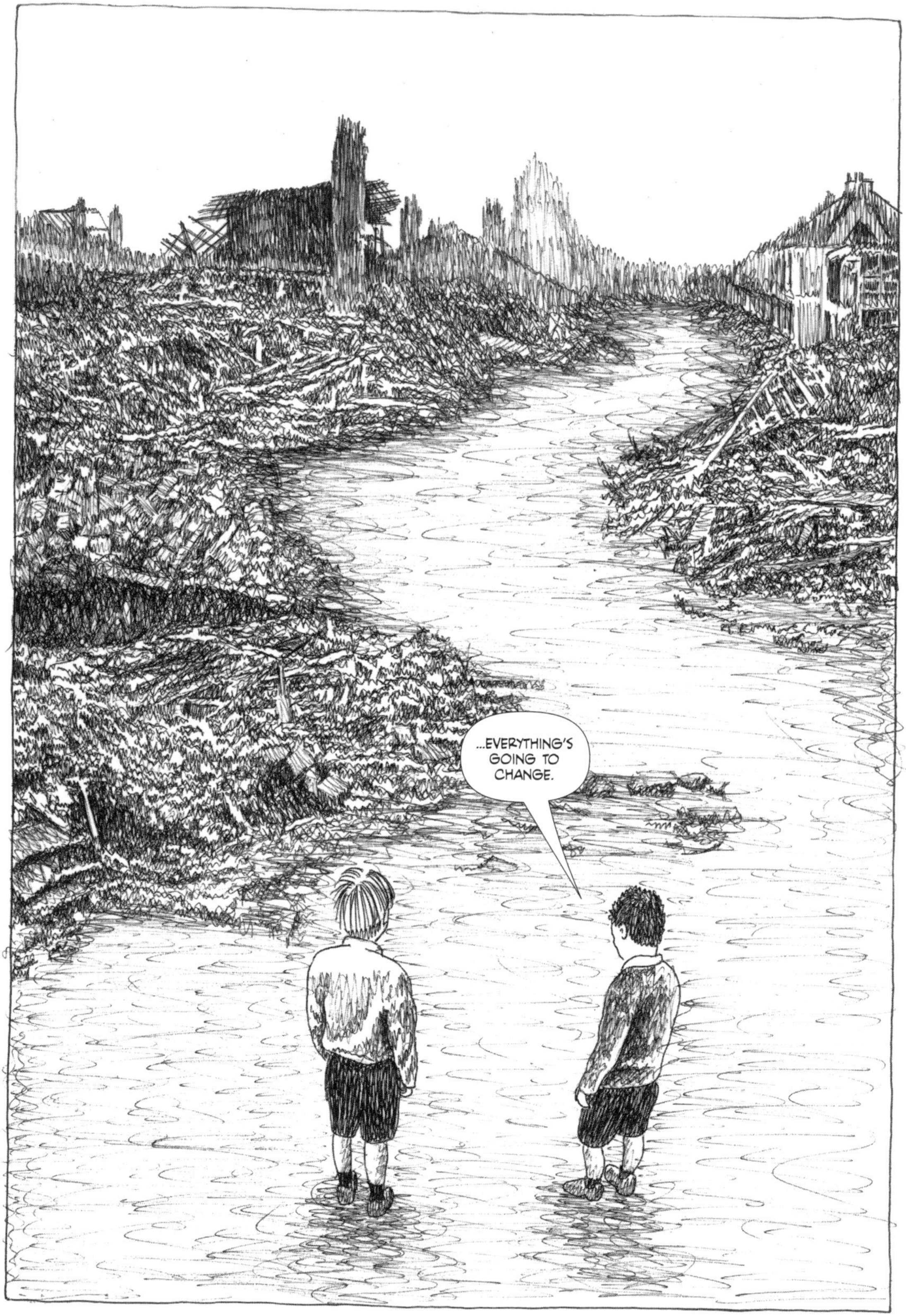
...EVERYTHING'S GOING TO CHANGE.

Author's note

The location of this story is never overtly stated because this is a story that could've happened anywhere in Britain. But it is set in a real place, namely the city of Bristol. Those familiar with the city will recognise many locations. However most of the primary locations of the story – and particularly the bomb-sites – are fictionalised, for the simple reason that I didn't want to upset anyone. Bristol was the fourth most heavily-bombed city during the war (after London, Coventry and Liverpool), and northeast Bristol – where Ralph's family live – was quite badly hit, due to its proximity to various factories. The families of those who died in those raids still live in Bristol, and many people still remember them. I did not want to cause them any distress. For this reason, I'd like to state that there is no such place in Bristol as Richmond Street (where the children's bomb site is located), and several other significant locations – particularly those with war damage – are either fictionalised or deliberately inaccurate.

I would also like to acknowledge Bristol Archives for their assistance during the early research I did on this book. Several images, most notably the opening double-page spread, were based on images found in Bristol Archives, and I would like to thank them for granting permission for me to use them as reference, and for their interest in the project. I would encourage anyone interested in the history of Bristol to pay them a visit.

Acknowledgements

The author would like to thank the following people for their help, advice, guidance and general support during the production of this book:

Corinne Pearlman, Dan Raymond-Barker, Juha Sorsa, Emma Hayley, Hannah Berry, Karrie Fransman, Shane Chebsey, David Lloyd, Gavin Mitchell, Paul Gravett, Peter Stanbury, James McKay, William Volley, INJ Culbard, Rob Davis, Benjamin Read, Jock, John Spelling, Dom Reardon, Lee O'Connor, Pat Mills, Charlie Adlard, Bryan and Mary Talbot, Bristol Central Library, Bristol Archives, and all my family and friends.

Special thanks are owed to the following for modelling for photo-reference: Pete Donnell, George Cole, Lou Taylor, Matt Jennings, Maria Cahill, Rory Walker, Delphine Guilemoteau, Hattie French, Oliver Droop, Laurie Ray, James McKay, Simon Gurr and John Barbour.

MORE GRAPHIC TITLES
New Internationalist

newint.org

myriad

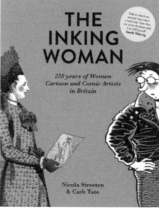

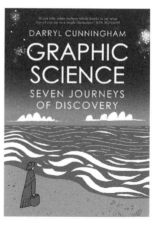

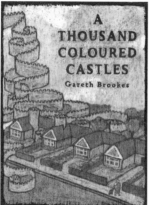

myriadeditions.com